The Crater Lake Murders

The largest, longest unsolved federal homicide case in Oregon

Monty Orrick

Genius
Book Publishing

Milwaukee Wisconsin USA

Published by
Genius Book Publishing
PO Box 250380
Milwaukee, Wisconsin 53225
Geniusbookpublishing.com

ISBN: 978-1-958727-12-6

230626 Trade

The Crater Lake Murders

Monty Orrick

Contents

Acknowledgments

A lot of people directly contributed to this book, for better or worse. Everyone alive whose name appears in it, I owe a debt of gratitude especially Keane Tupper, Alan Eberlein, Robert and Cheryl Cole, Steven Mark, Robert A. McNally, Cheryl Ousey, Tim Gordon, and Philip Culhane. Thank you all for your contribution, time, and patience with this long project.

My editor, Leya Booth, helped me whip my final draft into the book you're holding. She and her husband Steven had faith in this story which, to a writer, is about the greatest love of all. I appreciate that.

I'm also grateful for the motivation, encouragement and inspiration I received from several people no longer alive. Albert Jones, Charles Culhane, Frank Eberlein, Wallace Myers, Ken Kesey, and Mark Reisner.

The person who took the "for better or worse" part most to heart was my wife, Carolyn Arno. She regularly encouraged me about the worth of this story as I disappeared down the rabbit hole of research and writing for days, weeks, months, and years. She kept the lights on for our entire family in the last year while I bashed out the final drafts. Actually, that's the greatest love of all. This book would not exist without her. Thank you, dear. (Oh by the way, I just saw Jack Santo disappear down a rabbit hole. Can I take another year off?)

Prologue

For Spring Break 2011, I took my family on vacation to the only National Park in Oregon, Crater Lake, one of our favorite places. From Portland, it takes about six hours—seven if you're driving a Plymouth Voyager with small children, as we were on that trip. We'd booked a couple nights at Diamond Lake Lodge where I planned to take my daughters trout fishing. We'd also arranged to go on a snowshoeing tour with a ranger around part of the crater. Ah! Oregon. Snowshoeing in Crater Lake National Park will re-enter this story in a big way, but not for another nine years.

The first morning, the girls all slept in—perhaps a little tired from our ranger tour the day before. In the tiny kitchen of a rustic fisherman's cabin on Diamond Lake, I poured my first cup of coffee from a stained coffee pot and sat down on a scratchy, old sofa. Outside, the treetops brightened as the sun glowed behind Mount Thielsen. I thought about going back to bed, but it was so beautiful out. I grabbed my laptop instead. An annoying, chirpy jingle signaled

I had an internet connection, which surprised me. I typed the words "death crater lake" without thinking much about it. I'd read the book *Death in Yellowstone* by Lee Whittlesey. Reading about tourists getting into deadly situations in beautiful places satisfies a morbid curiosity of mine with a little natural history thrown in. It's good morning reading, educational and exciting. There are also a few lessons buried in the accounts, some wisdom, like watch your step.

It's hard to say which is worse, falling in a boiling hot spring or toppling ass over teakettle into a rocky crater. On a page managed by the Crater Lake Institute, there were plenty of descriptions of the latter. Falls make up the majority of deadly accidents at Crater Lake, along with winter visitors succumbing to the elements and the occasional disappearance. It went down well with my first cup. In the middle of it, a much longer account caught my eye.

1952
July 19

Albert Marston Jones, 56, of Concord, Calif. and Charles Patrick Culhane, 52, of Detroit, Mich. are found murdered on the South Road. 3.5 miles north of the south boundary. Both men were executives with the United Motor Service, a subsidiary of General Motors. The case has never been solved.

For the next several days, this brief description percolated in my imagination and started to bother me. It hit a little too close to home. The men had been on a fishing trip to a river I had fished before, Union Creek. That is what bothered me the most: These men were just minding their own business on their way to a weekend fishing trip and wound up dead. That the murders occurred inside a National Park and were never solved strained the imagination. The FBI was the lead investigative agency yet never named a suspect?! The sum of these elements make the story intriguing. That's how it struck me originally.

After we got home, I returned to my job as a photojournalist at KATU (the ABC affiliate in Portland). Before I ever thought of solving the case, I only wanted to find out more about it. I dug into the story a little deeper online and reached out to a few people who knew the subject.

A few weeks later, an important piece of the early research arrived. It was a term paper by a student at Southern Oregon University, Cheryl Ousey, written in 2001. Besides her twenty-page, double spaced thesis, her paper contained newspaper clippings, law enforcement records, and interviews—more information about the subject than existed anywhere outside the official inquiry by the FBI, which was unavailable. The newspaper stories from 1952 put the case in a historical context. It was a sensation, according to the headlines. Even after the story lost momentum, it would be revived on the anniversaries, reminding readers that the Crater Lake murders case was still active. Ms. Ousey's paper also had copies of a few pages of the FBI file. These were fascinating too, the holy grail of the unsolved investigation.

Eventually I decided I wanted to produce a TV story about the Crater Lake murders and, in the process, learn all I could about it. If only I could get hold of the elusive FBI file, but that was not a public record and even a Freedom of Information Act (FOIA) request would take years to satisfy.

At the time, I was employed as a photojournalist and, like most newsroom photographers, had little editorial control. So I did the next best thing. I started bugging my friend at work who did have control over which stories we reported. I recall driving down NE Broadway in Portland and telling Ian Parker about this amazing story I'd found. Something passed between us that afternoon and Ian became intrigued too. This is important because, if Ian had been too busy to listen, I'm not sure where the story would be today.

Prologue

Together, we drove the company car with all our gear to Crater Lake National Park in 2013 and shot our "sweeps piece" that June. Ian's script, which he batted out in a blazing hot Fort Klamath motel room, along with my photography and final edit, resulted in a fresh, accurate account that would serve anyone with an interest in the story.

For several years after, it was one of the first stories to pop up in internet searches. Then, after one of several server "crashes" at work during that period, Ian's and my piece disappeared, written on the wind, as they say in our industry. Our sweeps story and all the information contained in it became irretrievably lost. That might have been the culmination of my effort, but it wasn't.

Two and a half years later and three days before Christmas in 2015, Ian approached me in the newsroom. It was an ordinary workday, both of us turning in general assignment stories for the early shows. With an unusually large smile on his face for a Wednesday, Ian handed me three DVDs. Each bore an imposing imprint: Federal Bureau of Investigation. Our FOIA request had finally been fulfilled by some good people in Washington D.C. Only Ian knew how much I'd wanted to see that file. I could not have been happier if Santa had presented it in person. I did not wait until Christmas to open it.

The contents of the files were a little overwhelming. The hard copy of 2,137 pages stood over a foot high. I took the giant stack home and highlighted parts of it, then took notes—trying to arrange it into something easier to organize and digest intellectually. After a few months, I moved the four-pound stack of paper into the closet, beside my snow boots. Eventually, it found a place at the bottom of a file cabinet where it sat for several years—out of sight, but not entirely forgotten.

Time has a way of passing more quickly than you realize, particularly working full time in TV news with a growing family. Months turn into years and children graduate from elementary and high school in about half the time it took when you were a kid, or so it seems. On November 21, 2019, I got down on my knees in the back of the closet and dug through the effluvia of waders, gaiters, and boots until I could pull out the bottom drawer of the file cabinet and reveal its long-buried contents.

Inside it were seven, thick volumes bound with rubber bands. It was heavier than I remembered and no better organized. Surely, I could find a better way to arrange and examine these pages.

I came to this obvious conclusion on the couch with my laptop balanced on my knees and the hard copy on a pillow beside me. With relative ease I downloaded the seven PDF files into Google Docs and with relative ease put the pages in chronological order.

That was the moment of conception. Seeing the case as it played out in its logical order helped enormously. Also, I noticed it was a lot more interesting than I'd remembered it from three years before. For the first time, I saw the opportunity to cross-check the FBI file with records from several other agencies, like the Oregon State Police, Oregon Department of Corrections, and the Sheriff's Office in Klamath County where the murders took place. Within a few weeks, my requests from these offices began to arrive electronically and added slightly to the monster FBI file. Taken together, I felt there was a story here: retelling the circumstances of the case with all the new information made available by the FBI file. Even though the case would likely never be solved, it was still interesting, made even more so with new details.

Then an amazing thing happened. I say "amazing" because it was wonderful and horrible at the same time. The Pandemic hit and everything changed at work—including my workflow. One day managers brusquely announced that general assignment photographers and reporters were no longer allowed inside the building. I was relegated to waiting for stories to be assigned while sitting in the parking lot, inside my vehicle. There were other changes, as well. We were being assigned fewer stories in general, which meant fewer interviews and less editing, because we were disallowed from going inside the newsroom.

Suddenly, I found myself with a lot of time on my hands. My colleagues, also on the "outs," as it were, spent their idle hours walking around the neighborhood, standing together talking behind their masks, worrying about Covid and smoking. What was I to do? I don't smoke, enjoy walking, or like worrying about things I can't control. I enjoy talking to my friends at work, but I realized I had something more interesting to do with my time. I decided to spend the idle hours at work writing this story. At least, the story contained within the FBI file, which I had finally wrestled into shape.

The writing went pretty fast for the first few drafts and looked like it might develop into an interesting historical piece. At this point, I dared hope it would be accepted by my favorite historical periodical, *Oregon Historical Quarterly*.

Every source is consistent about who committed the crime, even if he was never brought to justice. The FBI, Oregon State Police, one victim's remaining family, and the intrepid Cheryl were all in agreement. Jack Santo, born in Medford and bad as they come, had to be the perpetrator—or one of his associates. In the midst of a Northern California crime spree where Santo participated in six murders and counting, he must have returned home to Southern Oregon in time to do the murders at Crater Park on July 19, 1952. That was the most popular theory for most of seventy years.

What a tantalizing figure he was. Irresistible and enigmatic—with a taste for violence and indifference to human suffering. He had all the criminal and sociopathic attributes necessary to kill two innocent businessmen on a weekend fishing trip.

Even without knowing his complete history, there was a big problem putting Jack at Crater Park on July 19, 1952. The motive seemed obvious, money. But what about the means and opportunity?

Questioned regularly about it after his incarceration for the other killings, he insisted he did not kill Jones and Culhane. Neither did any of his shady associates indicate knowledge of their boss' involvement, even in trade for lighter sentences in the other cases.

In 1955, Santo died in the gas chamber at San Quentin for the murder of a crippled Burbank widow during a botched robbery attempt. After his execution there was a sense of relief among followers of the Crater Lake case that the killer had been brought to justice—albeit for a different crime.

It does not do service to the story to give it away in the prologue, but within these pages is the argument why Santo could not have done it, supported by FBI documents.

At some point in the writing, I realized I was becoming the authority on the Crater Lake murders. Which meant I knew more about the case than the other five people alive who also remembered it. One was Al Jones' granddaughter, Alice Simms. Cheryl Ousey was another, if she still thought about it more than twenty years after writing her thesis. Alan Eberlein remains the last person alive who was present the day of the murders and has an abiding interest in it. (So does his brother, Neal.) Stephen R. Mark is the park historian and author of many good books about Crater Lake. He has also written about this case[1] and appeared with Alan in the KATU story. Then there was Ian Parker and me, the world's foremost authority on an unsolved murder case that had been virtually forgotten about.

After reorganizing the FBI file in early 2020, I saw something six pages from the end. Within a few pages of the file's last mention of Jack Santo was another man, two men actually, though I did not link them initially. Briefly mentioned, they came to light almost fifteen years after the murders and five years after their deaths. They were the last suspects of over two hundred whose names appear in the FBI file.

---

1 Mark, Stephen R. "A Biography of an Unsolved Double Murder at Crater Lake National Park" *Journal of the Shaw Historical Library* Volume 33, 2022

Prologue

These were individuals the Oregon State Police liked as well, after being contacted about them by the Marion County Sheriff.

Ten years after I became aware of the Crater Lake case and well into the historical piece I was writing, this new clue tipped the story sideways, knocking its entire contents into an area I had almost no experience with, personal or professional. Sometimes it is good that you don't know what you don't know. If I realized then how many obstacles stood in the way of completing the research and writing this story, I would have quit. Ignorant of it all, I clumsily persevered.

Based on publicly available information and original research, *The Crater Lake Murders* is the most logical explanation of the crime: the fullest narrative explaining how the murders went down, who did it, and why. And it comes with a few surprises, including finding the original scene of the murders whose exact location was lost to time. Taken together, it draws a picture of a quintessentially Western story—a heretofore unsolved murder that is both fascinating and highly inconvenient.

HAPPY VALLEY, OREGON June 2021

It's been more than a year since I left Oregon to finish this book. Since that time, there have been several rewrites and vetting of sources, all of which remind me of that beautiful state and the people there I miss. When I read this story and picture Crater Lake, I get a little lonesome. I can't help it. That is the spirit in which this book is offered: a letter home to my family and friends and the places I love.

RAYMOND, MAINE September 2022

Introduction

The Thing That Nobody Talks About

When a man lays dying, if he still possesses the energy and clarity to speak, he chooses his words carefully. He may be remembered by those last few words. If he forms a phrase particularly well, they may be his epitaph, carved into a headstone. Whatever those last words are before departing, he would be most fortunate to share them with someone he loves.

On December 9, 1966, the day Oscar Arrell died, he turned to his wife, Hazel, at their home in Silverton, Oregon. The words he spoke were not those of love, however. One of the last things Oscar communicated to his wife concerned a subject that made them both uncomfortable. Oscar reminded her about "the thing that nobody talks about."

Oscar's last few words concerned an incident that happened more than fourteen years before when two General Motors executives,

Introduction

Albert M. Jones

Albert Jones (left) and Charles Culhane (right) were found shot to death in Crater Lake National Park. Oscar Arrell claimed he knew who did it because they admitted it to him, as well as naming their accomplice. He implored his wife to take this information to the police, so justice might finally be done.

After the murders on July 19, 1952, the shocking details of the crime were splashed across the front pages of newspapers nationwide. A green 1951 Pontiac was found abandoned by a popular lookout just inside the park. Two days later, the two men were found dead in the woods less than a mile away. Graphic photographs of the murder scene appeared on front pages nationwide. Readers were intrigued, anticipating new information, more grisly details, and perhaps a suspect or two, but the killers left few clues. Despite the crime's unusual nature and the curiosity it generated, within a few weeks interest dimmed then blinked out altogether. Of course, the FBI worked diligently to find the murderers—until the end of the decade and, after that, another 35 years. Despite this effort, agents were not able to name a single suspect.

Charles P. Culhane

While Oscar Arrell's tip came too late for the killers to be held responsible, it did answer the fundamental question and enduring mystery of the case: Who did it? Of course, that would be just another theory, if the facts reported in the FBI file did not support it.

As it turns out, everything in the FBI file reinforces Arrell's accusation. Besides the FBI file, each law enforcement report and almost all the additional material (e.g. personal accounts and newspaper stories) supports the same conclusion.

Why has it taken this long for the story to come out? Most of the case facts contained in the FBI file were buried inside the lengthy document and had never seen the light of inquiry. Also, it has never been compared with the case files of other law enforcement agencies.

Why It Matters

The violent, senseless nature of these murders always bothered me. Two guys driving through Crater Lake National Park on their way to fish Union Creek could just as easily describe my excursions with friends to fish the same water. To end up like Jones and Culhane was unthinkable. It was also frustrating that the top law enforcement agency in the world never found the perpetrators, or even named a suspect. This failure denied the victim's families the small comfort of knowing who had killed their husbands, fathers, and sons. They deserve that, at least.

Researching the biographies of the two men who died, Albert Marston Jones and Charles Patrick Culhane, I learned each was a complex individual: hard-working, devoted to their wives and families, trying to enjoy a hard-earned day off when they were kidnapped and shot. The more research and information I collected, the greater my desire to write something that befit their honorable lives.

Introduction

Except being kept alive by the odd web article and a short podcast, the Crater Lake murders have otherwise been forgotten about. This has benefitted the law enforcement agencies tasked with solving the case, whose inadequacies solving it have never been much considered. After pulling off a perfect crime, the perpetrators successfully disappeared back into their lives—both cause and effect of the inattention.

A lot of history fades away because it's not interesting in the first place, but that is not the case with the Crater Lake murders. What happened and how, as described in the FBI file and Oregon State Police records, is as compelling as it ever was. The personal histories of the victims are easy to appreciate: each had a life story worth recounting. New details support a theory that goes further than any other in identifying who might have participated in the murders. Taken together, a story emerges. One may finally speak aloud "the thing that nobody talks about."

Section One: The FBI File

Page one of the FBI file—a teletype message to FBI Director J. Edgar Hoover the day before the victims were found. Hoover insisted these reports be one page long, thus their terseness and lack of expression.

14

1 | Deconstructing Tragedy

The seldom seen FBI report is the official document concerning the senseless murders of two General Motors executives in Crater Lake National Park on July 19, 1952. Exhaustive in its scope, the 2,137 page report is a window into history where one may see a different way of life, looser standards of law enforcement and blatant racial prejudice; but a lot of professionalism too and in many areas great attention to detail. The sum makes a fascinatingly complex story, unique to its time.

The file is a historical document. Ninety percent of it is dated from two days after the murders in July 1952 through 1957. It is entirely of its time. The language is, in many places, baroque and dated—like a character from the past, speaking a little too elaborately.

There are few people with a living memory of the Crater Lake murders. Reading through the file, one is reminded that every person whose name appears has passed away. Conversely, the places where the crime occurred, a busy canyon overlook and adjacent patch of woods, look almost exactly as they did seventy years ago. Neither has the unfairness of the crime aged either. The murders are as shocking now as they were then. The injustice done to the victims' families by never prosecuting or even naming a suspect has not diminished. In fact, it gets worse because everyone familiar with it assumes the case will never be solved.

Despite the bygone era, the futility in solving the murders, and the inevitable passing of everyone with personal knowledge about the case, there is an enduring curiosity. In all these years, only two people, the granddaughter of one of the victims and the author, have read the entire contents of the file. If that makes it sound intriguing, it is not. The story is damned interesting, but the file is mostly perfunctory reports, valueless interviews, negative ballistics reports, and descriptions of suspects lacking motive, means, or opportunity. The FBI file is not a page-turner. But to this writer, who has read it many times, it contains the outline of the greatest true crime story ever told.

Credit the bureau, who put everything they had into the investigation and extended enormous reach to solve it. In the first two months alone, over eighty agents' names were attached to the case—working it hard. Though they never produced a suspect, it was not for lack of trying. The net was cast widely—into nearly all fifty states, Canada, and Mexico. Before long, they had gathered the names of over a hundred potential suspects. The report is a rogues' gallery of all the most active criminals in America from 1952 to 1955, big time and small. Eventually, over two hundred individual names appeared in connection with the case; most were men with a criminal record. Surely someone in this group must have known what happened or was present at the murder. How did they avoid being caught by the most well-equipped law enforcement agency in the world at the time? And the largest question… Who did it?

Whether you want to look at the Crater Lake murders through the historical lens of the FBI file or a contemporary "likeliest explanation" theory, the starting place for both is the same, the victims' car.

... at a lookout point, they found the car used by the victims and on checking same found the key in the ignition, left front door open, the luggage and suit coats of both victims in car [*sic*].

FBI file. Volume 1 p. 1

How It Started

The above passage describes the moment that Saturday afternoon when Jack Vaughn, Frank Eberlein, and his 13-year-old son, Alan, drove up to the victims' car. Though they didn't know it yet, they were present shortly after the darkest moment of this mystery. The murders had occurred two hours earlier and half a mile away. The passage also represents the first of two great coincidences in this case. (The second comes at the end of the book.)

Before finding the Pontiac, Eberlein and Vaughn had completed their work week at Specialized Service, a busy automobile parts distributorship in Klamath Falls owned by Eberlein. That same morning, they had a short meeting with two General Motors executives visiting from out of town, Charles Culhane and Albert Jones, who had arrived neatly attired in suit and tie. They were on a business junket, visiting all the big accounts, including Specialized Service. Jones was the western regional manager out of Berkeley, California. He was a friend and frequent fishing partner of Frank Eberlein. Culhane was Jones' big boss out of Detroit, the General Sales Manager for many of GM's most important manufacturing parts. Before the meeting broke up that Saturday around 11 a.m., they all agreed to meet that afternoon at Union Creek just outside Crater Lake National Park where they'd spend the weekend fishing.

After leaving Specialized Service on Saturday morning, Jones and Culhane returned to their hotel and checked out, leaving Klamath

Deconstructing Tragedy

Falls at exactly noon. On their way to Union Creek, they planned to drive Jones' spacious Pontiac Chieftain around Crater Lake. Jones had made this tour before, including a few weeks previously with his wife. This was Culhane's first visit to Crater Lake and he was looking forward to it and the tour with Jones.

Vaughn and the Eberleins left town around 1:30 p.m., planning to drive directly to the cabin. According to weather reports, it was a glorious afternoon with summer temperatures in the seventies. Alan can still remember the day and the vehicle they drove, a 1948 tan Chevrolet pickup. Seated between his father and Vaughn, who was driving, they entered the park through the old south gate then referred to as the Klamath Falls entrance. Vaughn produced a season pass for Ranger Joe Hunt who had just arrived for his shift and waved them through.

Three miles up the road and a few minutes later, they recognized Jones' Pontiac parked at the overlook. Vaughn steered his truck beside it. Everybody got out expecting at any moment to see their friends walking along the trail or from behind the huge Ponderosa pines that lined the canyon rim. The Pontiac looked like it had just been parked there. The right passenger door had been left open. The car keys hung absently in the ignition. Their suit jackets were carefully folded on the backseat. Surely, Jones and his boss were nearby.

In this state of anticipation, the minutes ticked by. A dramatic precipice dropping a football field's length into the canyon formed by Annie Creek was just a few feet away—distracting and beautiful, attracting more cars and tourists to the overlook. The cool mountain air was fresh and scented of dirt and pine needles. Time passed quickly until, after forty-five minutes or so, one of the men realized something was dreadfully wrong. Their friends should have shown up by now, with a smile on their face and a story to go with it.

Less than an hour after they arrived at the park entrance, Frank and Jack returned to the south gate to inquire about their missing friends. Surely, there was some reasonable explanation. Misfortune could not visit two respectable businessmen touring a busy park in July. There wasn't enough time for trouble to have found them. The men had only been in town for a day.

Their Last Full Day

The day before was Friday, July 18, 1952. Albert Jones and Charles Culhane met in Klamath Falls to finish a business trip Culhane had begun that Monday. Though they had spoken over the phone to arrange their meeting, Jones and Culhane had never met in person before. Both men worked for the General Motors subsidiary, United Motor Service. Though it has since merged with AC Delco, this important division of General Motors produced and sold Delco batteries, AC spark plugs, and other GM parts. In 1952, General Motors was the largest automobile manufacturer in America.[2] Chevrolet was their most popular make. Culhane had been General Sales Manager for a little over a year. Responsible for sales throughout the United States, Culhane worked and resided in Detroit, Michigan but had never traveled west before in this capacity for UMS.

Jones was Zone Manager for the UMS office in Berkeley, California—a position he'd held for several years, responsible for accounts from Northern California to Southern Oregon. He'd worked for UMS for fifteen years in total. Before his trip with Culhane ended, they planned to visit Medford on Monday then drive to Eureka in Northern California and end up in San Francisco by Tuesday evening. Jones would drop Culhane off at the Fairmont Hotel on Nob Hill where his boss would spend the night before returning to Detroit the following day. After dropping off Culhane,

---

2 The second most popular vehicle make in 1952 was Ford, followed by Plymouth. Another popular GM make was Pontiac which was more expensive than Fords and Plymouths. A 1951 Pontiac Chieftain like Jones' retailed for $1,922 new.

Jones would drive across the Bay Bridge to his home in Concord. He lived there with his second wife Betty with whom he'd been married for a little more than a year.

Outside of work, the executives were very different people. Charles Culhane was from the Midwest, a dedicated family man who'd risen quickly at UMS to a senior position. A private person, Culhane had few outside interests. He was not known to associate much with coworkers outside the office.

Jones' attitude and lifestyle was altogether different. He'd been divorced. He was a Westerner with city tastes he'd cultivated living in San Francisco. He was gregarious at work and play—with a reputation as a man about town. Born in Canada, he changed citizenship when his family moved to Washington state. His upbringing in British Columbia and the Pacific Northwest gave him an appreciation of nature and wilderness. He was comfortable in the outdoors and went out of his way to explore them whenever his busy schedule permitted. Among his outdoor skills, Jones was an avid, skilled fly fisherman.

Another difference: Jones and Culhane were physically dissimilar. Autopsy records show Culhane was thin—five feet eleven inches tall and one hundred sixty pounds. Albert Jones stood about six feet and one inch tall. He weighed two hundred and ten pounds. The medical examiner described him as "a very large man."

Flying in from Detroit, Culhane's first stop on Monday was Spokane. For the rest of the week, he was driven throughout the state by Seattle Zone Manager Harold Weirs. After a whirlwind tour visiting parts shops and big distributors, the two men eventually made it to Eugene, Oregon on Friday. The weekend had finally arrived, but work wasn't over yet. Culhane was scheduled to meet Al Jones in Klamath Falls the next day.

It is a scenic two-hour drive from Eugene east to Klamath Falls. Up and over Willamette Pass, several unique Cascade features catch the eye of motorists on Highway 58. As Weirs and Culhane motored past, they could not have failed to notice Diamond Peak's jutting cone and deep, shadowy bowls filled with snow even in July. The snowmelt feeds Salt Creek which falls steeply down the mountain then, beside Highway 58, tumbles suddenly over sheer obsidian falls, 286 feet high. On the other side of the pass, the highway snakes around Odell Lake, another showcase for Diamond Peak. Motorists who stop beside its ample shoreline—on clear days when the water is still—can admire the peak's reflection in the lake.

Perhaps Culhane and Weirs stopped to look at Diamond Peak—the weather that day was clear—or, after a long week sleeping in hotels and being introduced to strangers, Culhane may not have paid much attention to his surroundings. On the last full day of his life, Charles Culhane may have simply looked forward to reaching Klamath Falls and getting some rest. He would complain the following day of feeling fatigued.

While Weirs and Culhane were driving over the pass, Jones drove north from the Bay Area in his company car, a light green 1951 Pontiac Chieftain. Among its features was a "268 straight 8" engine and Hydra-matic four speed transmission—a nice automobile for touring. Jones used the main highway through the state's Central Valley—old U.S Route 99. Like the interstate that replaced it in 1964, 99W was a straight shot. Jones stopped briefly in Redding, California to visit a client before heading east to Klamath Falls. The trip took all day.

The Klamath River drains an enormous basin, the Klamath Basin, extending from Crater Lake south and west into California. After flowing two hundred and sixty miles, the river empties into the Pacific Ocean by Requa. Another important feature of the basin is the Pacific Flyway, one of the planet's greatest bird migration routes. Besides the Klamath River, other local waterways that attract the birds are the Williamson River, Upper and Lower Klamath Lake, Agency Lake, and the Sprague River. All of these and seasonal creeks too numerous to mention feed enormous marshes which historically filled vast areas between the rivers and lakes. An enduring legend of this place is that in spring and fall millions of ducks, geese, and migrating waterfowl would cover the sky until the blue and bright sun behind it was no longer visible.

The most prominent feature in this area of the basin is Mount Scott to the north, almost 9,000 feet high. To the near side of Mt Scott is a smaller, darker mountain, deceptively insignificant. In fact, it's the epicenter of one of the most important events in recent geological history. This dark mound near Mount Scott was hollowed out by a cataclysmic volcanic explosion 7,700 years ago. Previously, this mound was a mountain, among the tallest in the Cascade Range, Mount Mazama. When a restless mass of gas and molten rock trapped below the mountain could no longer be contained, it exploded. Mazama's liquid core covered the area in lava flows and deep deposits of ash. Rocks from the blast were flung clear to Medford. A silica cloud created during the event reached all the way to Quebec in Canada. When the ash, lava, and noxious gas cleared, there was a big steaming hole or crater where the mountain had stood. Eventually, the crater cooled, and after thousands of years, filled with snowmelt—a lot of snowmelt. The lake that formed is almost two thousand feet deep. Renowned for its clarity, depth, and emerald blue color, Crater Lake is the most beautiful lake in Oregon; also, its only National Park.

Friday Evening in The Falls

In 1952, the nearest town with accommodations for tourists visiting Crater Lake National Park was Klamath Falls. This is where the three executives met on Friday, July 18th. Weirs and Culhane arrived first, then Jones. They all checked into the Wi-Ne-Ma Hotel downtown. From the hotel, Jones called Specialized Service to set up the meeting for the next morning. In his fifteen years at UMS, Jones visited

Specialized Service several times a year and had struck up a close personal friendship with Frank Eberlein. During the season and when they weren't doing business, the men enjoyed fly fishing the trout streams around Klamath Falls. Besides talking business and meeting Culhane, plans were firmed up for the weekend and where they would fish.

The fishing opportunities would be excellent. The snowmelt and flows had come down after the spring runoff. The weather was warm and the bugs were out. Perfect conditions for fly fishing. They'd fish Union Creek outside Prospect just west of Crater Lake, and stay at Union Creek Resort. Hopefully, the big boss would join them.

Sometime before five o'clock, Jones drove to The Gun Store on Main Street. He spent $15.33 on a fishing license and some tackle. The out-of-state license was $5. Whatever else Jones bought, it likely included a few Bucktail Coachman flies. These were Frank Eberlein's favorite flies for the waters they would ply with hook and tackle.

One last detail of Jones' trip to The Gun Store is mentioned briefly in the FBI file. Frank Eberlein recollected in one of his many interviews with the bureau that Jones' boss, Charles Culhane, accompanied him during his visit to The Gun Store. This small detail is inconsistent with the FBI file that has Culhane and Weirs arriving in Klamath Falls around 6:30 p.m. A Gun Store employee said Jones came in alone.

That evening, Jones, Culhane, and Weirs enjoyed a drink together at the hotel. After that, Weirs went out around eight to visit friends in town. Jones and Culhane stayed in and had dinner. When Weirs got back around midnight, he stopped by Jones' room for a nightcap.

In his interview, Weirs said he did not notice anything unusual that night or the following morning. All three UMS salesmen went to bed that night without any premonition about what would happen later that day.

Saturday July 19, 1952

Early Saturday, Weirs headed back to Seattle, leaving Jones and Culhane to finish the trip.

After breakfast, they made two quick business stops in Klamath Falls. The first was to Moty and Van Dyke, a repair and parts shop. Culhane gave their top salesman a special pin with a Delco battery insignia. Around 10:15 a.m., they went to Specialized Service to meet Frank Eberlein. Sales manager Jack Vaughn was also there. Vaughn was Eberlein's top man and a close friend. He was also friendly with Jones. On a previous visit, Jones had joined the Vaughns for dinner in their home. Vaughn would be the third member of the fishing party that weekend. Like Jones, he made plans to stay at the Union Creek Resort.

The resort is still there today and, like so many places in this story, remains virtually unchanged. Just west of Crater Lake on Oregon Route 62, Union Creek flows under the highway near the resort. The creek boasts of some of the best small water trout fishing in the state—then and now. Frank Eberlein was particularly enthusiastic about the dry fly fishing in Union Creek—one of many feeder streams of the Rogue River. Jones' favorite Rogue River tributary was Foster Creek, a few miles away. Besides the Rogue River, the north fork of the Umpqua is also in the vicinity. It is a world famous steelhead destination, popularized in the early 20th century by the western writer Zane Grey. The resort is still popular with anglers.

All of these fisheries have a special charm, especially the smaller and less preferred fisheries like Union Creek. Seldom deeper than a few feet and easily waded across, each is a little different from the other and can hold the imagination of a trout fisherman for as long as the spell lasts. The pine forests they twist through are full of impressive, large trees. In July 1952, the snow was off the ground and the rivers had just come down, ideal conditions for fly fishing. Lurking under the cutbanks and in the deeper pools, colorful rainbow trout called redsides are fairly numerous and occasionally grow quite large, exceeding two pounds or better. The specific knowledge required to catch them on a fly is limited to locals and the occasional out-of-towner who knew his stuff, like Jones.

While Jones was thinking about the trout fishing he'd soon enjoy, his boss was preoccupied with work.

One reason for Culhane's coming west was to examine how business was being conducted. He had recently expressed dissatisfaction about excessive travel expenses being charged to the company by salesmen like Jones. Jones' regional manager, Ira Kennedy, was taking the brunt of Culhane's dissatisfactions regarding the bottom line. The FBI interviewed several people, including Culhane's wife, who said Kennedy and her husband did not get along. This may have put Jones in a good position. The several days of travel to get acquainted with Culhane might have been an opportunity for Jones' promotion, depending on the boss' level of dissatisfaction with Kennedy.

However much Jones wanted to make a good impression with his boss that weekend, it was not going to happen. At some point Friday or Saturday, Culhane complained of not feeling well and elected not to join the fishing party for the weekend. Perhaps he was just tired. From Jones' room in the hotel on Friday, Culhane called the exchange. The operator connected him to the Hotel Medford where he made his reservation for Saturday and Sunday.

Culhane was not the type of boss who enjoyed dry fly fishing or drinking and relaxing in a mountain cabin with coworkers. According to his wife, his one personal indulgence was visiting museums on the only day he reserved for himself, Sunday.

So the new plan for Saturday was that Jones would play tour guide and drive Culhane to the lake and possibly around it. After that, Culhane would take the Pontiac and head straight to Medford— dropping Jones with his host at Union Creek along the way.

Jones must have been a little disappointed. He would not have the chance to schmooze his boss around the fireplace or show off a bit, casting flies to big hungry trout. It would just be the four of them: Jones and Vaughn, Eberlein and his son, Alan, fly fishing for trout in idyllic surroundings—with nothing to bother them until Monday morning when Jones planned on taking the bus from Klamath Falls to Medford to meet Culhane there.

In a three page, single-space account he wrote about the events of July 19th, Frank Eberlein described it this way:

> Since their next appointment was in Medford on Monday, they decided to do some sightseeing since Culhane had never been out West. Jones was familiar with the area around Crater Lake and Union Creek, having spent some vacation time in the area previously.
>
> *Frank Eberlein*
> *The Crater Lake Murders of July, 1952*

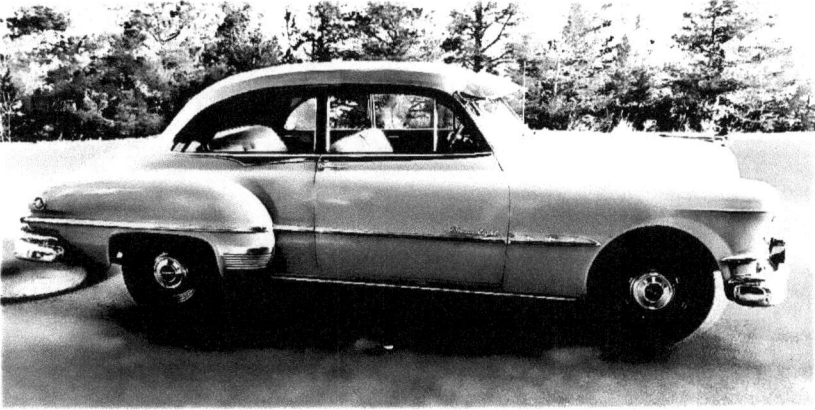

1951 Pontiac Chieftain

A Beautiful Tour

That was how they left it on Saturday at the offices of Specialized Service. It had been a long week, especially for Charles Culhane. Everyone was looking forward to enjoying a little time off, each in their own way. It was a beautiful summer day—almost seventy degrees out. No one could know the goodbyes they shared were final when Albert Jones and Charles Culhane drove off in the Pontiac at 11:15 a.m.

After they collected their bags and left the hotel, their last stop in Klamath Falls was for fuel, recorded on a gas station receipt totaling $3.83 at 12:01 p.m.

After filling up, Jones gripped the column shifter in the Pontiac and put it into gear. From the gas station, he drove north through town. The trip from Klamath Falls to Crater Lake begins unremarkably, but the scenery improves quickly. In an hour and a half, it is possible to drive to the edge of an enormous steep-sided bowl filled with water bluer than the sky.

Crater Lake was their destination, but the only lake they would see that day was Upper Klamath Lake, the largest lake in Oregon.

27

Deconstructing Tragedy

Highway 97 curved around thirteen miles of the eastern shore, affording a view west to Mount McLoughlin, over 9,000 feet high. The smell of desert sage was in the air. If the windows had been cracked, for an Easterner like Charles Culhane, this would have been a unique sensation—the pleasant sting of sharp, desert perfume.

The big Pontiac roared down the road. Inside it, they rested on a commodious bench seat with heavy springs and deep padding, but no seat belts—not in 1952. The polished enamel dashboard was inset with an ashtray and cigarette lighter. Radio sounds emitted from a round speaker with a clock inset. An almost empty carton of Parliaments lay on the seat between them, in case either man needed a fresh pack.

Highway 62, approaching CLNP south gate

A few miles north of Upper Klamath Lake, they would have crossed one of its main tributaries, the Williamson River. Spring fed at its source, it drains almost two million acres in fifty miles before being consumed by the lake. By mid-July, after the heavy winter of '51-'52, the Williamson was just coming into shape. The fly fisherman in Jones likely took a quick look over his shoulder driving over the bridge.

Somewhere between leaving Specialized Service and reaching their final destination, both men removed their coats, folded them neatly and placed them on the backseat. This simple action has always stood out. Common to disappearances or untimely deaths, small acts performed in the last hours appear larger. A bath drawn, but never taken. Or a sport coat laid out smoothly to avoid wrinkles, but never worn again.

Just past the river, Jones read the sign for Crater Lake National Park. The big steering wheel turned easily in his hands as the Pontiac left the main highway onto Oregon Route 62. Within a few minutes, they were in Fort Klamath whose most famous resident has been dead since 1873.

Captain Jack, or Kientpoos[3] to his people, is the famous Modoc warrior whose tribe inhabited what geographers call the Intermountain Region of California—from Mt Shasta to Tule Lake. They lived here from time immemorial until the 1870s. At that time, the federal government decided they needed to be moved north to cohabitate with the Klamath Tribe. When the Modoc would not be moved, a war broke out. Many died in this conflict, shot, or in Kientpoos' case, executed. His headstone and three other monuments bearing the name of Modoc warriors mark the spot. When Jones and Culhane wheeled past it on the left, they were only a few minutes from the Klamath Falls entrance to the park.

They made pretty good time. After their gas stop in Klamath Falls, it only took an hour and four minutes. Hindsight suggests

---

3 The other common phonetic spelling of the Modoc Chief is Kintpuash.

haste may have led to their undoing. Had Jones decided to wet a line at the Williamson Bridge, their entire future might have changed in those few minutes. Since Jones apparently drove as fast as he could, they could not have arrived much sooner. Had they driven just a few minutes slower or stopped anywhere on the way, their day and lives may have gone as planned.

Slowing to pass through the Klamath Falls entrance.[4] Jones bought a day pass for a dollar. Just like tourists entering the park today, he received a sheet filled with park information and a map of the lake. In 1952, it was called the *Crater Lake Bulletin*. Jones put the *Bulletin* on the seat next to the Parliament carton. The ranger jotted down his license plate number and the time of day.

When pressed later by the head ranger and FBI, Dick Marquiss could not remember who was driving the Pontiac or give any details of their meeting. In fact, he did not remember anything about the men or their vehicle. They arrived at the end of his shift and before his replacement, Joe Hunt, took over. The best Marquiss could recollect was that he did not notice anything suspicious around that time. During the exchange, Marquiss read Jones' round-cornered, gold-on-black California license plate and wrote the number in his log, 6A16762. Next to that, he wrote 1:05 p.m. He issued them a permit, 49803. Though he never remembered

---

4 This entrance has since been replaced by the south gate entrance, several miles up the road off highway 62 by the Annie Creek Campground.

anything, Marquiss was almost certainly the last person who saw Jones and Culhane alive, aside from their killers.

Three and a half miles uphill from the old Klamath Falls entrance to the park is a viewpoint, the Annie Creek Canyon Overlook. It is the first remarkable view tourists come upon inside the park. Here, tourists look across a chasm to the opposite side—a 90° cliff face of gray, volcanic ash. What most don't realize is that they are standing on a cliff face equally extreme. If you're brave enough to stand at the edge, you can see all the way to the bottom, three hundred feet down. There, the tiny creek that carved this steep, narrow canyon meanders through a strip of willows and trees fallen down from the canyon above.

There are several turnouts on the highway along Annie Creek Canyon. The first one inside the park is the overlook that figures in this story. Today, it looks almost exactly like it did in 1952. Its surface is unpaved. The dirt is smoothed every season by thousands of tourists and their vehicles. More recently, a paved strip was added—near the highway. In 1952, there was a low wooden barrier along parts of the perimeter near the road, but that has since been removed. Other than the old fence and the paved pullout lane, nothing else has changed in more than seventy years. The Annie Creek Canyon

SLAIN MEN'S CAR FOUND-The car in the picture above is parked on the exact spot where Culhane and Jones' car was first found shortly before 1 p.m. on Saturday, July 19, 1952. This viewpoint is located about six miles north of the old ranger check station at the south entrance to Crater National park.

A photo that accompanied a ten-year retrospective of the Crater Lake murders in the *Medford Mail Tribune* on October 11, 1962.

31

Deconstructing Tragedy

Overlook remains most tourists' introduction to Crater Lake. A preview of the coming attraction.

The overlook and the dirt parking area next to it appear almost ordinary from the highway. But there is something about it, a tiny temptation. It beckons for one to come closer and see what all the excitement's about. That is why a thousand people stop here every week during the season. They get out of their cars, take a few steps, and the sudden, precipitous edge comes into view. This is where parents freeze and look around nervously for their children. The brave among them step closer. People with a fear of heights never get out of the car, sensing the danger. You don't see a three hundred foot straight drop every day—not with dirt under your feet.

Compared to the Grand Canyon and the ancient processes that created it, Annie Creek Canyon is a newborn. Seven thousand years is a geological blink of the eye. The canyon walls are devoid of any horizontal lines or strata representing different times in prehistory. There is only one layer—representing one moment—when Mt Mazama exploded into the stratosphere and Crater Lake began forming. But most tourists don't think about that. They just know it's steep as hell and to keep a tight grip on the kids.

When the tourists clear out, it's easy to imagine Jones and Culhane pulling up in the big Pontiac... slowing as it turned off the highway, dirt crunching under the polished whitewalls. Rolling to a stop, both doors swung open and the men stepped out. Inhaling the cool mountain air, they ambled in the direction of the overlook—exactly like a hundred other park visitors that weekend. Or this weekend.

But what happened next to Albert Jones and Charles Culhane? No one knows.

The First Great Coincidence

After Jones and Culhane drove away from the gate at the Klamath Falls entrance in the direction of the lake, they effectively vanished for two days. What happened next in the timeline at the overlook is truly fantastic. According to Alan's recollection all these years later, Vaughn was driving when the pickup arrived at the overlook. They parked beside the Pontiac on the canyon side.

Frank Eberlein described the moment in a paper he penned about the dramatic events that weekend.

> . . . much to our surprise, we came upon the Jones Culhane car. The right front door was open, the keys were in the car, and everything in the car appeared to be in order but no passengers were in sight. We assumed they must be nearby so we waited for them to appear.

> **Frank Eberlein**
> **The Crater Lake Murders of July, 1952**

It was incredibly good luck when Frank Eberlein and Jack Vaughn saw Jones' Pontiac parked beside the road at the overlook. Fortuitous, if they could take advantage of their good timing and find their friends, which seemed possible. If they had not noticed Jones' car on their way to Union Creek, who knows how long it might have sat there before someone looked for the owner.

The only connection to them was their car. It was always one of the first items mentioned in law enforcement reports and newspapers. The unhurried way the Pontiac was left at the overlook created as much mystery as the men's disappearance. This seemingly abandoned expensive automobile became the centerpiece of the search and every story about it.

Deconstructing Tragedy

The first newspaper report appeared Monday July 21st in the local paper and it focused on the Pontiac. This was two full days after Jones and Culhane had disappeared. The newspaperman got a few details wrong, but you can't blame him. He was describing something he hadn't actually seen. Plus, the Pontiac had been moved by then. Nevertheless, the description had a matter-of-fact immediacy.

The Abandoned Pontiac

> From all appearances, the car had been left by persons intending to stop only a few minutes. The car windows were down, keys were in the ignition switch and the right door was standing open. Inside the car was the two men's luggage, fishing gear, briefcases and their coats were on hangers in the rear seat.
>
> But there was no sight of Culhane and Jones.... And they have not been reported since.
>
> *Wallace Myers*
> *Klamath Falls Herald and News, p. 1*

The FBI and Oregon State Police reports detail exactly what was inside the car. In the backseat, the men's suit coats were neatly folded alongside their luggage—not on hangers. There was a Brownie camera too, but no film was inside it. Jones had his fly-fishing gear in the back with a copy of the latest *Sports Afield*. In the middle of the front bench seat lay a Parliament carton with two packs inside, and the *Crater Lake Bulletin*.

The Pontiac was in a completely undisturbed state, at least according to John Vaughn, but he saw something out of place.

VAUGHN stated that as they were examining the tracks of the victims' car, they noted tracks which appeared to cross the tracks of the victims' automobile, and it would appear that this car had made a fast start as the gravel on the shoulder was dug up some. The left front door of the victims' car was closed tightly.

FBI File, Vol. 1 p. 264

After driving through the Klamath Falls Entrance to the park at 2:20 p.m., the Eberleins and Vaughn arrived to find their friends' unattended vehicle parked at the overlook. After waiting another forty-five minutes or so at the overlook, according to Frank, they "grew very concerned." They had all been together in Klamath Falls just a few hours before. Now, with their car parked at the edge of a precipitous cliff, the two General Motors executives were nowhere in sight.

The old south gate or the "Klamath Falls Entrance" to CLNP through which Jones and Culhane entered and their killers likely exited.
Courtesy: Southern Oregon Historical Society

Had their friends fallen into the canyon? Frank and Jack discussed this frightening possibility.

In the midst of all the confusion, one person had the presence of mind to attempt to determine how long the Pontiac had been parked. Thirteen-year-old Alan Eberlein pushed his hand through the open chrome grill to feel the radiator. Though it does not appear in the FBI or OSP reports, his father repeated Alan's observation in his three-page statement. He said Alan (below) found the radiator "quite warm" when he touched it. It is a clue that confirms the accepted sequence of events—that the Pontiac had been there since Jones and Culhane entered the park. When asked about it sixty-eight years later, Alan Eberlein recalled the moment. Could the hot engine block of a 1951 Pontiac parked in a sunny spot on a warm afternoon remain hot to the touch after an hour and a half?

"That's how we took the temperature of our farm equipment. It was a very warm day. The car wouldn't have cooled down real fast."

While Alan was taking the temperature of the Pontiac, his father and Jack Vaughn were realizing their friends might be in a lot of trouble. They climbed back into the tan pickup and returned to the Klamath Falls entrance hoping for some information that might explain everything.

Another ranger, Joe Hunt, had replaced Dick Marquiss since Jones and Culhane had passed through. He recorded the time when Eberlein and Vaughn arrived to report their friends missing. It was 4:40 p.m. Standing around the tiny south gate booth, Eberlein and Vaughn talked it over with the ranger then returned to the overlook at five o'clock. Between the time the men left and then returned to the Pontiac, something odd happened to Alan. It was a momentary event which, in the intervening years, has acquired some significance. Many believe the perpetrators returned to the scene.

After his father and Jack Vaughn left to find a ranger, Alan stayed behind to keep an eye on the luggage and gear. It was late afternoon. Shadows were lengthening across the parking area. He decided to wait in the car. Behind a steering wheel big enough for a tugboat, there was plenty of room on the wide bench seat. With nothing else to occupy him, Alan pulled Jones' copy of *Sports Afield* from the back. Leafing through the pages, he became distracted by images of big game hunting, fishing scenes, and advertisements for the most modern fishing and hunting gear. Looking down, he ignored the hum of automobiles to his left entering and exiting the park. It was a brief interlude of calm in the upsetting afternoon. Suddenly, from the direction of the highway, Alan heard something that caused him to look up from his reading.

"A car came up fast, crunching gravel," Alan recalled.

The vehicle pulled up very near the driver's side window, but only for an instant, then drove off. According to his father, Alan "saw the taillight disappear behind the big pine tree." The only piece of vehicle information he could glean from that fleeting moment was its color, black. The thirteen-year-old's account is described in his father's report.

> Alan remained with the Jones Culhane car. He reported that while positioned in the driver's seat of that car another car approached from the North, crossed over to the left side of the road, pulled alongside but instead of stopping, accelerated and continued South.
>
> *Frank Eberlein*
> *The Crater Lake Murders of July, 1952*

For our TV story in 2013, reporter Ian Parker and I interviewed Alan beside the overlook. He was seventy-four years old then. Could he recall who was driving the car that pulled up next to him at the overlook? During those crucial few hours after Albert Jones and Charles Culhane disappeared, could it be the perpetrators returning to examine the contents of their victims' car? Alan was an uncommonly observant boy, but he never saw who was driving that day.

"It all happened... fast. By the time I looked up, the car was behind me. I saw it for a few seconds... then it disappeared behind this big tree."

It took only a few seconds, but something had happened.

What did it look like to the occupant or occupants of the other vehicle? They were in a car driving southeast just before five o'clock. The sun would be behind them—below the trees, fully illuminating the overlook and the Pontiac. Looking in the direction of the other vehicle from the Pontiac would be looking towards the sun. It was an advantageous position for the car that approached the Pontiac and may explain why Alan didn't see much.

The question is, why didn't the other vehicle see Alan in the front seat before they pulled beside him? A thirteen-year-old boy hunched over in a large automobile behind a big steering wheel might be difficult to see—until they were side by side.

Many believe these were the murderers coming back to plunder the contents of the Pontiac. If so, it reveals a critical piece of information. They drove away from the overlook in the direction of Fort Klamath via the exit just down the highway.

No one knows what type of automobile the killers drove that day. Alan could not recall any distinguishing details of it, which suggests the car was not flashy or expensive. More likely, it was an older model and a common make, like a Ford or Plymouth. Anybody that needs money badly enough to rob two strangers inside a busy park is not driving a high-value automobile.

This plain old jalopy may not have belonged to the perpetrators either. They might have borrowed it. If it was registered to them, it was not one of the 466 vehicles recorded in the park that day and whose owners were interviewed as part of the FBI probe.

How did this mystery car avoid having its license plate recorded entering the park? Dick Marquiss recorded Jones' license number when he bought a pass. Joe Hunt did not record Frank Eberlein's license plate number because he had a pass, purchased earlier in the season. Besides pass holders many others could come and go without any record of it. Park employees, contractors working inside the park, and local tribal members all avoided having to pay a fee and have their license recorded. After producing a pass or identification that showed they belonged to any of the above, they got waved through—entering and leaving the park anonymously. It is also possible the driver of this mystery car entered with a pass he had stolen. Or he may have switched license plates. About 50 of the 466 plates recorded in the park on July 19th could not be traced. Finding every tourist driving through the park that day was impossible and the FBI knew that early on.

North Gate, East Gate and Klamath Falls Entrances in 1952

Snowpack measurements around Crater Lake National Park in 1952 reflected one of the heaviest winters on record. The west and south gate entrances were open all year. The road from Diamond Lake to the north gate was plowed and opened on July 12th. The road from the east gate into the park was plowed during the third week of July. It opened for the season on July 19th, coincidentally, the same day as the murders. The Park Service released the information where it was picked up by at least one local paper the day after.

> MEDFORD (U.P.)—All entrances to Crater Lake National Park were open to two-way traffic Saturday and visitors facilities were in operation... the State Highway Department reported that snow clearing operations Had been completed on the north and east entrance roads. The north entrance had been open to one-way traffic for a week.
>
> *The Eugene Guard July 20, 1952 p.10*

The east entrance was closed to traffic permanently in 1956—partly because it was the least frequented by tourists. Most visitors drove or arrived by bus via the north and south entrances because of their highway access. Locals living in towns east and north of the park along highway 97 preferred the east entrance. Anyone who used the east gate on the day it opened in 1952 was likely a local person, because that information was not widely known—for at least another day—until it appeared in *The Guard*. If one ascribes to the theory that a local person or persons did the murders, it would make sense that they used the east gate to enter the park that day.

The Search Begins

After Eberlein and Vaughn reported their friends missing to the Ranger Hunt, they drove back to the overlook. Eberlein and Vaughn were shortly met there by Chief Ranger Lou Hallock. This was not the Chief Ranger's first search and rescue. Before taking the job at Crater Lake National Park, Hallock had been Chief Ranger in Yosemite and Carlsbad Caverns; both have had their share of visitor mishaps.[5] Logic dictated that the men had either gotten lost in the

---

5 Grand Canyon N.P. is the most dangerous, followed by Yosemite then Great Smoky Mountains Nat'l Park. Falls are the most likely cause of death in Crater Lake National Park and in National Parks overall.

woods or fallen into the canyon. In either case, finding them quickly would increase their chances of survival if, indeed, they were in peril. Someone produced a map. To see the area from above, the canyon looks like a flat, gray snake. Running roughly parallel to it, Powerline Road is a thin dirt line scratched into the forest.

Hallock got things moving in a hurry. It was early in the evening when two search parties were formed. The first group consisted of a dozen or so men, mostly park employees, who walked together through the woods on the opposite side of the highway. There was much shouting of the men's names and looking for anything that might stand out from the ordinary. The forest was extremely plain. Medium size lodgepole and fir rose to the shoulders of a few larger Ponderosa pines. There are no trails or landmarks whatsoever in this southern strip of the park. The southern boundary of the national forest is less than a half mile away. The only manmade feature here is

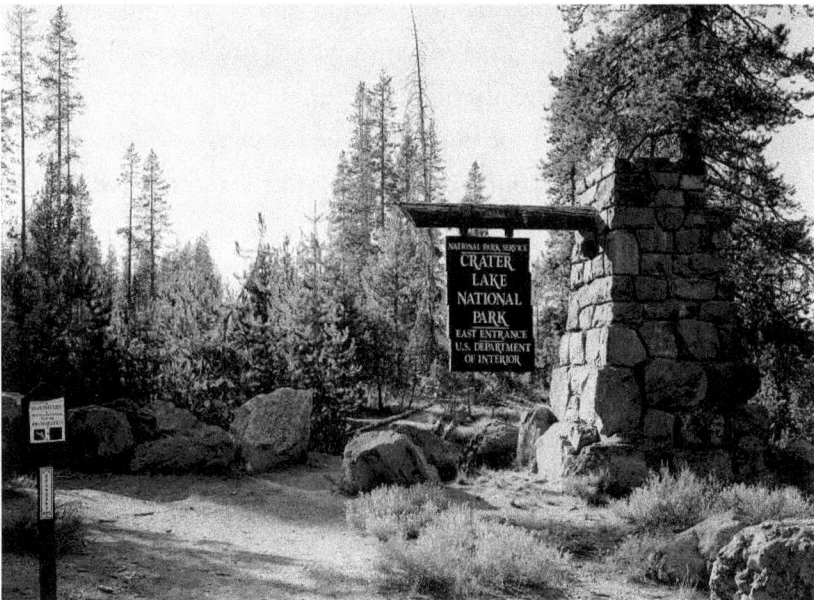

Before the east entrance closed to all motor traffic in 1956, it was popular with locals visiting Crater Lake.
Courtesy: Crater Lake Institute

a dirt road running underneath the power lines. It delivers electricity to this side of the park, including the headquarters and lodge complex. This one lane road is fairly maintained, but not marked. Its two entrance points are difficult to recognize from the highway. Because of the power lines, there was no reason to invite tourists in there. It was a no man's land at the edge of the popular park—an empty corner. In the waning light of a bluebird day on July 19, 1952, it would see more activity than it ever had before.

All the shouting and commotion implied that there was reason to believe the men might be out there, hopelessly turned around in the nondescript woods or walking on Powerline Road. This was the best case scenario.

The second big search that day was opposite the woods in Annie Creek Canyon, steep-walled and potentially dangerous for climbers. Searching it required a technical descent with ropes and a harness. Two rangers with special training were assigned. Their mission was to look for and, it was hoped, rescue anyone clinging to the canyon wall. Then there was the alternative: Climbers would recover Jones and Culhane's bodies at the bottom of the canyon.

This grim, second outcome became the most favored theory among searchers that evening. It's easy to understand why. The Pontiac was parked by the edge. The park had a history of deadly falling accidents. Awful as it sounds, mishaps involving two visitors falling simultaneously have occurred there.

It was possible one of the men had tumbled over the edge and the other, in an attempt to save him, fell too.

The man Hallock assigned to search the precipitous slope was Assistant Chief Ranger Bernie Packard. In the late afternoon, he and a climbing partner were lowered over the wall. Dangling from the edge, they combed the steep, loose ground looking for a man clinging to a shrub—just out of earshot or too tired to call out. Eventually, they descended the entire three hundred feet.

At the bottom of the canyon, they found themselves standing next to a boisterous stream barely a foot deep and several feet wide, Annie Creek. They spent the rest of the late afternoon and evening searching the ground between the walls. There was a lot to search: melting snow drifts and the waist-high strip of willows lining the creek. For Packard and his partner, they were ready to find two lifeless bodies down there somewhere, but that did not happen.

After a few hours it began to grow dark. The sun set around 9:00. There was no moon. The canyon darkened until the only thing visible from the bottom was the starry night sky between the walls. All that met the senses down there, besides the starlight, was the constant, low gurgling of the creek. The climbers were forced to quit. Preparations were made for them to stay overnight.

> ... because of the hazard involved in retracing their steps in the dark... Bedrolls and food were lowered to the party and they bedded down for the night.
>
> *Chief Ranger Lou Hallock,*
> *REPORT OF MURDER OF C.P. CULHANE*
> *AND A.M. JONES IN CRATER LAKE*
> *NATIONAL PARK ON OR ABOUT JULY 19,1952*

Back at the rim, a searcher turned the keys in the Pontiac's ignition, to see if it would start. The six-cylinder engine turned over immediately. Car problems did not contribute to the men's predicament. Neither did they run out of gas. The fuel gauge registered full.[6]

That evening Jack Vaughn phoned his wife in Klamath Falls and asked her to check the two area hospitals. Neither had admitted Jones or Culhane.

---

6 One might speculate, based on this observation, that the men stopped for fuel on the way. Alan Eberlein believes it's more likely Jones and Culhane had not traveled far enough for the gauge to come off the full mark. They arrived at the south gate in one hour and three minutes from their previous gas stop in Klamath Falls, which also suggests they made no stops in between.

Deconstructing Tragedy

The old Park Headquarters where Frank Eberlein and his son, Alan, spent the night of July 19, 1952. Today it's an administration building, part of the complex that includes the visitor center.
Courtesy: NPS

Unlike the canyon search along Annie Creek, the ground search by the highway was not technical. The volcanic, sandy ground does not support much vegetation between the trees, which are not dense. Sight lines are good. The ground here slopes several degrees downhill in a southerly direction toward the park boundary on the other side of Powerline Road. At least, that is what it looks like in 2022.

It's hard to know exactly how these woods appeared seventy years ago, but photographs of the area taken around 1952 look indistinguishable from today. Many features would not have changed at all, like the ground slope or the composition of the larger trees.

In these sparse woods beside the overlook, there are two small, several acre sections of older, larger trees. One lines the highway opposite the overlook. It gives the impression that the woods hereabouts are dense and beautiful, which they are not.

The second woodsier area is a quarter mile from the highway. From ground level, it does not stand out from the woods surrounding it, but when viewed from overhead, a slightly greater density of trees is apparent. This second stand was a little farther than crews could reach before it got dark on Saturday.

Eventually, all the searchers except Packard and his partner returned to a staging area on Highway 62. The missing men were still presumed lost or fallen into the canyon. Nothing about the Pontiac indicated a crime had been committed, or any violence either. Jack Vaughn drove Jones' car back to Klamath Falls in the hope that it would be returned to its owner the following day. Frank Eberlein and Alan drove to the Park Headquarters where a core group planned for Sunday. The Chief Ranger described their deliberations that night.

> A discussion was held in the Ranger Office… in an attempt to find a possible solution to the disappearance of Jones and Culhane…. It was decided to reinstitute the search shortly after daylight enlarging the area examined as the search progressed. Early Sunday morning the party in the canyon researched the area of the canyon floor immediately beneath the overlook. They then proceeded upstream and searched an additional one fourth mile of the canyon floor. The search parties on the West side of the highway were enlarged and continued the search of the forest land North and South of the Overlook. A portion of the area searched by these two crews had been previously searched late Saturday afternoon and the duplication was purposeful in order that no possible clue be overlooked.

> *Chief Ranger Louis M. Hallock*
> *REPORT OF MURDER . . .*

That evening, Frank Eberlein called UMS Area Manager Ira Kennedy in San Francisco. Kennedy had worked with Al Jones for many years. They were friends. After receiving the call from Eberlein that the men had gone missing, Kennedy attempted to book a flight into Klamath Falls Municipal Airport for Sunday. He was not successful but he was able to book one for the following day.

Before he fell asleep that night, Frank Eberlein sat on his cot and looked over at his son lying in another cot in a dark corner at Park Headquarters. Eventually he laid down and tried to sleep, but when he closed his eyes, he did not replay images of an enjoyable afternoon fishing with his friend, Al Jones. Whatever went through his mind was not the stuff of pleasant dreams.

Sunday July 20, 1952

The sun appeared bright orange above the east rim of Crater Lake, bathing the wall on the opposite side in a velvety light that fell like a glowing curtain until it reached the lake, illuminating the shallows. Inside the park, it was fifty-two degrees at six a.m. Another beautiful day was forecast. The morning sun helped the searchers warm up as they re-worked the same section of forest they had walked through on Saturday—making certain they hadn't missed anything in the excitement and half-light the previous evening. When searchers found no evidence of Jones or Culhane by going over the same ground as the previous evening, they enlarged the area south to the boundary and west in the direction of the Park Headquarters.

After a short and not particularly restful night, Frank and his son drove to the overlook first thing on Sunday morning. Alan is the only person alive who remembers the search that day. He described it once in a paper.

> The woods search, comprised of a 12 man trail crew, was spaced 20 feet apart combing the area.

> *Alan Eberlein*
> *The Crater Lake Murders of July, 1952*

In order to keep the ground search organized and know roughly where on the map they were walking, crews used compass directions as a point of reference. They walked, as much as possible, north to south between the highway and Powerline Road then reversed course when they reached the area of the road.

Despite searching all day and evening, by Sunday night the dozen men found no sign of the missing executives; neither did they reach the more distant stand of larger trees by the powerlines.

The rangers who spent the night in Annie Creek Canyon resumed searching the pinched river bottom early Sunday. Unlike the woods above them, this was a limited space, less than a football field wide. Snowbanks in the shady canyon were deep enough that July to have hidden a body. Their surface was flat but dirty with a coating of ash and pine needles raining down from the cliff face. A two-hundred-pound object falling several hundred feet would have created an obvious disturbance. Nothing did. Neither had the men fallen into the creek or willows.

Once Packard and his partner determined that no one had fallen into Annie Creek Canyon, this information was passed back to Hallock who notified Oregon State Police. It was eleven a.m. that Sunday.

(l to r) Frank Eberlein, Chief Ranger Louis Hallock, and United Motor Service Representative Ira Kennedy
Courtesy: Klamath Falls Herald and News

There was one other dangerous search performed that day. Immediately west of the overlook is a steep, slippery slope—just above the south canyon wall. The search was undertaken for thoroughness, but with limited expectations. It was difficult and dangerous. The steep sandy edge curved sharply to a freefall more than twenty stories high. After returning to the rim that afternoon from the canyon bottom, Ranger Packard was asked to search this slope. He roped up one more time. Results were the same. The two executives were not there either.

The person most perplexed by the events of the last two days was Frank Eberlein. He'd known Jones for fifteen years. They had fished the local waters together. Eberlein knew his friend was an experienced outdoorsman and comfortable in the woods. It did not make sense that he would venture into this easy-to-navigate little forest with his boss and get them both lost.

The events of Saturday and Sunday did not become public until Monday when the *Klamath Falls Herald and News*

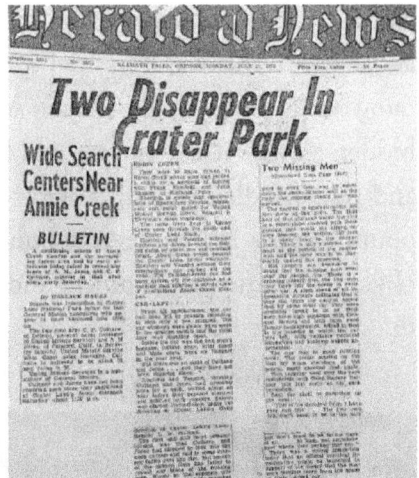

printed the first story about it. It was written by Wallace Myers who stayed with the story thereafter. His account related the confusion and wonder, particularly in a quote from Chief Ranger Lou Hallock.

"This is the darndest thing I have ever run into. The two men just don't seem to be in the park at all. At least, not anywhere near where they parked that car."

If there was any silver lining on Sunday, it was that the men had not fallen into the canyon, which had seemed possible the day before. And they were not wandering around in the woods—not within earshot. There was a third theory gaining traction among the searchers. Hallock, Eberlein, and the other organizers had the same idea. Did the missing men meet with some criminal element? The fact that Jones and Culhane had not fallen into the canyon made this third theory more likely. In a way, it was even more worrisome.

After Sunday dinner at Crater Lake Lodge, guests wandered outside to the enclosed patio. From a table there, at the edge of the crater, they could see its full circumference: the sublime spectacle that greets tourists almost every day during the high season. It was uncommonly mild that evening—even warm. Like the day before, the sun set around nine. In the waning light, two objects appeared above the rim, at first indistinct then brighter. Against the moonless night sky, Jupiter and Saturn hung like Christmas lights, and reflected calmly in the laketop.

Five miles from the contented lodge guests, a dozen searchers in the middle of the woods decided to quit. Beside the Powerline Road, the searchers' flashlight beams became a little cluster darting between the trees. There was yelling as the men huddled up. All were quickly accounted for, a dozen or so. The group turned their backs to the road and headed to the highway where the other searchers and organizers were waiting. The little nucleus of light marking the march back quickly disappeared.

Near enough to have been touched by the distant beams, an unusually proportioned fir tree stood just up Powerline Road. The trunk was split five feet off the ground, creating two trees, slightly off-center, almost parallel.

Below the split, deep shadows covered the forest floor and everything on it. Invisible at this hour were the bodies of two men lying at a right angle to each other just a few feet apart. The record shows that they would not be discovered for some time yet—certainly not in the inky blackness of a moonless night. The only intrusion to the senses was the distant hum of cars on the highway and a gentle wind in the trees. From the shadows, an inaudible question hung in the breeze. How did these men come to be here and why?

2 | Monday July 21

The Woods Opposite the Overlook

The strip of woods beside Annie Creek Canyon near the overlook is deceptively remote, despite being near Highway 62. Whenever a tourist pulls over and steps out of their car—to stretch and breathe and take a look around—they walk to the canyon side. Except for emergency bathroom stops or to give a dog a break, no one crosses the road. And no one goes further than a few trees deep, if they do. Venture beyond that and you will invariably be standing by yourself in the middle of the woods.

There is no sound out there except the wind in the trees, bird calls, and the occasional distant downshift of an eighteen-wheeler. It is a no man's land, without any of the lake views or weird volcanic features inside the park. Though the woods by the overlook have never been logged, it is not particularly ancient-seeming. There are some old trees here, but it doesn't feel like an old growth forest. The ground is too dusty. The big trees are fairly far apart. On a list of attractive places to visit at Crater Lake National Park, the woods opposite Annie Creek Canyon Overlook are near the bottom. In fact, they're not on any list at all.

Though these woods are thin and plain, visitors driving up or down Highway 62 by the overlook would not know it. Rather dense and attractive trees line the highway here. To enthusiastic newcomers, it looks like there could be a campground or a hiking trail on the other side. There are interesting destinations just up the road like Annie Falls, Park Headquarters, and the campground.

Finding the Murder Scene

Walking toward the Powerline Road, the men on Monday's search crew were talking, each to the man walking nearest him, as they combed the woods that morning. Two questions preoccupied them. Where are the missing men? Sunday's all-day search answered this question. Jones and Culhane were nowhere to be seen. Few of the searchers believed as they did the day before—that the two men had either gotten lost or fallen into the canyon. But nothing had turned up to indicate either outcome. If the men had gotten lost, they would have been rescued by now, and if they'd fallen into the canyon, Ranger Packard would have found them at the bottom.

The second question searchers asked themselves Monday morning occupied most of their conversation. What had happened to Jones and Culhane? As they combed the woods, anyone's guess was as good as another's. One thing most of the searchers agreed on... whatever happened to the motor executives did not look good.

If they were kidnapped and taken from the scene, as was being speculated, Jones and Culhane could be anywhere—as far away as a car might drive in two days, including Mexico and Canada.

Monday July 21

There was not much anyone could do about this possibility.[7] There weren't photographs available of either man yet—to reproduce and distribute for possible identification by a witness. Despite the revised speculation about Jones and Culhane's fate, without any other leads, the woods adjacent to the overlook remained the only place to search for them.

Like the previous two days, search conditions were ideal—mild and sunny. The crew was slightly larger than the day before—around twenty men. The group this day must have been ready for anything. It took about six hours before they found it. A Klamath Falls man, Rex Ash, reportedly came upon two bodies underneath a large, uniquely configured fir tree just off Powerline Road. It was Jones and Culhane. Both men were dead.

One account has it that, upon finding the men, two warning shots were fired—the same two sounds that had emanated from the spot on Saturday.

The ranger in charge of the group, Charles Kasling, sent word of finding the men to Chief Ranger Hallock who received it around noon at his office in Park Headquarters.[8]

When the message came in, Hallock was on the phone with Wallace Myers, the newspaperman from the *Klamath Falls Herald and News* who'd been assigned the story and whose first few reports would be reproduced by newspapers all around the country. Myers was in the process of offering and helping organize the services of the Klamath Air and Search Rescue Unit, which Hallock had accepted. Myers was in the middle of writing out a teletype summoning the KASRU when the radio call came in from Ranger Kasling.

Hallock jumped in his park service truck and sped down the mountain to meet the search group. Kasling waited for him by the

---

7 The APB (All Points Bulletin) system had been in use since 1947, but was not employed during the search for Jones and Culhane.
8 The FBI file has it several hours later, 2:50 p.m., which was closer to when they arrived.

highway. Shortly after, they were walking down the hill to an area just inside the park boundary near Powerline Road. It took a few minutes before they arrived at a small group of searchers—gathered away from the crime scene but in sight of the bodies. The original scene as described by Frank Eberlein when he saw it was quite shocking: The manner in which both Albert Jones and Charles Culhane's bodies were left was different from later photographs. Though he witnessed it, Hallock failed to describe it in his report, only that he "tentatively identified the two men as the missing Jones and Culhane."

Hallock had the search crew secure the area, then drove back to the Ranger's Office. He notified the FBI, OSP, the Klamath County Coroner, and Frank Eberlein. Eberlein was needed to positively identify the victims, though there was little doubt about it.

Once he received a call from Hallock, Frank Eberlein left Klamath Falls with Ira Kennedy who had arrived by plane that day. Kennedy brought Jones and Culhane's official UMS portraits. These became the images we are most familiar with today (see Introduction). Together, Eberlein and Kennedy drove Jones' Pontiac (which Jack Vaughn had driven back to Klamath Falls on Saturday night), retracing the route the deceased men had taken forty-eight hours earlier. The plan was for them to drop the Pontiac off at the garage in Fort Klamath where the FBI, who was taking control of the case, might search it more thoroughly.[9]

Upon arriving at the roadblock, Hallock brought Eberlein into the woods. According to Eberlein, Sheriff Red Britton was also present. These three men were at the scene about half an hour before everyone else began to arrive. Hallock brought in a second group around two fifteen that afternoon. It included representatives of Oregon State Police, the FBI, members of the Klamath County Sheriff's Office,

---

9 It sounds odd that such a key piece of evidence, like the victim's car, was driven before being thoroughly examined for fingerprints and clues, but modern forensics and concepts like secure crime scenes and evidence collection were new in 1952.

Monday July 21

District Attorney D. E. Van Vactor, County Coroner George Adler, and Ira Kennedy.

In the confusion and high excitement before everyone arrived, one member of the search crew, John Owings, took advantage of the moment and snapped several photographs of the scene to sell to a true-crime pulp magazine that was popular back then. After receiving the Chief Ranger's phone call, local FBI agent Willard Linehan drove to the park and straight to the scene. Once he discovered Owings' ambitions to sell the photographs for a profit, Linehan confiscated the film. Even though Owings' intentions were selfish and potentially painful to the victims' families, the images might have been valuable. They showed the bodies when searchers found them in their original positions, critical to understanding the moment when the murders occurred. It is assumed that Linehan destroyed Owings' images as they have never been seen or heard about since. Unfortunately, there is no law enforcement record of how the scene looked before the bodies were moved; neither the FBI nor Oregon State Police photographed the scene in its original state. The only record and way to understand it is Eberlein's written description.

Given its proximity to the scene, Powerline Road was considered as a route the killers might have used, going in or out. The road was blocked off on both ends. Plaster casts were poured into tire tread impressions at the south end by the Oregon State Police. It turned out that the marks were left by a park electrician, Paul Koehler, during a scheduled inspection a few days prior.

Another person present during the commotion that day was Albert Jones' wife, Betty. She had gotten in a car and started driving up from Concord on Sunday. She told the UMS driver who accompanied her that she had a strong feeling that her husband was already dead. The reason, she felt, was that Albert was too skilled in the outdoors to get himself and his boss lost; for that reason, she believed something bad had happened. Whether it was logic or intuition, her premonition proved correct. Whatever feelings she had for this beautiful spot her husband and she once enjoyed together had been betrayed.

Official photos from Monday in wide, medium, and close-up shots show Albert Jones and Charles Culhane lying dead at the base of a large tree. Less obvious are two smaller trees—about twelve inches wide—next to their waist. In some of the photos, each man appears by himself; in others, they are photographed together. In one wide shot (see cover), they are surrounded by rangers, law enforcement, and county officials.

Laid out on their backs with their arms at their sides, both of the deceased look like they went for a hike then decided to take a nap. In the grainy black and white image, the executives appear out of place: dressed in fresh-pressed shirts and ironed slacks. Jones and Culhane do not fit in visually with the other men at the scene who are almost all dressed informally. All the images are peculiar and deeply unsettling.

There are four official accounts describing the crime scene that day. Within the two-thousand-page file, the FBI produced a fifty-page report devoted to the scene and events. In his three-page account, Frank Eberlein described his impressions of the investigation, including the physical orientation of the bodies before anyone else arrived. There is also Ranger Hallock's factually titled *REPORT OF MURDER OF C.P. CULHANE AND A.M. JONES IN CRATER LAKE NATIONAL PARK ON OR ABOUT JULY 19, 1952.*

The fourth written account is from a Private with the Oregon State Police who filed a four-page Officer's Report submitted on Wednesday July 23, 1952 titled *MODE OF OPERATION.* Trooper Lawrence Bergmann was beginning his career with OSP. In what was possibly the most important report he ever filed in his career, Bergmann described the scene and made several key observations.

The body of Mr. Culhane was found lying on his back, legs outstretched, with right arm and hand across chest, left arm alongside torso. Victim was clad in a white shirt and blue slacks, in stocking feet, no shoes, and gag was in the mouth, tied around the face with the victims [*sic*] necktie, very tightly.

The gag consisted of an undershirt, torn in two, ½ being in Culhane's mouth and the other in Jones's mouth. The victims [*sic*] upper denture was found in his shirt pocket.[10] Body was lying with head to the south and feet to north. The body of Mr. A.M. Jones was found lying about 5 feet away from Mr. Culhane and more at a 45 degree angle, with the stocking feet pointed at the middle of Culhane's torso, and head to the west. Body was face up, legs outstretched, arms to side. Torso was clad in a white shirt, tan slacks, red socks, no shoes. Glasses were on his face and his upper plate dentures were found in his shirt pocket. Victim was gagged in same manner as Mr. Culhane with his necktie tied tightly over the piece of undershirt and around the mouth.

L.G. Bergmann,
Private Officer's Report

The Federal Bureau of Investigation's representative, Agent Willard Linehan, took over as soon as he arrived that day. Because the murders occurred on federal property or a "government reservation" as the FBI describes it in the file, they had jurisdiction. Linehan was the bureau's lone representative in Klamath Falls. Eventually two other agents arrived from the Portland office, Special Agents Tandy Jack Fleming and Ronald Sherk. As the case gained national prominence,

---

10 According to the FBI Report, Culhane's dentures were in his front trouser pocket. The salient point regarding the dentures is that Culhane was given time to remove them and the crime was still a robbery/assault at that point.

it drew immediate attention from Director J. Edgar Hoover. Though his interest in the case waned, the investigation continued through 1995. Eventually, well over a hundred agents would become involved in this case in some form or another. Initially the Special Agent in Charge of the Portland Field Office, J. B. Poster took the lead in the first weeks and months of the investigation.

When he described the crime scene in his teletype of July 23rd, two days after the bodies were discovered in the woods, Willard Linehan did not mention the position of the bodies in their original state or any other.

> BODIES OF BOTH WERE LOCATED IN CLNP ON THE AFTERNOON OF JULY TWENTY ONE LAST. BOTH VICTIMS WERE SHOT THROUGH THE HEAD, HAD GAGS IN MOUTH WHICH WERE HELD IN PLACE BY NECKTIES TIED AROUND THE MOUTH AND NECK

> *SA Willard T. Linehan*
> *TELETYPE, July 23, 1952*

The FBI's fifty-page synopsis was authored by Asst. Special Agent in Charge W. H. Williams from the FBI's Portland Field Office. He was not present the day the bodies were recovered, but described them in the report.

> The body of CULHANE was lying face upward beside a small pine tree approximately four inches in diameter with his head toward the southeast... The body of JONES was lying face upward beside another small pine tree approximately six feet from the tree beside which CULHANE lay.

> *FBI File Vol. 1 p.245*

Monday July 21

At least nine men, besides the FBI and search crew, arrived to document the scene below the big fir. All were there in some professional capacity: Chief Ranger Hallock, Ranger Kasling, Frank Eberlein, Ira Kennedy, Special Agent Linehan, Sheriff Britton, Klamath County District Attorney Van Vactor, Klamath County Coroner Dr. Adler, and OSP Trooper Lawrence Bergmann.

Before the day ended, the number of visitors to the scene swelled to include ten more, at least. State Livestock Investigator Chester Liechty was with Trooper Bergmann when the call came in. They rode together to the park and joined the group surrounding the scene, which now included CLNP photographer Francis E. McIntosh, Park Superintendent John Wosky, Assistant Director of Park Services Thomas J. Allen, Asst. Chief Ranger Bernie Packard, OSP Trooper Les Harroun, Klamath County Deputy Sheriff Del Reed, one other unnamed photographer, a reporter from the *Medford Tribune*, and Wallace Myers from the *Herald and News*.

The photograph on this book's cover is a wide shot of the scene. Within the frame, ten individuals are present and appear to be working. Everyone performed their job with the utmost seriousness. For many of them, this was the most eventful day of their career.

The bodies were removed and the scene cleared about 7:00 p.m.

Before everyone left that evening, the big fir tree south of Charles Culhane's head was "blazemarked." That's a knife cut that removes the bark in a square or rectangular shape large enough to be seen from a distance, like a trail marker. It was necessary because investigators returning the following day might have a hard time finding the location of the murders. It remains difficult to find even today.

FBI and OSP accounts are consistent regarding the final position of the bodies underneath the big fir tree. Charles Patrick Culhane, lying on his back, had his right elbow and torso touching a pine tree ten inches in diameter. The blood collected around his necktie gag indicated he was shot once in his head, but not straight on. The shot that killed him was delivered at his right rear jaw and exited through his neck—effectively severing his brain stem. His shoes had been removed, yet his socks were perfectly clean on the bottom. It would be discovered during the autopsy the gag in both men's mouths had been fashioned from Culhane's undershirt, torn in half. Culhane's gag was held in place with his necktie—stretched across his mouth— knotted tightly behind his neck in almost the exact place he was shot. The belt holding Culhane's neatly tucked shirttails had been re-buckled slightly off center.

Both law enforcement agencies and the coroner shared the same language in their reports that the men's outward appearance showed "no sign of a struggle."

WARNING: GRAPHIC IMAGE

Given each victim's almost identical proximity to a jackpine at his elbow, it has been speculated the killers attempted to tie Albert Jones, foreground, and Charles Culhane, background, to the trees. Courtesy: OSP

Monday July 21

Culhane's watch was missing from his wrist. His wallet had been rifled through and dropped near his body. Whatever cash he carried had been stolen. His elegant brown Florsheim wingtips, noted by several people in his meetings on Saturday, were also missing from the scene. They were never recovered, even after a careful search of the woods. His dress socks were completely clean and free of any pine needles, dirt, or debris.

Culhane wore two partial dental plates, one upper and one lower. Both were found in his shirt pocket. This last detail indicates some interplay between the killers and victims: a level of concern by the perpetrators while the gags were being tied. If they left the dentures in his mouth, one could fall out and cause Culhane to choke. At the moment Culhane removed his dentures, he might have believed he could survive the robbery. Why else would they bother to have him remove his partials?

Albert Marston Jones' body was in a very similar position a few feet away, angled with his feet pointing toward Culhane's torso. Like his boss, Jones was shot behind the ear and through the brain stem, but without an exit wound. Underneath the place where Jones was laid out, a decomposing log pushed up under his shoulder blades. Like Culhane, Jones was shoeless. His brown Bullock and Jones wingtips were discarded nine feet from their owner. His socks were also clean and free of forest debris.

Another similarity between the two men's positions in the woods were two ten-inch diameter lodgepole pines. One was quite near Jones' right side where his pinkie finger nearly contacted it. Culhane's right elbow rested on the jackpine he leaned against. In some newspaper reports, the men were mistakenly described as having been tied up or "bound" when they were found. Though it was incorrect, it made sense given the proximity of the trees. Many witnesses that day noticed the nearness of both men's hands and back to the trees and speculated about it.

Even on their backs, in their pressed dress shirts and trousers, the victims looked like they might carry a lot of cash. It turned out they did. Between them, Jones and Culhane probably carried between two and three hundred dollars, the equivalent of two or three thousand dollars today. Culhane, it was assumed, carried most of it. He began the trip with twelve hundred dollars. Jones did not carry as much money when he traveled for work. He preferred to make out checks when he needed cash and probably had less in his wallet. All of this is pure conjecture, based on the file. No one knows how much money the men had before they were robbed and killed, except the killers.

Like his boss, Jones' wallet had been emptied and tossed aside. There were a couple of spare keys and credit cards inside. An empty fold indicated the absence of several cards. Like his boss, Jones had removed his partial dental plate and placed it in the breast pocket of his shirt. This must have occurred before any fighting or the gags had been set. He still had forty-one cents in change. Albert Jones' cigarette lighter, engraved with his initials, lay next to him in the dirt.

Death Struggle

Culhane's ripped T-shirt—which was used as a gag and found in the mouths of both victims—is a detail with a question mark beside it. Why would the perpetrators have Culhane remove his T-shirt, tear it in half, and make two gags from it if they didn't intend to tie them up? It doesn't make sense to leave their hands free to remove the elaborate gags. These men were going to be tied up.

The gags suggest another question. Why bother with them at all, if you intend to kill your hostages? Everything at the scene suggests the robbers planned to tie them up, gag, and rob them. Shooting them in the head was not the plan. It became the last piece of violent punctuation because something else happened. But what? For Jones and Culhane, fighting to breathe through a T-shirt stuffed into their mouth while being tied to a tree might have looked like a life or death situation. And may have motivated Jones' fighting instinct.

Both victims' autopsies revealed bruises around their groin. Jones' injuries were particularly severe. Delivering a hard kick in the groin is an act of violence that is very personal. You must stand face to face—smelling for at least a few seconds the other man's breath and body odor. In a street fight, a blow like this is delivered to subdue an opponent completely. When you receive it, catching your breath can take a while. There is no fighting back. Another reason to kick an opponent in the groin is to get him on the ground. With Jones seated, he could be controlled and tied to the tree. Then Jones took another heavy blow, this time to his head, fracturing it.

Jones was tall and heavyset. When provoked, he was a fighter. In his last minutes on Earth, he fought back, but not hard enough. Whoever got the best of him was tough, strong, and comfortable with extreme violence.

Photos from the murder scene show Jones' shirt tucked into his slacks which were held up with suspenders. It is not possible that a big man like Jones could fight hand to hand without his shirt coming untucked. His neat shirtfront suggests he was shot shortly after being punched and kicked. So Jones' struggle ended quickly, if not immediately after it began. That his eyeglasses were still firmly on his head, even after being struck hard enough to crack his skull, is another indication he did not fight back much. His original posture in death, which will be discussed shortly, emphasizes these points.

It is Charles Culhane's part in this story that is the most difficult to imagine. He had no business being out there. Of everyone in the park that day, he was among the most upstanding—a model citizen whose success was forged by hard work and strong character—which makes his last few moments a travesty, justice unfulfilled. This good man did not deserve what was coming.

If they killed Jones first—likely given his injuries—then Charles Culhane watched the struggle, saw the gun pressed to Jones' neck and fired. In the next instant, Charles Culhane took a brutal kick to the groin or perhaps he had already taken the blow and was seated the entire time, willing to take his chances of being tied to a tree when the fight broke out next to him.

Once they shot Jones, Culhane's fate was sealed. The same gun touched his neck, long enough to discharge. There would be no witnesses.

Jones and Culhane's treatment suggests an animosity that was greater than most stranger on stranger homicides.[11] What about these two ordinary-looking businessmen touring the park provoked the terrible beating they took before being shot in the head? What motivated two murders that likely started as a carjacking?

Seventy years later, the brutality is still appalling. What could be worse? That the perpetrators got away with it. The sudden, awful violence they created would never be vindicated in their lifetimes.

Now that we have answered the question of what happened to these men in death, let's take a moment to discuss who they were in life.

---

11 Timrots A.D. and Rand, M.R. "Violent Crime by Strangers and Nonstrangers" Bureau of Justice Statistics, 1987

3 | The Missing Men and Their Friend

Charles Patrick Culhane Senior—Top Executive, Family Man

Charles Culhane had been employed by General Motors, specifically United Motor Service, since 1935, and his loyalty had been rewarded. He climbed the corporate ladder steadily at UMS. In May 1951, he was promoted to General Sales Manager, responsible for UMS sales across the country. At the time, Delco batteries and AC Spark Plugs were household names, widely advertised in the burgeoning entertainment technology called television.

The year before he died, Culhane earned a salary of $18,000 plus bonuses and $35,000 in General Motors stock. He was what people in corporate America used to refer to as "a very big man." One of the biggest fish in the pond at UMS and General Motors. Given his status, it is difficult to figure out how he got mixed up in a random double murder two thousand miles from his plush office in Detroit.

He was about the least likely individual in 1952 to wind up that way. Yet he did.

Did Culhane engage in risky behavior outside of work? Was he the type of guy who invited trouble when he wasn't in the office? Was there anything about Charles Culhane's life that might have predicted his outcome?

The FBI interviewed many of Culhane's colleagues, a few superiors, and office staff looking for anyone or anything at his workplace connected to his murder. They followed up each rumor and morsel of office gossip. What they found was that Culhane was a well-respected professional who was dedicated and even-tempered to a fault. One colleague went so far as to call Culhane "stone faced." Another said he had "no close friends" at work. This may have contributed to a degree of resentment and professional envy. He had risen from middle management to the highest echelon at GM in a relatively short time. The FBI interviewed a few who were candid in their dislike.

While Charles Culhane was not described as a particularly warm individual, at least at work, no one harbored any desire to kill him for it. Or knew of anyone that might feel that way. Neither did any of the blue-collar types he dealt with in labor negotiations wish to kill him. They described him as tough and professional, but not underhanded in a way that might have created enemies.

Of everyone Culhane worked with, the one who most caught the FBI's attention was his personal secretary, Catherine Braunsdorf. Besides knowing his work relationships, she knew his private business too—including how much money Culhane had with him the day he flew to Spokane. According to her, before leaving, Culhane withdrew one hundred and fifty dollars in cash from his personal account.

Naturally, the bureau looked into the possibility that Culhane and his secretary might have a more complicated, romantic relationship, but Culhane was squeaky clean. When the bureau looked into Braunsdorf's personal life, however, they discovered a complex family drama that involved her spouse.

Braunsdorf's husband sold pianos and played bass viol in the Detroit Symphony Orchestra. The file describes his daughter by a previous marriage as being "mentally deficient." One day, Eugene Braunsdorf "fatally shot" her in order to "relieve her suffering." He was charged with manslaughter and the case went to trial. Eugene Braunsdorf was eventually found guilty, but given a suspended sentence. The court concluded that Braunsdorf was "innocent by reason of insanity." On May 23, 1950, the *Detroit Free-Press* ran the front page headline, "Father Cleared in Mercy Killing."

It must have occurred to the agent investigating this that anyone crazy enough to shoot his daughter might contemplate killing his wife's boss—if she were sleeping with him. But she wasn't. Culhane wasn't that type of boss. There is no connection between the Braunsdorf family tragedy and Charles Culhane's untimely death.

Though unintentional, the FBI renders Mrs. Braunsdorf colorfully. She shares a lot of opinions about her former boss, but the most intriguing was her characterization of the petty squabbles and jealousies around the office while Culhane was in charge. She told the FBI about her coworkers' feelings toward her boss and even speculated who might want to kill him and why. The FBI file describes her theory.

> The murders were not the "result of a bona fide robbery". She was of this impression from information

she had obtained from newspaper articles pertaining to the murders. She stated that she had learned that there were expensive items belonging to both victims left in the victims' automobile after they had been killed. She stated that it was the general consensus of the clerical and stenographical personnel as well as her own opinion that the motive must have been a "company job". She stated that she was unable to furnish any information that would specifically indicate her feelings other than that Mr. CULHANE was disliked by IRA KENNEDY due to the fact that Mr CULHANE had been appointed General Sales Manager in preference to Mr KENNEDY.

FBI File Vol. 7 p. 155

One area where Charles Culhane's wife and his secretary agreed was that West Coast man Ira Kennedy harbored some resentment. He did not appreciate his boss' rapid ascendance at UMS, they said. Moreover, Culhane had recently criticized Kennedy's office for excessive charges to the company credit account.

Kennedy was interviewed about the murders and his potential involvement in them. Kennedy had an alibi, of course. He was in San Francisco the day of the murders at the UMS office. The idea that Kennedy had hired a hitman to follow Culhane to Klamath Falls to kill him and another innocent person while touring Crater Lake was too farfetched. Plus, Al Jones was a friend of Kennedy's. It did not add up.

Many other details eliminated Kennedy as a suspect. Frank Eberlein called him at home the night of the disappearance. Kennedy said he had known Culhane for many years and considered him a friend. Further, he added that he was not passed over for the promotion Culhane received. Kennedy said he declined to take the job because he enjoyed living in San Francisco, and didn't want to move to Detroit.

The Missing Men and Their Friend

The only known disagreement between Culhane and Kennedy was about travel expenses, which Culhane brought to the attention of other managers in Detroit. Hardly the kind of rift that causes one top executive to kill another. Kennedy did not succeed Culhane as General Sales Manager at UMS and retired two years later.

Culhane grew up in the Midwest with two brothers and four sisters. Eventually, five of them moved to Chicago. Charles married Irene LaFond in 1929. They had two sons, Charles Jr. and David, ages 23 and 21 when their father died. The family resided outside Detroit on West Outer Drive near Highland Park—a modest home of 1,100 square feet. A coworker said that his family was his hobby. Outside of work, it was his only other activity. He didn't play poker, go to church, enjoy gardening—none of that. He enjoyed being home with his family, but work and travel took most of his time. He walked that line professionally where a man must be away from the family he loves in order to make them as comfortable as possible. This dedication to his job and the travel it required may have created a void in his family life, according to the file.

> Upon removal of the family to Detroit, the father had been away from home a great deal of the time due to job responsibility as Sales Manager at various levels within the organization. They estimated their father to be away from home at least half the time. For that reason, they were not too closely acquainted with him.

FBI file Vol. 2, p. 236

After their father's death, both sons pursued careers in journalism. David Culhane was the *Baltimore Sun* Bureau Chief in London from 1960 to 1966. His newspaper career must have taught him a great deal because he left it for another very high profile position. In 1967 until his retirement in the 1980s, he worked for CBS News, the gold standard for TV news at the time. During his tenure there, he was a frequent correspondent on the *CBS Evening News with Walter Cronkite*—later with Dan Rather. In a career full of notable assignments, David Culhane is perhaps best remembered for his work on *Sunday Morning with Charles Kuralt*, segments of which still find their way into journalism curricula today, including his Emmy-winning piece on VietNam veterans. These are the sort of accomplishments any son and father would enjoy sharing, but that pleasure was denied them when their dad was murdered. According to his son Philip Culhane, David is now ninety-two years old and lives in Larchmont, New York.

Charles Culhane's other son, Charles Jr., has since passed away.

The FBI described Irene Culhane's condition following the murders as "prostrated with grief." She was unable to be interviewed for months. This made investigation into her husband difficult. Motivated to find out all they could and as soon as possible, the FBI derived most of their personal information from Culhane's sons. David and Charles Jr. tried as best they could to recall and describe the personal effects their father had on him the day he died, like his wallet, watch, and shoes. The sons' desire to assist the investigation while their mother was convalescing made a favorable impression on agents. Their conduct and description of their father was consistent with everything else the FBI learned in the weeks following the murders. Charles Culhane Senior loved his family and was respected and loved in return. His attitude and reputation at work was above reproach. There was no reason anyone would want to kill him.

A few months later, Irene was well enough to be interviewed about her husband. His life insurance and other personal finances came to light then, but revealed nothing more than a man who had looked after his family, even from the grave.

Six years later, Irene wanted to participate further and asked to see the FBI's roster of visitors in Crater Lake National Park the day her husband was killed. Irene made a startling recognition that seemed significant at the time. From the list, she identified two people whom she knew personally that were present in the park on July 19th. It seemed an intriguing clue—something that might turn the case in a new direction, which it desperately needed in 1958. The FBI reached out to these acquaintances of the Culhanes who were at Crater Lake the day Charles died. It was confirmed that their presence was merely a coincidence.

Her husband's death negatively affected Irene Culhane's life in many ways. Active in her church, she naturally sought solace there after becoming a widow. Unfortunately, her church regarded her in a less benevolent light because of the violent and criminal way Charles had died. Though she had nothing to do with it, the episode had left a stain on Mrs. Culhane's character in the eyes of her parish. She sought to attend a new church to practice her faith, but leadership there did not welcome her there either. In a personal letter to FBI Director J. Edgar Hoover, she asked for official clearance in the case. On the face of it, this would seem like a good opportunity for the bureau to do something nice for the widow of a man whose murder they had not solved, and looked like they would never solve. However, Hoover would not officially clear Irene Culhane in the case at that time, citing protocol.

Outside of her family, no one knows how she felt about the investigation into her husband's death, which was effectively dropped after 1967. Irene LaFond Culhane died on February 19, 1979.

There is one item in the file that stands out against Charles Culhane's quiet family life and busy career. He may have had a kind of premonition about the end of his life. Catherine Braunsdorf recalled something her boss told her the day before his final plane trip that in retrospect sounds foreshadowing.

He mentioned casually that he had a feeling that something had been left undone.... He felt possibly that he should not go on this trip inasmuch as some work was not taken care of which should have been. In the succeeding week MRS. BRAUNSDORF stated she did not come across anything which he had not handled.

FBI File Vol. 2 p. 249

Albert Marston Jones—Successful Traveling Salesman

Between Jones and Culhane, Jones had a more colorful history and personal life. As his marriage dissolved and he became divorced, he courted a number of girlfriends. He also had disagreements with a few men over the years. The FBI looked into all these associations for anyone with a possible motive to kill Jones, so he fills out considerably more space in the FBI file than Culhane. Jones' bio includes more than twenty interviews with friends, two former enemies, girlfriends, business associates, a bitter ex-wife, and a grieving widow.

How different Jones was from his boss is exemplified by an ex-girlfriend he met at Bimbo's 365 Club.[12] She was a swimmer in the "fishbowl" at the restaurant's original location on Market Street in San Francisco. The fishbowl was a special feature above the bar at

12 Established in 1931, it is one of the oldest and most famous drinking establishments in the city. It moved once—to its present location at 1025 Columbus Avenue.

Bimbo's. Around a sunken fish tank, mirrors were creatively placed which made the girls appear naked as they swam. This intriguing display assured a bar full of male patrons, and it was a frequent hangout of the soon to be divorced man-about-town, Albert Jones. Jones and his fishbowl girlfriend only went out a few times; none of his friends could recall her name. The agent who pulled the long straw and went to Bimbo's to inquire about her identity came up empty. In the file, he wrote about the failed attempt with disappointment. But did he really think a semi-nude barmaid would be of use solving a complex double murder four hundred miles away? If nothing else, it demonstrates how little progress was being made into areas that might solve the case.

In San Francisco, Jones was a sophisticated bon vivant—an epicurean who patronized the best restaurants in the city. If he enjoyed his meal, he would call the chef over, compliment his culinary talent, and tip him five bucks.

Albert Jones was married twice, first to Alice Jones whom he married on New Year's Eve, 1919. Early in their marriage, the Joneses had a son who was born with spinal meningitis and died two years later. Later, they had a daughter named Virginia—later Virginia Jones Cota. Albert and Alice divorced in 1950. In her interview with the FBI, she recalled their marital discord with elaboration that was helpful at the time. In the divorce decree, the reason for their split after thirty-one years was Albert's "extreme cruelty" or infidelity. Before she would grant him the divorce, Alice insisted Jones give her a $20,000 life insurance policy naming her sole beneficiary. Having already met his second wife, Betty, and wishing a new life for themselves, Jones complied. This generous life insurance policy, likely with a double indemnity payout for accidental death, caught the attention of everyone who knew about it. The FBI looked into it for anything underhanded, but it turned out to be another sad coincidence. Jones' hefty insurance claim did not figure as a motive in the investigation—just an unforeseen windfall for the ex-wife with whom he'd shared most of his life and a surviving child. He had also considered his current wife in the event of death. Jones had a policy in Betty's name for $5,000.

Jones remarried the same year Alice divorced him. He met his new wife at the office, working the UMS switchboards in Berkeley. After they were married and living together on Gill Drive in Concord, he often remarked how happy he was with his new wife, Crilla, whom everyone called Betty. The FBI report concluded she had nothing to do with the events of July 19, 1952. Her coworkers described her as "a pleasant, smart woman."

Albert and Betty enjoyed traveling together on his regular business excursions around California and southern Oregon, including Crater Lake on several occasions. In fact, the Joneses were in Klamath Falls less than two weeks before Albert was killed. They had dinner with Jack Vaughn and his wife on Tuesday July 8th. Two days later, they drove to Medford. Betty did not indicate if, that day, they took highway 62 through Crater Lake National Park or the more direct route via highway 140. At Jones' funeral, Betty told an attendee that she and her husband had visited the overlook before; when she drove up to be present during the investigation, she was familiar with the place already. That must have been very strange.

Betty described Jones to Special Agent Linehan at Frank Eberlein's house the day after the bodies were recovered. Among his personal effects, she identified his shoes, which Linehan had brought that day after retrieving them from the crime scene. Recounting her husband's character, Betty told Linehan of several occasions when Albert would enter a drinking establishment and buy a round for the house. Besides being a cheerful good-fellow, she said her husband could be a bit of a showoff. While they were courting, she had seen him flash money around, peeling five spots off a roll. Agents were left to conjecture whether or not this tendency might have attracted the wrong attention on July 18th or the day he died.

Investigators also became interested in two occasions when Jones was out drinking and fought with another bar patron. Several people interviewed in the file noted that whenever Jones had too much alcohol, he could be both overly friendly and easily provoked.

One of these bar fights occurred in Klamath Falls two years before, but was mostly a shouting and shoving match. John Vaughn was present and described it as small-town stuff. He knew the man Jones scuffled with and volunteered his name to the bureau who immediately located and questioned him. Anthony Pasaretti must have wondered why the officers were making a federal case out of a little bar fight. Naturally, Pasaretti said that Jones had started it, which Vaughn corroborated.

Suggesting Pasaretti had waited two years to kill Jones for poking him in the eye was grasping at straws, but the FBI's case was weak. They had little evidence, no suspects, and no good leads. That's why an argument in a bar two years before had any significance. There was nothing else to go on.

Regarding Jones' two bar fights: A lot of men in their youth or early middle age have this aggressive streak. They go to bars, become slightly inebriated, and get into a scuffle. It's not admirable behavior— but it isn't against the law, if no one gets hurt. And his infidelities? Fooling around outside an unhappy marriage isn't unusual either, or against the law.

What drew the bureau's attention was his inclination to fight if he was challenged. Had it contributed to the circumstances of his death and his boss', Charles Culhane?

That he would not back down, if he or someone he knew were challenged, is unusual for a man in his fifties. This kind of attitude usually subsides before middle age. But not with Jones, apparently. His current wife, Betty, had only known him for a few years. Her first interview in the FBI Report leaves no doubt that his tendency to physically defend himself or others was deep-seated.

> She explained that after she ascertained that her
> husband had received a fractured skull that the picture
> had possibly become clearer to her. She explained
> her husband is a powerful man she knows would not
> stand by and see some other person or persons attack
> CULHANE but would rather would throw discretion to
> the wind and do what he could to protect CULHANE.
>
> *FBI File Vol. 1, p. 290*

It's an odd phrase to describe a man fighting for his life as one who would "throw discretion to the wind." Jones' fighting instinct inspired much conjecture in the file and there is a lot of physical evidence from the murder scene that suggests Jones fought back. His autopsy showed heavy bruising in the groin area. He also sustained a deep fracture to his head separate from the gunshot that killed him.

In contrast to his personal life, Jones' professional life was exemplary. In all his business dealings, he exhibited a high standard. He was honest and hardworking.

Jones was born in Victoria, British Columbia. Later, he became a U.S. citizen after his father moved the family to Bellingham, Washington. Early in his career, Jones had a tool company that went bankrupt. According to a former partner, he "sold almost all of his personal belongings and eventually paid back all of his debts."

He began working for United Motor Service in Seattle in 1933 before moving to the Zone Office in San Francisco in 1935. While they lived in San Francisco, Jones and his wife Alice socialized with Floyd Arthur "Bill" Boss who was also employed at UMS. This was when Jones experienced turbulence in his marriage.

Jones wrote Boss a letter of recommendation for a job in Honolulu, which Boss accepted in 1940. Sometime after that, the two men had a severe falling out. Boss went out of his way to tell the

FBI some unflattering things about Jones' behavior while married. Boss was candid that Jones fraternized with other women and that he, Boss, sometimes provided Jones' alibi for the late nights. According to Boss, Jones resented his knowledge of the infidelities. This soured their friendship. Of all the people interviewed about Jones, only Boss and Jones' ex-wife spoke negatively of him. Traveling salesmen had a reputation in those days of meeting women on the road and engaging in relations outside of marriage. It was a popular stereotype of the day, and, according to Alice Jones and Bill Boss, this cliche' may have described Albert Jones—at least, for part of his first marriage.

Besides the resentful, personal recriminations that came out about Jones, another personality trait of his came to light. It was not a failing, but the sort of behavior some find admirable. It was described by yet another ex-girlfriend and another man who was a friend of Jones and liked him. They both agreed that Albert Jones did not like to get pushed around. An occasional drinking partner named Reginald Pitzer said if either Jones or his friends were challenged, he would "fight like a tiger." Another friend said almost the exact same thing about Jones—that he "would not back down if challenged."

Buried inside the stories of Jones and Culhane are questions about their last day that were never adequately understood, then forgotten about altogether. In those last few hours together before arriving at the park, what was their attitude toward each other? Though they had at least one close business associate in common (Kennedy), they were complete strangers to each other before they met on Friday at the Wi-Ne-Ma Hotel. Because their names frequently appear together in all the newspaper accounts and the FBI file, readers assume a familiarity that did not exist.

What was Jones' attitude toward his boss? Might it in any way have contributed to Jones's aggressiveness during the kidnapping and lead to their demise? Jones must have felt that if he made a good impression on Culhane, it might help him professionally. Perhaps he might gain some advantage and, with Culhane's approval, move onto a faster career track. Jones's career track suggested he was ambitious.

Could a desire to impress or protect his boss have caused him to behave more aggressively during the kidnapping and robbery? The skull fracture revealed that Jones was beaten down severely. The only blow Culhane received was the one that killed him. If Jones hadn't been with his boss, would he have acted as aggressively?

❦

In 2002, the daughter of Virginia Jones Cota, Alice Simms, investigated her grandfather's murder and wrote about it in a research paper entitled "Two Men Cruelly Gagged, Robbed, Killed… Who Did It?.... Why?" As the title indicates, neither Alice Simms nor her mother felt there was closure around the untimely death of the family patriarch.

Simms' paper is largely concerned with her theories—developed over her lifetime, through family experience, and compiled after an investigation she conducted. She also had access to the same FBI report that this book is based on. It's not clear if she got all 2,137 pages. Nevertheless, her conclusions were emphatic.

In her eight-page report, she "strongly felt" one suspect in particular was responsible for her grandfather's death. He was the same man the bureau investigated for years and takes up large sections of volumes four through seven in the FBI file. His name was Jack Santo. Simms felt strongly enough about his culpability to end her report accusing him of the murder of her grandfather and his boss, Charles Culhane.

Frank Eberlein's Critical Crime Scene Observation

Besides the backgrounds of the two missing men and how they died, there is a third character who shapes our understanding of the case. Mostly this is because Frank Eberlein knew so many details leading up to the disappearance and because of his close relationship to Jones. He knew more than any other single person about what happened. Owing to his extreme closeness to the event and one of the men who died, he might also be considered a victim.

Like his friend Albert Jones, Frank Eberlein worked hard to promote himself in business while improving his family's situation. Early in his career, Eberlein and a partner pooled $700 to purchase enough inventory to open a parts shop, specializing in radiators and electrical repairs. The operation at 11th and Main in downtown Klamath Falls expanded constantly. Specialized Service grew to become one of the largest car parts distributors in southern Oregon.

It is through his business dealings with United Motor Service that Eberlein and Jones came to be friends. The men had much in common: both were self-made, sold auto parts, and enjoyed the outdoors. Their relationship grew beyond business. They knew each other's families and, whenever they could, enjoyed fly fishing rivers and streams around the Klamath Basin.

Frank Eberlein was a substantial person in Klamath Falls with an impeccable reputation. Besides his skill in business, he was trustworthy, loyal to a fault, smart as hell, and an expert fly fisherman. If you counted yourself a friend of his, like Al Jones, you likely possessed some of these qualities yourself.

Jones thought enough of his friend Culhane that, when one of United Motor Service's top executives flew in from Detroit for business, he wanted Culhane to meet Eberlein. It was, sadly, the first and last time they would ever meet. All of these last few interactions left an impression on Frank, made indelible by having to recount them constantly for the various law enforcement agencies involved. The memory that lasted and troubled him most was the loss of his friendship with Al Jones.

Among the first people Chief Ranger Hallock notified was Frank Eberlein. He came with Ira Kennedy and was the first person Hallock took to the scene, along with Sheriff "Red" Britton.

Of all the county officials, police officers, and G-men active in the search, the only civilian to write about it at length was Frank Eberlein. He authored a three-page, single space account that is consistent with the others, except for one significant difference. Frank Eberlein disagreed completely about the original body positions of the deceased. In all three official accounts, both men were described as lying flat on their backs. Frank Eberlein witnessed something alarmingly different. In fact, neither victim was originally on his back.

> Nothing had been disturbed and no one was permitted past the ribbon barrier… Each body was near a small tree a foot less in diameter about fifteen feet apart. Albert Jones was in a sitting position, hunched forward but still upright with a bullet hole in the rear center of his head… The body of Charles Culhane was sprawled on the ground, lying partly turned sideways… against a tree.
>
> *Frank Eberlein*
> *The Crater Lake Murders of July, 1952*

The awkward, upended body positions of Jones and Culhane gave each the appearance of having just arrived there—unsettling, to say the least. Despite the vast discrepancy between the official reports and Frank Eberlein's, his account of the original scene has never been challenged. According to him, Willard Linehan and/or the other two agents who drove down that day from the Portland Field Office moved the bodies.

> "No bodies were moved until the F.B.I. men arrived."

> *Frank Eberlein*
> *The Crater Lake Murders of July, 1952*

At least some members of the bureau witnessed the deceased in their original state, according to Eberlein. Yet this key piece of information about the bodies did not make it into Agent Linehan's report or any other. Whether or not the Oregon State Police saw the original scene is not known. In his report, Trooper Pvt. Lawrence Bergmann described both men as lying flat on their backs.

Years later, Frank Eberlein explained the discrepancy in a letter to Southern Oregon University student Cheryl Ousey for her thesis.

> Some of the pictures may appear to differ from the written details because the pictures were taken after the bodies were moved. I was there before the F.B.I. or the photographer-reporter, had at least ½ hour to view the undisturbed situation while awaiting their arrival.

> *Frank Eberlein to Cheryl Ousey, 2001*

Shortly after Eberlein was allowed in, Jones and Culhane were laid out flat on their backs under the big fir tree. From his original sitting position, Al Jones was laid down with a decomposing tree limb pushing up slightly under his shoulders. Arms at his side, his right hand came to rest palm down. The knuckle of his pinkie finger was almost touching a ten-inch diameter lodgepole pine. He appeared in a state of repose.

Investigators moved Charles Culhane slightly to the side of the tree that he was originally lying sideways against. In his second state, he was wedged against the small lodgepole. The tree contacted him at his waist and right elbow. His forearm lay across his stomach, giving him the appearance of having just fallen asleep.

In these new positions, the shocking nature of how the men had fallen after being shot was erased. No longer did the scene reflect sudden, deadly violence. On their backs after being repositioned, the corpses appeared at rest, without much harm or terror inflicted.

The families of Albert Jones and Charles Culhane mourned deeply the sudden loss of their beloved husbands, fathers, and siblings. In the background, Frank Eberlein lost something substantial by the overlook that Saturday, but he never got a sympathy card or any closure. He had to live the rest of his life having witnessed and knowing about some of the most disturbing aspects of this bloody, double murder.

> To see his friend with a bullet hole in his head left
> an impact on my Dad. He didn't want to talk about it.
>
> *Alan Eberlein*
> *Interview, March 31, 2020*

From the outset, Eberlein was frustrated at the way law enforcement investigated the murders. He was dismayed when he saw the "FBI men," as he referred to them, moving the bodies before the scene was photographed.

But why were they moved? This was before crime scene preservation techniques were used that we take for granted today. No one intentionally wanted to remove vital clues, or make the case more difficult to solve. In all likelihood, the motivation to move the bodies came out of pure practicality. Changing the original death scene made it easier to work around psychologically, because it was less disturbing. Also, it presented photographs that were easier to view. The family would have appreciated this if they ever saw the pictures in a newspaper. The rearrangement of bodies this way rarely occurs at crime scenes in the 21st century.

The Chicago Police Department in the late 1940s began using crime scene techniques we'd recognize today—evidence collection, preserving a scene, photographing it in the original state, and so on. When these techniques helped convict criminals, other large urban police departments adopted them. In the early 1950s, the University of California (Berkeley) became the first college to offer a bachelor's degree in criminology. It would take a few years for the burgeoning science to filter down to smaller police and sheriff's departments. This included remote areas of the West.

Because all the official reports describing the murder scene wrote that the men died on their backs, there was never any official consideration of how they died based on their original positions, each of which tells a story.

Jones died seated—with his legs out in front and his torso leaning forward. It is unlikely, impossible even, for him to have been shot standing up and then expire in this position. He had to be seated when he was shot. Also, he had to be wearing his shoes in these last moments then had them removed after he died because his socks were clean. It is possible his hands were tied behind his back when he was shot. If his hands were free in those last moments, he would have pulled at his gag

Frank Eberlein

82

which was found firmly in place. When his killers removed Jones' shoes, the jackpine probably supported his back. Otherwise, he would have fallen backwards. It makes sense that Jones had his hands tied behind the jack pine the entire time—then was cut loose after having his shoes removed. This explains why his gag was in place, the absence of any debris on his socks, and his being found in a seated position with his legs stretched out in front of him, toddler-like.

Eberlein believed Culhane might have been standing with his hands free when he was shot.

> Culhane was wearing a white dress shirt and the bleeding pattern indicated he was standing with his right arm raised with his hand over his heart until he fell to the ground.
>
> *Frank Eberlein*
> *The Crater Lake Murders of July, 1952*

There are no bleeding patterns on Jones in the crime scene photos that might confirm or discredit this observation. Once again, we have to accept the redoubtable Eberlein at face value.

If he were not standing, there is another explanation how blood got on Culhane's right arm. When he was shot below his right ear in the back of his jaw, the bullet exited on the left side of his neck. If he were tied with his hands behind him, his arms and shirt sleeves were directly below the back of his head and neck. Blood may have fallen on his shirt sleeve in this position.

In the aftermath of the murders, Frank made himself available to anyone who needed information or help concerning the murders: the Federal Bureau of Investigation, the Oregon State Police, the National Park Service, local newspapers—even Jones' widow, Betty, who stayed with the Eberleins while they made preparations to return her husband's body to the Bay Area for burial. Frank had a strong

WARNING: GRAPHIC IMAGE

Even after being moved, each victim is lying against a ten-inch diameter lodgepole pine.
Courtesy: OSP

sense of duty to Jones. He wanted to know who killed his friend. But justice never came.

If a death or tragic incident involves a member of your own family, there's a word for it: grief. Though difficult, it is something that people can wrap their minds and emotions around. There's an appropriate reaction from people you know—condolences, sympathy cards, and heartfelt wishes.

It's different when you see your friend murdered. The reaction of people is not the same. They talk about it openly and ask questions. It is the kind of idle, distasteful behavior that families of the deceased are usually spared. Frank Eberlein would not have been able to avoid it. Customers at Specialized Service inquired about the murders and Frank's experience for many weeks after—wanting firsthand information about what happened and what the murder scene looked like. That mental snapshot would never be deleted from his memory.

Besides his family, Eberlein's other refuge from this traumatic episode was his cabin at Union Creek. Unfortunately, getting there required driving west on highway 62 along Annie Creek Canyon, passing by the overlook and adjacent woods. The Eberleins still own the cabin. Now Alan, his brother, and their families drive by the overlook whenever they visit Union Creek to fish and relax on the weekends and vacation. Do they think about the events of July 1952 when they drive by? Of course they do.

4 | The Autopsies

Albert Jones' Autopsy

The bodies of Albert Jones and Charles Culhane were removed from the park around seven o'clock that Monday night and driven to Ward's Funeral Home in Klamath Falls. By nine o'clock, Klamath County Medical Examiner Dr. George Adler began his examination, starting with Jones. The report starts by describing what the doctor observed in the woods that afternoon.

> There was no evidence of struggle.... The clothing in general was hardly disarranged.... Jones was still wearing his glasses and in his stocking feet, the soles of which were not soiled or torn.

> *Dr. George Adler*
> *Autopsy July 30, 1952*

Next, Adler described the bullet wound. Its entrance was two inches left of Jones' backbone and even with his left earlobe. The "puncture" was a quarter inch wide, surrounded by a smaller, black ring. The hair on his neck just outside the black ring was not burned, indicating the gun rested there when it discharged.

There was no exit wound—a conundrum that the Medical Examiner would have to answer. Where had the bullet come to rest? The next day, Adler moved Jones to Klamath Valley Hospital where an X-ray was performed. The black and white transparency displayed a bright solid object suspended above his right molar, which had cracked his tooth and stopped the bullet. Adler described how he extracted this crucial evidence.

"An incision was made along the border of the jaw and the bullet removed readily."

The bullet traveled left to right, "ranging slightly upwards." It passed through his brain stem and "completely divided it." The tiny lead slug became the first important piece of evidence in the case. It would have been Exhibit A if a suspect were ever charged and if there was a trial. Agent Willard Linehan was standing in the room with Dr. Adler during the autopsy when he collected the slug. The ammunition type was .32 ACP.[13] It was in remarkably good condition, which would be important if the murder weapon was ever found. Linehan wrote "Q3" on its flat bottom and placed it in a small container. It quickly made its way to the FBI's Ballistics Lab in Washington D.C. Forty or so other bullets were eventually compared to "Q3" by microscopic comparison. None were a match. Q3's whereabouts today are unknown.

Besides the gunshot, Jones sustained additional trauma to his head. According to Adler, Jones had his skull fractured by his right temple.

---

13 This caliber round, .32 Automatic Colt Pistol (aka .32 Auto) could be fired by either a .32 or 7.65mm semi-automatic pistol. Some revolvers shoot .32 ACP, but that is less common.

The Autopsies

> There was no connection between this fracture and other skull injuries produced by the bullet.

The blow that caused the skull fracture left an indentation in Jones' skin just under the top of his right ear where his eyeglass frame rested.

> ... other evidence of violence was seen around the right ear... Behind this ear was a deep groove that had some of the appearances of a burn... a heavy blow had been struck across the ear and the peculiar mark behind the ear was due to the driving of the earpiece of the glasses into the flesh.

> *Dr. George Adler*
> *Autopsy July 30, 1952*

What could have collided with Jones' head hard enough to leave a dent? It's difficult to imagine a fist packing that much force. A gun butt is heavy enough—even from a weapon as light as a .32. The most inexpensive .32s weigh twenty-six ounces or so unloaded, half again more with a full clip—almost two and a half pounds.

It was pretty easy to guess how long the men had lay there in the woods before arriving on Dr. Adler's autopsy table, but Medical Examiners try to avoid guessing, especially in reports they know the Federal Bureau of Investigation will scrutinize. Adler wrote he felt "with a high degree of accuracy" that Jones had been in the woods for 36 to 48 hours. Then he noticed something odd in Jones' groin area.

Across the left side of the scrotum was an abrasion about two inches long and about one quarter of an inch in width. There was little evidence of hemorrhage or reaction around the wound and it may well have been inflicted at the time or [*sic*] death or immediatley [*sic*] thereafter.

Dr. George Adler
Autopsy July 30, 1952

Even though the skin abrasion did not show a lot of bleeding, Jones' scrotum was badly bruised ("very ecchymotic"). Without putting too fine a point on it, whoever kicked Jones in the groin did not hold back. Reflexively, Jones bent over when he got kicked or perhaps fell on the ground.

Among the other findings, there was a small hole in the front of Jones' pants. The Medical Examiner did not elaborate, but there is reference to the hole and the wound in the OSP report.

There was a small round hole in the front of Jones's slacks and also through the underwear shorts and a small blood stain to indicate that probably the victim stumbled or fell against a twig which made the puncture that caused the bruise and contusion on the left testicle.

Trooper E.G. Bergmann
Officer's Report

How did Jones get a hole in his slacks that produced a blood stain? Did it occur during or separate from the kick to his groin? Neither the Medical Examiner's autopsy nor the OSP report lend much clarity.

Besides the puncture/contusion to his groin, Jones also sustained a few fresh, minor abrasions on his hands and one or two "very minor" scrapes on his shin above the ankle. The hand abrasions were described as "not defensive." The "few minor abrasions... on Jones' hands" might have been sustained in the process of being tied to the tree. He may even have been tied to the tree for a short time. Details in the autopsy suggest this possibility—though there is no direct evidence of it, like ligature marks on the wrist. (That the men may have been briefly tied up will be discussed when we consider their original positions in death in Section Two of this book.)

Charles Culhane's Autopsy

While not your average postmortem examination, Charles Culhane's autopsy was more straightforward than Jones'. There were also several similarities. The first was the coroner's recognition that the victim showed no outward signs of struggle. Adler seemed to be going out of his way to confirm what the scene photographs suggest and the FBI also stated: Jones and Culhane did not die violently. There was "... no evidence of a scuffle, the clothing of the deceased was disturbed but little."

Adler may have arrived at the scene too late to see the bodies in their first state, which looked like both men died in a sudden, violent rampage. The way they were laid out, after the FBI arrived and moved them, gave the deceased an appearance of quiet repose, quite different from their original positions. It sounds like there was some effort to minimize the violence and terror that took place—perhaps to spare the families further grief. Alternatively, it may have been unintentional, just a natural, human response to try to minimize something awful.

After these visual observations, Dr. Adler put his hands on Culhane's face and worked his finger around the gag in Culhane's mouth, which was still tied in place.

> ... the throat was not obstructed by the gag. There
> was no obstruction to nasal breathing. The man was
> able to get sufficient air through the nose to prevent
> suffocation.
>
> *Dr. George Adler*
> *Autopsy July 30, 1952*

This suggests that if Jones and Culhane had lived through the beating and allowed themselves to be tied to the trees, they might not have suffocated from the gags. They also would not have died of exposure immediately. That Friday's and Saturday's nights were cold at that elevation, but not freezing. If they hadn't been shot, Jones and Culhane might have lived long enough to be found alive by searchers.

Charles Culhane was shot in his right cheek one inch behind the corner of his mouth. The bullet exploded through the teeth in his lower jaw and exited "the back of the neck." The bullet was never found and may still be somewhere in the woods. Dr Adler determined that he "died instantly."

The gun was pressed against Culhane's cheek when it fired and exited in exactly the same spot where the bullet entered Jones' neck: two inches left of his spine and even with his left earlobe. Although they go in an opposite direction, right to left for Culhane and vice versa for Jones, the bullet paths are on almost the same line; the shot that killed Jones angled slightly upward in its path, while Culhane's traveled nearly horizontal. The similarities show the gunman was not struggling with the victims. He had time to place the gun to the back of each victim's head before he shot them. Neither was his aim arbitrary or accidental. He knew that by severing the victims' spines, they would be immediately subdued. Like so many other aspects of the crime, there was thought and method in its execution.

Jones and Culhane were each shot in an almost exactly similar way, suggesting strongly that one person shot both men. The shooter seemed to know that firing a bullet between a human's ear and spine would kill them instantly. If he hadn't any experience killing humans this way, which is likely, where did he gain this knowledge about how to place a bullet to put down a living thing with one shot from a relatively small caliber firearm? In what type of occupation or endeavor does one learn how to subdue and kill an animal at short range? An experienced hunter or trapper might. Also, ranch work requires that animals be put down occasionally.

There's a reason why the perpetrator is usually referred to in the plural, even though autopsy evidence suggests a single individual shot both victims. This was the most popular theory at the time. Within the FBI file, several agents noted in their reports the strong likelihood that at least two men carried out the crime. More than four years after the murders, Portland's daily newspaper interviewed an agent from the FBI's field office about the likelihood that there were two people involved.

> It is entirely possible that one man could have committed this crime, but in all probability two or more were involved.

> **_Special Agent Joseph Santoiana_**
> **The Oregonian _October 1956_**

This same question was at the heart of the most famous murder case of the 1950s and the subject of the true crime book _In Cold Blood_ by Truman Capote. It occurred at the Clutter farm in Western Kansas, seven years after the Crater Lake murders. A prosperous farming family was shot to death by an assailant whom authorities could not connect to the crime. The Kansas Bureau of Investigation considered the possibility that one hateful, disturbed person might have killed all four members of the family. In the book, Capote described KBI investigator Alvin Dewey's quandary.

... Dewey was undecided. He still entertained a pair of opinions—or, to use his word, "concepts"—and, in reconstructing the crime had developed both a "single-killer concept" and a "double-killer concept."

Truman Capote
In Cold Blood

The Crater Lake murders share an unfortunate consonance with the case of the Clutter family—before Perry Smith and Dick Hickock came to light. How many men were involved?

Consider it both ways at Crater Lake. Could one robber with a relatively small gun force two men to march several minutes over rough ground? It's hard to imagine a brawler like Jones would allow one person to dominate both him and his boss in that setting.[14] That two men performed the kidnapping and murder makes a lot more sense.

---

14 Homicides involving multiple offenders and victims is very unusual, according to recent studies. See Bibliography. Cooper and Smith, "Homicide Trends in the United States, 1980-2008" USDOJ 2011

WARNING: GRAPHIC IMAGE

Charles Culhane, his right elbow pushed up against the jack pine. What appears to be a blood pattern on his left arm is inconsistent with his body position. Note the clean socks on both men.
Courtesy: Oregon State Police

5 | The Crime Broken Down and What It Reveals

Breaking the Crater Lake murders into distinct parts and examining each is helpful for understanding the killers' type and personality. Each says something different about the perpetrators, teasing out possible character traits.

It is possible to separate the crime into five stages, including the commission of the murders, which will be examined in a bit.

Here are the other four stages.

- The Stickup
- The Kidnapping
- The Forced March
- The Getaway

The Stickup

Hard-boiled fiction and true crime have a tendency to overlap, in story and language. One phrase quite popular in hard-boiled fiction and crime dramas in the 1940s and '50s was describing any injured party as "a victim of foul play." Nowadays, we would say "criminal activity." Lou Hallock used the more colorful term four times in his report when it was determined Jones and Culhane had met with it.

> It was decided to reinstitute the search the following morning over an enlarged area and to exploit the theory of foul play as fully as possible.
>
> **Chief Ranger Louis Hallock**
> **"Report of Murder..."**

Everything around and inside the Pontiac suggested that Albert Jones and Charles Culhane arrived at the overlook unremarkably. Their vehicle and the ground around it gave no indication of a struggle. Whatever transpired was decided without a fight—or so it appeared to everyone on Saturday. After it was ruled out that the men had neither gotten lost nor fallen into the canyon, the undisturbed state of the Pontiac began to tell a different story: its occupants were the victims of foul play, in a stickup that was not premeditated.

The perpetrators had to be comfortable with the location to attempt something so brazen and out in the open. At any moment, a carload of tourists might have stared directly at the kidnapping in progress or pulled into the turnout during it, but this did not happen. The stickup was perfectly executed. The robbers must have been familiar with the overlook, Highway 62, and its traffic flow. Some level of comfort with all these variables was necessary to pull this off.

The Crime Broken Down and What it Reveals

If there had been other tourists and vehicles at the overlook during the carjacking, there would be witnesses. Fate left Jones and Culhane by themselves above the massive gray chasm shortly after one o'clock. Then what happened?

The crime was set in motion when the kidnappers pulled up next to the Pontiac. (It's less likely the kidnappers were waiting at the overlook and Jones parked next to them.) Whether Jones and Culhane were already outside the Pontiac or seated in it, the stickup came like lightning out of the blue: unexpected, sensational, and frightening. Before they knew what hit them, they were hustled into the robbers' vehicle, subdued, and driven a short distance away from the Pontiac. We know it happened quickly because no one saw anything, and cars were driving by constantly. Like two trains running toward each other on the same track, there was something inevitable about the Pontiac and the kidnappers' car coming together at that exact moment. A minute or two later or earlier and there would have been witnesses. When that second car peeled out with Jones and Culhane inside it, the destinies of everyone inside changed forever.

Sitting by itself at the overlook with the passenger door swung open, Jones' car was a curiosity. The first local reporter to describe it said the owners "vanished into thin air"—which is a fairly good description—especially considering he never saw the Pontiac in that state. He heard it described two days later. After this bit of hyperbole, he wrote a few key details he'd gleaned from officials—including one kernel of speculation at the end.

> There is a growing theory that the two men may have left the scene in some other car. A close check of all information strongly indicates that if they did leave the canyon scenic spot by some other car, they were probably forced to do so.
>
> **Wallace Myers**
> **Klamath Falls Herald and News** *7/21/52*

The Kidnapping

Consistent with this kidnapping theory was an observation made by one of the first people at the overlook scene. John Vaughn believed he saw tire tracks directly in front of the Pontiac. It looked like a car had pulled out quickly and left impressions in the roadway. In retrospect, this sounds fairly significant—something law enforcement should have noticed and reported as well, but it does not appear in either the OSP or FBI files. Its only mention is buried in Frank Eberlein's short paper. It may be important in considering the initial interface between the robbers and the executives. Vaughn's observations suggest the robbers pulled in front of and blocked the Pontiac, then they hustled the victims into their car—probably at gunpoint to make it go quickly.

The men were driven a short distance up the road, just out of sight of the overlook and the Pontiac. How do we know this? We don't. But we know the robbers didn't waste any time by the overlook. And the area where Jones and Culhane were eventually found was straight down the hill from the turnaround just up the highway.

As soon as they drove away with the victims from the overlook, another serious crime occurred. According to current Oregon law, it began as second-degree kidnapping when Jones and Culhane were driven off against their will.[15] It rose to first degree kidnapping whenever violence first occurred.

It only took half a minute to drive up the hill and around the corner. In 2022, there is a paved turnaround and short term parking area two hundred yards uphill. This area existed in 1952, but was neither paved nor improved. Fewer tourists stopped there, then as now, because access wasn't as convenient as the overlook. Also, the overlook view is more inviting.

---

15 ORS 163.225

Once removed from their vehicle and riding with their kidnappers, Jones and Culhane were likely threatened again; warned not to try anything or risk being shot. All the perpetrators wanted was money and a gold watch or two. As soon as the traffic cleared, they pushed the two frightened executives out of the car and into a thick band of woods that lined the highway.

This was the only other moment, after the initial encounter at the overlook, that Jones and Culhane might have run or in some way foiled this kidnapping. However, they did what most of us would do with a gun at our back. They went along with it to avoid being shot.

The Forced March

Just as they were familiar with the overlook and highway traffic, the robbers had to know the woods where they brought Jones and Culhane. They knew they weren't going to encounter any more tourists, which was possible almost everywhere up the road, but not there. All four moved in unison, briskly stepping between the rocks and downed limbs, motivated by urgent, angry commands and a gun. For the two executives, fear and confusion likely mixed with hope. If they could all keep calm, they would survive. It was broad daylight in a National Park in July, not a back alley.

Both businessmen wore dress shoes and the flat leather soles probably slipped constantly on the pine needles and uneven ground. Quick stepping through the woods kept the executives off balance.

Though he'd never visited this remote area, Jones was familiar with other places in the park and was probably aware of his proximity to them: the lake, the lodge, and Park Headquarters. It is possible he was keeping his wits about him, looking for some way to save himself and his boss. Culhane, during this short walk, could not have been more out of his element. He may have been terrified.

Five minutes later and a quarter mile from the road, the group arrived at a large, unusually formed fir tree—two trees really, about three feet wide each, growing out of a single trunk. This big split fir is not what drew them to the location. They chose it because of two ten-inch-wide lodgepole pines, ten feet from each other. They were each thick enough at the base and tall enough to tie up Culhane and Jones without any chance of them freeing themselves or each other.

That the robbers selected this spot to tie two men to a tree says something about them. Just as they were familiar with the traffic flow by the overlook—and they knew there was no chance of being discovered in these woods—at least one of the robbers was comfortable being able to bind a man by his hands to a tree.

Jones and Culhane had to be scared. Neither had ever known a situation like this. Until their gags were tied, they were likely yelling and pleading, afraid for their lives. Experiencing something so frightening with an almost complete stranger—seeing naked fear in their eyes—was a terrible way to die.

Privilege and desperation collided that day in the worst possible way: Two innocent men lost their lives, while the two men responsible walked away. They left with a few hundred bucks, two wristwatches, and a pair of shoes, but their lives would never be the same. From that day forward, they were burdened with an awful secret and the pressure of keeping anyone else from knowing it. Their lives depended on it.

The Getaway

Underneath the split fir, the killers turned their backs on the bloody, gagged victims and most likely walked away as quickly as they could. Emerging from the shadows into the open woods, the killers carried key evidence linking them to the murders: the murder weapon, both men's watches, two of Albert Jones' gas cards and one pair of expensive dress shoes.

One of the great unknowns of this case is how the killers left the scene of the murders and made their getaway. They had robbed and beaten two innocent men, shot each in the back of their heads, then returned to the highway in a state of excitement and agitation. The robbery had gone completely wrong. Two men were dead. It was just a matter of time before police became involved. If the killers were found out, they and their families' lives would never be the same.

The killers had something going for them, too. Something they must have realized as soon as they got back inside their car. They were going to get away with it. Fleeing would be easy. No one had heard the gunshots or suspected anything. They had never seen their victims before that afternoon, so there was no way to connect them.

If one accepts Alan Eberlein's brush with the perpetrators while sitting in the front seat of the Pontiac, it is possible to time the killers' movements. After getting away with three hundred dollars or so, the contents of the Pontiac was another prize that might be unwrapped. Inside it, perhaps something of even greater value—more cash perhaps or jewelry—lay inside a briefcase. To the man that stole Culhane's new wingtips, the '51 Pontiac must have looked like a gleaming, green treasure box. But they could not risk being seen inside it or even near it, because it might look suspicious.

The offenders had already pulled off a kidnapping at the overlook with no problem. Grabbing anything of value inside the Pontiac would be even easier. But they would have to time it right. So they likely kept their distance—keeping a watchful eye on the Pontiac—and waited for an opportunity. The area of the turnaround was just close enough to the Pontiac through a narrow strip of woods, for them to have a lookout without risking being seen. In the meantime, other park visitors had arrived to enjoy the view—unaware that two tourists had been kidnapped from the same patch of gravel just a short time ago. Any activity at the overlook and near the Pontiac discouraged the killers from swooping in. So they waited and watched.

About an hour and a quarter after Jones and Culhane were kidnapped, the Eberleins and Jack Vaughn parked their tan pickup by the Pontiac. It was 2:25 or so. Initially, they were excited to see their friend's car—then by turns confused, anxious, and worried. This cycle took about forty-five minutes, according to Alan. After that, the two men drove the pickup back to the south gate and reported their friends missing, leaving the boy to keep an eye on things. Joe Hunt recorded the time that Eberlein and Vaughn contacted him as 4:40 pm.[16] This would have been the approximate time of Alan's encounter and the mysterious drive-by.

The overlook (OL) is the bare patch of dirt. The turnaround (TA) is the approximate area where the kidnappers took Jones and Culhane before forcing them into the woods opposite the highway.

Although the sightline is good, the turnaround is two hundred yards from the back of the overlook. It would have been difficult for the killers to realize the occupants of the tan truck, among the other tourists coming and going, were friends of the victims. When Alan slipped into the driver's seat of Jones's car to wait, the killers probably did not notice that either.

---

16 Frank Eberlein and Jack Vaughn must have spent more than an hour at the K Falls Entrance with Ranger Hunt.

The Crime Broken Down and What it Reveals

Sometime after that, the overlook cleared out. The killers saw their opportunity and quickly closed in, pulling alongside the Pontiac. They must have been surprised to see an adolescent boy behind the wheel reading, not paying attention—then they sped off in the direction of the south gate where Frank and Jack, at that moment, were speaking with Ranger Hunt.

It only took a minute or two before the nondescript coupe was at the stop sign and exit next to the booth. The driver and passenger would have noticed the tan pickup and two fishermen they had previously observed at the overlook, now speaking with a ranger. Hunt was only concerned with cars entering the park. Deep in conversation regarding their missing friends, none of them paid attention to late afternoon outgoing traffic.

As they rolled up to the stop, the perpetrators probably saw and understood this event in a way no one else could, or ever would. It is easy to imagine, the driver tapping his foot lightly on the gas as they departed. As he drove away, he would have taken one last look in the rearview mirror to see the men outside the booth getting smaller and smaller in it. Slumped in their seats, the two men likely sat up a little and took a deep breath. They had gotten away—with murder.

The stickup and kidnapping, followed by a forced march into the woods and the successful getaway, were carried out with a level of skill that says something about the men who did it. They were not discouraged by the stream of tourists and cars in the immediate vicinity. When the robbery got out of hand, they quickly dispatched Jones and Culhane before either could struggle much. They left the park without being seen. Though they probably waited several hours after killing the executives to actually drive away, they attempted to return to the Pontiac to check its contents one last time. The perpetrators knew what they were doing. They weren't scared and they probably knew they could get away with it because no one saw anything. All of it, taken together, demonstrates a degree of criminal sophistication, experience, or maturity that is different from almost all the suspects who would appear in the FBI and Oregon State Police files—virtually all of whom were small-time, twenty-something fuckups like Bill Russell.

J. Edgar in the Wild West

Something about the robbery and murders at Crater Lake seemed inconsistent with the time. IBM's UNIVAC computer was rolling out for consumer use. *I Love Lucy* was on TV. Movies were widescreen. Contrast that to the victims being marched into the woods then attempting to tie them up with a gag in their mouths. What happened out there sounds like a bygone era. Something in black and white or kinescope, not Cinerama. Stealing their shoes was the feature most out of step with the times, like something from the Gold Rush or Oregon Trail.

That the facts of the case fit a Western theme sparked the public's imagination in newspaper accounts of the murders. In 1952, America was obsessed with cowboys and Indians. *High Noon* won three Oscars that year.

Besides contributing to the crime's sensational aspects, the Wild West element is a clue to the perpetrators. The shoe stealing and attempt to tie up the victims demonstrates their mindset. They were not from the city. They weren't watching *I Love Lucy*. It is not a coincidence that elements of this crime lagged behind the times. The individual to whom all the evidence points as the shooter practiced a profession many equate with the Wild West. For many years, he worked as a ranch hand on a property not far from the murder scene.

The FBI found itself using modern scientific crime-solving techniques like ballistics and fingerprint and biochemical analysis (taken from soil at both scenes) to investigate old-fashioned road banditry. On the cusp between the Wild West and modern times, newspaper accounts also straddled that line. They could sound thoroughly contemporary.

> Two General Motors executives on a business trip to Southern Oregon were kidnapped and murdered a quarter mile from their car inside Crater Lake National Park.

Then, in the same story, use language like this.

> After two days, the men's bodies were found each with a gag stuffed in his mouth fashioned from his necktie. Before being shot, each was in the process of being tied to a tree. Both victims were found without their shoes.

The second description reads like the set-up of a Bret Harte story before the bandits are forced to cross the desert on foot. Add to it the cruel treatment of the victims and desperation all around. Was this 1852 or 1952?

This story exists simultaneously between two worlds, the Old West and Modern Day. A crusty, old sheriff in cowboy boots (Lloyd Low) had as much to say about it as the most modern, scientific crimefighter of his day (J. Edgar Hoover).

A Case Like No Other

To make any story, fiction or nonfiction, understandable, we unconsciously compare it to other stories we've heard before and look for signposts to guide us. For example...

The Crime Broken Down and What it Reveals

The killers waited inside the house for the victim to return.

A fingerprint impression lifted from the window matched the suspect.

When police made the arrest they found several items stolen from the victim's apartment.

And so on.

If we enjoy these stories in the first place, we remember pieces of them to make sense of new stories.

The problem with the story inside these pages is that most of what happened is unusual, from the stickup and robbery to the murders and getaway. Despite all the interactions between criminals and victims, there is an almost complete lack of clues connecting them—also unusual.

The coverup by the killers and those who knew or suspected them is atypical. Someone usually says something, but not in this case. The location where it happened is also weird: The entire crime occurred within a busy National Park on a Saturday in July. And the circumstances—beside being a busy tourist attraction—the kidnapping and murder took place in broad daylight. The way Jones and Culhane died and how they were found (as described by Frank Eberlein) is strange too. Anyone reading about the Crater Lake murders for the first time will have to use his or her imagination because there is no popular or familiar story that compares.

It isn't so much that a narrative must be a square peg. It could be any shape, but it is helpful when it fits a hole with a familiar shape, a story or even a fable. What we know from Little Red Riding Hood is that it's dangerous to wander alone in the woods at night. We take solace knowing that we would never do anything so careless. We enjoy scary stories we know could never happen to us.

Little Red Riding Hood is the story most similar to this narrative, superficially. Sure, the victims died in the woods, but Jones and Culhane didn't wander carelessly into them before they met the Big Bad Wolf. They were driving to a well-known fishing spot on a busy highway in the middle of summer inside a busy National Park. They didn't make any great mistake of judgment or naively trust someone they shouldn't. There is no easy corollary to help guide or comfort readers trying to understand this story.

The only conventional part of the narrative is that it's based on official documents submitted by law enforcement professionals. From here on, the plot diverts from something recognizable and is taken over by actions, players, and circumstances unlike other stories.

6 | No Clues, No Suspects, No Activity

The abandoned Pontiac and the murder scene offered few clues for the FBI. There were no fingerprints on the car. Other than one bullet and two cartridges, there was no physical evidence that could be linked to the perpetrators. There was not a single eyewitness during the crime's first two stages, the holdup and kidnapping. No one witnessed the events under the split fir either. Small wonder authorities were baffled—from the beginning and for another fifteen-plus years and beyond.

Despite the dearth of evidence, the bureau felt the killer or killers would be caught. Surely, someone would talk. The other key to solving this case lay in the way the crime was carried out and what that revealed about the triggerman and his accomplice. It was a unique calling card. The bureau knew it. Within the file, they devoted a great deal of space to detailing the components of this unusual crime. But beyond describing the stickup, kidnapping, robbery, and murder, there was little consideration given to what special skill it took to pull it off or the sort of individual that might possess it.

The field of criminal profiling did not come along until the 1970s. Before modern techniques could be applied, big federal cases were solved by an agent or team who took it on and saw it through to the end, like Special Agent Melvin Purvis who organized the sting that captured and killed John Dillinger. In the Crater Lake murders, the file suggests there was no spearpoint, but more of a local effort. Agents from the Portland Field Office pursued the case, particularly Special Agent in Charge, J. B. Poster, for the first year or so. After that, and when the case began to lose steam, other agents and names became more prominent in the file. When Jack Santo became the focus of the investigation, FBI offices and agents in California took over this new phase.

The perpetrators had little in common with Santo. Personal information about both offenders gathered from interviews with family, law enforcement records, and newspaper items suggest neither was a serial offender in his later years or would travel to commit crimes in other jurisdictions like Santo did. They seldom left the area near their home in Southern Oregon. The wide net cast by the bureau worked against their solving this extremely localized case.

Agent Linehan was the only FBI man working the case locally and his name did not appear in the file after September 1952. In hindsight, we can now know this case was solved by local investigators, but the source with the necessary information leading to this discovery would not occur for fifteen years. This source lived a few hundred miles from Crater Lake in Marion County. She initially contacted the sheriff there.

Since the late 20th century, it is not unusual for homicide cases to be solved months, years, or even decades after the original crime was committed. These late outcomes are often achieved using modern forensic techniques that rely on computers, like DNA matching. In

No Clues, No Suspects, No Activity

1952 and all the years before it, if a murder was not solved in a fairly short time, it was seldom solved—unless someone later admitted witnessing it or, after living too long with a guilty conscience, a participant confessed.

Without a witness who could describe the perpetrators or their car, there were no suspects or vehicle descriptions. The victims and their assailants were complete strangers to each other; there was no linking them through past or mutual associations. Alan Eberlein's apparent brush with the killers, as reported by his father, did not make it into the FBI file and was not a consideration. That left the fir tree and the path to it as the only places where investigators might find something linking the killers to the victims or the two scenes.

Any murder committed in the woods is inherently more difficult to solve. You don't have security cameras. There usually aren't people around. Evidence disappears into the ground or can become scattered by animals. Trees don't retain fingerprints. Pine needles cannot preserve a shoe impression.

Besides these obstacles to gathering evidence, the Crater Lake case had other issues, as well. Because the photography taken at the scene failed to record the original position of the bodies, this made bleeding patterns confusing while erasing information about the struggle.

The lack of good fingerprints on the Pontiac surprised and disappointed the FBI. The prints found on two discarded credit cards at the scene were not considered of high value; that is, it probably was not the killers who left their fingerprints on the cards. Some bloody pine needles were collected and transferred into ice cream containers and never mentioned again. There were two spent shell casings and one slug. Fortunately, the slug was in good shape and retained the distinctive lands and grooves for microscopic comparison. This was the bureau's best opportunity to solve the murders—if it could lead them to the murder weapon.

One Spent Bullet

Besides the spent bullet removed from Al Jones' jaw, two shell casings recovered at the scene were also distinct; each had specific marks around the rim where they ejected from the .32. They were labeled Q1 and Q2. Firearm experts know that a .32 caliber weapon has a European equivalent, the 7.65mm. Bullets fired from either are indistinguishable. Much time was taken to consider these three pieces of evidence: Q1, Q2 and the bullet, Q3.

Four days after the bodies were found, FBI Director J. Edgar Hoover described Q3 in a teletype message to the Special Agents in Charge at the Portland and Butte, Montana Field Offices.

> SUBMITTING TWO CARTRIDGE CASES FOUND NEAR BODIES AND BULLET FROM VICTIM JONES... BULLET FROM VICTIM JONES HAS RIFLING IMPRESSIONS FROM SIX LANDS AND GROOVES WITH RIGHT TWIST AND SIMILAR TO TYPE PRODUCED BY 7.65 MM (.32 AUTO) NO LATENTS DEVELOPED IN CARTRIDGE CASES. OTHER EXAMINATIONS REQUESTED BY PORTLAND...
>
> HOOVER

FBI file Vol. 1, p. 46

Hoover had Q3 analyzed and compared it to other bullets from .32 and 7.65 caliber weapons seized in other crimes—in 1952 and for the next several years. There was a strong belief they might come across the same gun that fired Q3 being used in another crime.

At the time of the Crater Lake murders, the science of ballistic comparison had been around for almost a hundred years. A Chicago jury in 1929 convicted several members of Al Capone's gang after seeing microscopic images of bullets fired during the St. Valentine's Day Massacre.[17] Three years later, the FBI opened the Criminology Laboratory in Washington, D.C., refining techniques in the science and strategies for its use at trials.

The analysis determined the distance between the lands and grooves.[18] Lands are the raised portion. Grooves are the indented portion between lands. Both are created when the bullet is shot through a barrel. In the manufacturing process, a broach is inserted in the barrel and drawn out, twisting it slightly to create a unique set of spiraled striations called "rifling." The striations cause a fired bullet to spin slightly while it goes down the barrel and continue spinning through the air. This rotation causes it to fly straighter and be aimed more accurately. The bullet's brass casing also acquires unique marks when it is discharged. In this case, when firing a semi-automatic .32 caliber handgun, the ejector strikes the shell and the recoil forces it through the port, ejecting it and leaving a distinct impression. (Bullets fired from revolvers leave their casings seated inside the cylinder, not ejected.)

In just the first two months after the murders, more than thirty handguns were tested—as many .32s as 7.65mms. The bureau kept up this pace for another several years. Virtually, every gun of those calibers used in the commission of a crime anywhere in the United States wound up being shipped to Washington for comparison to Q3. They all had an identical outcome: ballistics reports filed "without result."

A .32 is one of the least expensive and most common firearms—now or seventy years ago. Gun collectors covet several versions, like the Walther PPK James Bond carries in books and movies. Most .32s are ordinary and quite cheap. A used Beretta or Targa costs about $100. The gun is light, compact, and easily concealed. It is popular

---

17 Mostly, hammer indentations on the rim of shotgun shells ejected during the shootout.
18   Measured in millimeters with a comparison microscope.

with gun owners in states where it is legal to carry a concealed weapon. Professional law enforcement officers typically carry higher caliber weapons. An American-manufactured .32 is generally less expensive than a European manufactured 7.65mm, but the ammunition is interchangeable. The two bullets used in the Crater Lake murders were a brand known as "Western," which are still sold today. In most gun stores and big box retailers with a gun counter, a box of fifty .32 ACP Western cartridges costs around ten bucks today. Analyzing guns and the criminals associated with them takes up more space in the FBI file than any other subject. Apparently, the FBI thought a ballistics match was their best chance to make a case and solve the murders. As time wore on and the investigation stalled, finding the gun that fired Q3 and tracing its ownership could still make the case.

Comparing every .32 Auto or 7.65mm used in a crime to Q3 took a lot of time and effort. Consider shipping more than thirty weapons from all over the U.S. one at a time to Washington, D.C.— then taking each into a lab, firing them into a water-filled chamber, putting the spent round under a microscope, and carefully comparing it to Q3. And that happened in the first three months; they tested a lot more weapons after that. It is a testament to the thoroughness of the bureau to try to find a match for the murder weapon. In hindsight it is clear that, no matter how many guns the bureau seized and how many expert analyses they performed, unless they were seizing and testing guns from the immediate region around Crater Lake, they would never find it. In fairness, the .32 may have been destroyed or gotten rid of right after being used on Jones and Culhane in the woods. The assassin knew it was virtually the only way he could get caught. He would have been smart to dispose of it immediately.

As widely accepted theories like fingerprint analysis and carpet fiber matching have come under greater legal scrutiny in the 21st century, ballistics testing and bullet matching can also be problematic in legal settings. All these areas of forensic analysis have been spearheaded by the FBI Laboratory aka Laboratory Division of the bureau. The FBI has trained perhaps hundreds of individuals in their methods who then appear in court as experts, usually giving testimony to help the prosecution. While all these theories use scientific procedures and terminology, the scientific rigor we associate with university labs or the medical field are not applied. Unfortunately, the FBI lab and Justice Department have resisted offers from the scientific community to blind test or audit their cases. Thus, the problem persists and seems to be getting worse.[19]

Two Gold Watches

For years afterwards, the FBI tried to locate Culhane's gold Glycine wristwatch (with the matching Speidel band) and Jones' more common Hamilton. The bureau reached out to pawn shops and jewelers throughout the country to be on the lookout for the timepieces. Culhane's Swiss-made Glycine was distinctive in its features and seemingly easier to trace. It was never located.

Though not quite as expensive as his boss', Jones wore a sporty Hamilton—popular with aviators, American-manufactured with a Swiss movement. When he left his position at United Motor Service in Seattle to go to California, Jones' coworkers chipped in and bought it for him. This was the custom of the day, a proper sendoff to a valued employee and friend. It bore a personal engraving inscribed on the back, "To A.M. Jones from UMS."

On page 2,035 of the FBI file, seven years after the murders, a jeweler in Grants, New Mexico claimed he saw Jones' Hamilton wristwatch with its unique inscription. The jeweler's name was redacted, but his account is recorded.

---

19 Lander, Eric S et al "Forensic Science in Criminal Courts: Ensuring Scientific Validity in Feature-Comparison Methods" President's Council of Advisors on Science and Technology (PCAST) Sept. 2016

After reading about the murders in an FBI bulletin distributed to pawn shops and jewelers in New Mexico in 1959, the jeweler thought he remembered working on Jones' gold Hamilton. He recalled peering through his jeweler's loupe and seeing the tiny, distinctive UMS engraving. At first, he thought these initials stood for the United States Marine Corps then realized they were different. That's why, he said, he remembered repairing it. Also, he said the engraving on the back had been hidden with a leather watch band, different from Jones' original. After creating all this intrigue, neither the jeweler nor shop owner was able to find any record of the watch in their files. Given that the circular went out seven years after the murders, the bureau's timing could have been better.

The Colton Credit Card

Among the several items taken from the murder scene were a couple of gas cards snatched from Jones' wallet before the robbers tossed it in the dirt. This little detail was part of most newspaper accounts in the days and weeks after the murders. As a whole, the Crater Lake murders story, however incomplete, was sensational. It lit the public imagination for weeks afterward. This inspired private citizens with no connection to the case at all to contact the FBI, trying to be helpful. There were so few good leads, the FBI was forced to follow up any credible tip. It was all well intended, but never produced a single piece of information leading to a suspect.

One tip got everyone's attention, temporarily. It came out of Southern California less than two weeks after the murders. In the file, a teletype to FBIHQ records the moment. The urgency in the message suggests the agent who wrote it believed the perpetrators, or someone connected to them, used one of Jones' cards.

In a little town called Colton, Jones' Shell card turned up at a gas station transaction there. After this exchange, the owner said he saw the vehicle associated with the card leave in the direction of the Arizona border. He also recalled its make, model, and license plate number. This was critical information that might provide investigators with their first good lead. Clearly, the agent who took the statement and fired off the teletype felt this information could crack the case. Writing in the clipped, all caps style typical of FBI teletype messages, one senses Special Agent Carson's excitement (see Photos).

> ... SUBJ PROCEEDED EAST ON HIGHWAY NINE DRIVING CRYSLER [*sic*] TWO-DOOR SEDAN YEAR AND COLOR UNKNOWN BEARING OR LIC. ONE NINE THREE... PHOENIX ADVISE ARIZ. STATE POLICE THAT FEDERAL WARRANT HAS BEEN ISSUED TO HOLD ALL SUBJECTS...

FBI TELETYPE August 3, 1952
SA Carson

Among the jargon, abbreviations, and awkward conjunctions specific to FBI reports is one discouraging note written in cursive beside the seven numerals given as the car's license plate number.

"**Incorrect** Oregon plates do not go that high."

The unnamed agent who scribbled the notation was correct. A stamped 1951 Oregon license plate had six numbers separated by a dash.

Another problem was the Colton Shell station owner. When asked about the make and model of the car in question, he could no longer recall it. In fact, he said, it was one of his employees who had interacted with the driver and run the card. When the FBI inquired as to the attendant's whereabouts, the owner claimed he had quit and left no forwarding address. According to Colton Police, the filling station owner had made false reports in the past. Investigators could not catch a break. The public attention was hurting more than helping at this stage.

The Ghost Car

On Saturday, July 19, 1952, the park was full of tourists excited to see one of the West's great natural wonders, Crater Lake. It was estimated more than a thousand people came through the park that day. Was it possible one of them had seen Jones or Culhane being stuffed into a car or being led into the woods?

Thus began the monumental task of matching license plates to the vehicle owners. Between 6 a.m. and 2 p.m. that day, the park registered five-hundred-twenty-three vehicles entering the four gates. License plate numbers were traced to four-hundred-sixty-six registered owners. Each was contacted by an agent of the Federal Bureau of Investigation. These contacts and interviews generated a great deal of reportage, none of which contained any useful, new information. The statements take up considerable space in the first volume of the file. Perhaps the most important fact gleaned from this effort was recognizing how difficult it would be to do a complete job on it—impossible even.

Subtract four hundred sixty-six from five hundred twenty-three—that leaves fifty-seven—the number of cars whose plates were recorded entering the park that day whose owners could not be traced. If you figure about two people per car (on average), the identities of more than a hundred park visitors remained unknown. Another large unknown were the vehicles whose plates were never recorded in the first place—those who had season passes, worked for the park, and members of the local Native American tribe who were not required to have a pass, only a tribal card.

In 1952, Crater Lake National Park could be accessed from four entrances. The east, west, north, and south gates. Jones and Culhane entered by the south gate or Klamath Falls Entrance. The north entrance was heavily used, then as now. The west gate was popular with visitors driving from Medford (before Interstate 5). The east gate was popular with locals who didn't want to drive through Fort Klamath to the south gate.[20]

Whichever entrance the perpetrators used to get into the park, it was another example of how careful they were—too smart to drive a vehicle that could be traced to them. That demonstrates possible intent and premeditation. They may have entered the park intending to rob a tourist. Find an easy mark, someone who looked like he might be carrying a lot of cash. That opportunity presented itself when Jones and Culhane arrived at the overlook.

Less Convenient Theories: Premeditation

Given the casual appearance of the Pontiac when Frank Eberlein found it—the men's sport coats neatly folded across the backseat and passenger door swung wide open—the presumption was that the men left the vehicle and strolled towards the canyon. It is a convenient starting place to reconstruct whatever happened afterward. At the same time, it infers that something about their physical appearance, attitude, or vehicle made them targets. This scenario also suggests that whatever happened outside the car occurred suddenly and without premeditation, but that might not be correct.

What if Jones and Culhane had been forced from their car while they were still inside? Frank Eberlein found something odd about the Pontiac that led him to believe his friends were inside it when they were held up and kidnapped. He thought it unlikely that Culhane would leave the passenger door open. This would cause the dome light to be illuminated and drain the battery. To Frank Eberlein,

---

20 It has been closed for many years. Unimproved and blocked, remnants of the blacktop mark its course today.

professional automobile men like himself or the victims would never leave a door swung open, no matter how irresistible the scenery.

There was also an oddity about the other door, which John Vaughn observed. Shortly after they first got to the overlook, he noticed that the driver's side door was "very tightly closed," or slammed shut.

Both Eberlein and Vaughn believed the car doors indicated that Jones and Culhane were surprised by the robbers while still seated inside the Pontiac. Each arrived at this conclusion using different data, which makes the case stronger. Surprisingly, neither the OSP nor FBI mention Eberlein's or Vaughn's observations about the car doors. Its significance was not appreciated nor shared in any report—other than Eberlein's.

It's very possible that the robbers found Jones and Culhane sitting in the front seat of the car, pulled over, yanked them out of the Pontiac, and shoved them into a second vehicle. All of it totally spur of the moment—a crime of opportunity. It is also possible and worth considering that some level of premeditation occurred and that Jones and Culhane were not targets chosen randomly.

It is unlikely the perpetrators followed the Pontiac into the park. This would have risked being recorded by Ranger Marquiss or someone remembering their car entering the south gate at the same time. What seems most likely is that the perpetrators were parked along the highway inside the park when the Pontiac drove by, or they were parked at the overlook before the robbery and kidnapping commenced. Either way, Jones and Culhane could have been inside the car then removed from it.

Highway traffic had temporarily subsided. At that moment, there were only two cars at the overlook–the Pontiac and an old black sedan or coupe. During the kidnapping, the passenger door was left open. The driver's door was slammed shut. This second violent action caused the Pontiac to rock gently back and forth on its air suspension for a few seconds. That was all the time it took to hustle the executives into the suspect's vehicle before it peeled out in a spray of gravel and dust.

There's another possible theory considering premeditation. Might the perpetrators have followed the executives from Klamath Falls intending to rob them at the first opportunity, which presented itself at the overlook? But why would a local hoodlum become interested in two General Motors executives in town for less than a day? Klamath Falls had its share of professionals driving around in nice cars; Jones and Culhane wouldn't have stood out.

Jones and Culhane spent Friday night at the Wi-Ne-Ma Hotel. It may have been the nicest hotel in Klamath Falls at the time, but it was not the Fairmont. Could a hotel employee have seen them and tipped off the robbers who followed them the next day? The FBI could not find any hotel employees who recalled anything unusual about the men.

The Gun Store in Klamath Falls

Another episode, documented from interviews and a receipt, was Jones' visit to the local sport shop. When he arrived in Klamath Falls on Friday afternoon, Jones paid a quick visit to The Gun Store around 4:30 p.m. The receipt in Jones' wallet reflected a total of $15.33. Jones spent five dollars for an out-of-state fishing license (if he hadn't bought one earlier that season) and the balance on tackle, probably fly fishing gear: leaders, flies, fly dope, etc. This is probably where Jones acquired the *Sports Afield* magazine that was found in the Pontiac the following day. It probably got thrown on the counter too. Ten dollars in 1952 is like a hundred bucks today. Spending that much on flies and leaders takes a while. Fishermen take their time. They linger, solicit advice. An impressive shop like The Gun Store had advice to share. Jones was the outgoing type with a tendency to show off a bit, a real sport. It's easy to imagine him talking it up with anyone in the store that day. The FBI file indicates that he did.

An agent discovered Jones' remarks in the store on July 18 ranged further than fly selection and river conditions. Jones went out of his way to brag about what a "big man" his boss was, according to counterman Bill Kennedy. He said Jones told him he was "taking his boss fishing and kept making remarks indicating that CULHANE was a very important man." Was anyone else present when Jones was bragging about his boss? Perhaps a patron with bad intent who might see an opportunity to fleece a tourist or two?

Kennedy did not recall any other patrons in the store at the time.[21]

Were Jones, Culhane, or Culhane's Washington guide, Harold Weir, anywhere in town where someone could get the mistaken impression they were carrying large amounts of cash? It's unlikely anyone at Moty and Van Dyke or Specialized Service would have let

---

21 This last detail is odd. Stores that specialize in hunting and fishing are typically busy from lunchtime to closing any Friday during the season. Plus, Jones had to be in the store long enough to spend at least ten dollars, which could take a while in 1952. It does not make sense that Jones was the only patron in The Gun Store shortly before it closed on Friday July 18, but that's what Kennedy said.

A meeting with United Motor Service executives including Albert Marston Jones (far right) and Ira Kennedy next to Jones.
Courtesy: C. Ousey

slip that dangerous falsehood. They were not giving out cash awards during their business calls in Klamath Falls. Salesmen at Moty and Specialized received Delco pins, flair for their shop coveralls.

Could either Culhane or Jones have done something to motivate an organized killing? The FBI floated that question. Culhane's secretary, Catherine Braunsdorf, thought that a contract killing was the most likely explanation. She told agents it was a "company job." She had a long time to think about it—seven years before she was interviewed in 1959. She claimed that other UMS employees agreed with her, but the bureau found nothing concrete in her allegation.

Additionally, the murders did not resemble a mob hit. The .32 caliber weapon was too small. Hired guns don't shoot victims in the neck/spine. Hit men don't steal wingtips or attempt to tie their victims to trees. Most especially, mobsters avoid FBI jurisdictions.

What about professional jealousy? Irene Culhane and Catherine Braunsdorf were in agreement. There was friction between West Coast man Ira Kennedy and Charles stemming from the latter's dissatisfaction with a too liberal expense policy at Kennedy's office. But the FBI ruled out Kennedy early in the investigation.

Braunsdorf offered another potential assailant to satisfy her "inside job" theory, but he was hardly the type. When the FBI caught up to General Sales Manager Harold Potter in 1957, he expressed he had been "fearful of the possibility Mr. Culhane might succeed him." Not exactly a motive to kill someone. Just a little professional jealousy amplified by a nosy office secretary spreading gossip.

The FBI did not find any substance in the rumors. Neither Kennedy nor Potter had any connection to the terrible events at Crater Lake. Kennedy came to the park the day Jones and Culhane were found as a representative of UMS. He described Charles Culhane as a "friend" and was, no doubt, affected by the loss of Al Jones with whom he worked closely. It's unfortunate that innuendo cast Ira Kennedy as potentially malevolent when nothing he said or did suggests it.

Following the Pontiac and its occupants with the intention of robbing them implies premeditation. Nothing in any of the official reports suggests this is what happened. Both the Oregon State Police and the FBI believed the initial encounter was spur of the moment, without premeditation or "prior intent."

Eye and Ear Witnesses

Four hundred sixty-six registered vehicle owners in the park on July 19th were contacted by the FBI. Only two provided information that pertained to the investigation. Harry Cole and his wife were retired and living in Florida. For summer vacation in 1952, they planned to take their new RV, an International Metro House Car, across the country. The House Car was one of the first recreational vehicles sold in America, but more closely resembled an old bread truck. Still, you could sleep and cook in it. Pretty nifty.

No Clues, No Suspects, No Activity

Their tour was to include several national parks, culminating in several days visiting Crater Lake National Park. When the Coles finally reached the park on Friday July 18th, they entered through the South Gate then drove five miles up the hill to Annie Creek Campground where they planned to spend the night.

The FBI interviewed the couple eight months after the murders—in February 1953—and were interested to know if they had heard or seen anything unusual. It turned out they had heard something in the early afternoon of July 19th, right around the time Jones and Culhane entered the park.

The Coles wanted to check out another campground in the park and were getting their gear and House Car in order when, while seated at the picnic table in the middle of their campsite, they heard something that stuck out in their memory eight months later.

> ... two gun shots... in rapid succession. It was his estimation that they were several miles from his camp.
>
> *FBI Report*
> *Vol. 4 pps. 3-4*

After they heard the shots, the couple looked at each other, but didn't say much more about it. They left the park four days later. After reading about the murders of Jones and Culhane, they contacted the FBI. Of the six hundred ninety interviews with visitors and park employees, only the Coles and a single park employee had information about the murders. Why it took eight months for the bureau to interview the Coles is not clear from the report.

The split fir is four and a half miles as the crow flies from Annie Springs Campground—a long way for the report of a small caliber gunshot to travel. There is also an eight-hundred-foot elevation gain.[22] Nevertheless, the Coles' account is compelling and consistent.

---

22 Sound travels omnidirectionally, so the eight-hundred-foot difference in altitude shouldn't't cause the purported gunshot noises to be diminished.

Perhaps the most important detail in their recollection is that the shots went off "in rapid succession." Like the stickup and kidnapping at the overlook, it was another element of the crime that occurred very quickly.

Jurisdiction and the FBI

The federal government technically owns all National Parks and the land within their boundaries. These are sometimes referred to as "government reservations." That is why the FBI has law enforcement responsibilities in National Parks though they are not always called upon. More often, they share those responsibilities with local law enforcement and/or park rangers.

Today, rangers in National Parks like Crater Lake possess broad authority to enforce the law within park boundaries, but not in 1952. In those days and before, rangers did not investigate crimes.[23] Until then, law enforcement within Crater Lake National Park was provided by Oregon State Police who patrolled the roads and highways. The local police or county sheriff's deputies assisted in emergencies like forest fires or to arrest someone. For the FBI to investigate a crime committed in a national park was unusual, then and now.

It might be argued that the lead agency in the Crater Lake murder case was the least likely to solve it. The Oregon State Police and the Klamath County Sheriff's Office had troopers and deputies all around the region. The bureau had one agent in Southern Oregon and a Field Office in Portland. Having such little presence did not help. Given these geographic challenges, one might assume the bureau would request assistance from local agencies, but that was not the case. The Seat of Government, as the FBI refers to itself, is not an easy collaborator. It was not unusual then for the bureau

---

23 They became sworn law enforcement officers in the 1970s, after a ranger was shot and killed at Point Reyes National Seashore in California.

to keep smaller, local agencies in the dark about investigations they were all working. Even large agencies, most famously the Central Intelligence Agency (another branch of the Department of Justice), had difficulty sharing information with the FBI.[24] In early 1967, the Marion County Sheriff and Oregon State Police provided compelling new information to the bureau about a suspect who had allegedly admitted to doing the murders. Perhaps because of the source of this new lead, the FBI briefly collaborated with OSP to investigate it.

After a second fruitless day looking for Jones and Culhane, Chief Ranger Louis Hallock knew this would not be like other searches he'd conducted. The men were neither lost nor had fallen into the canyon. Whatever their outcome, Hallock knew he needed expertise outside his own. That afternoon, Louis Hallock contacted the Oregon State Police and the FBI's resident agent in Klamath Falls, Willard Linehan. It certainly made sense.

In those parts, any town large enough to support a post office has a colorful tale or two of bandits robbing stagecoaches, pony riders, and unsuspecting gold miners. In many ways, this crime was just an updating of the story with the victims riding in an automobile instead of on top of a saddle. Whatever you call the perpetrators— murderers, kidnappers, or road bandits—they all implied a crime serious enough to involve the FBI.

There are cases larger than the Crater Lake murders where the FBI chose not to participate directly and deferred to state and local law enforcement. For example, the 1981 Trailside Murder case in Marin County, California involved four people found dead inside Point Reyes National Seashore. Though the killings occurred in two separate incidents, all four bodies were discovered the same afternoon. In his book, *The Sleeping Lady*, Robert Graysmith describes how the FBI opted out of the Trailside Murder investigation to the

---

24 The 9/11 Investigation is the most well-known example of federal agencies withholding information from each other.

disappointment of the local sheriff's office. As the bodies piled up at Point Reyes and nearby Mt Tamalpais, many believed the FBI should assume the lead role. Their office in San Francisco seemed well situated—just an hour from the seashore park.

Though the FBI provided some assistance, they deferred to local authorities and courts to adjudicate the crimes. Eventually, the Marin County Sheriff's Office connected serial killer David Carpenter to the killings and solved them in a dramatic fashion, as described in Graysmith's book. It seems inconsistent that the FBI took the lead for the Crater Lake case with so little presence in the area and then opted out of the Trailside Murders investigation with a big field office an hour away. Perhaps, after thirty years, Director Hoover had learned something that reformed his attitude about localized crime and homicide.

The FBI file does not offer insight into why J. Edgar Hoover decided to head up the Crater Lake investigation. It is well known that Hoover enjoyed high-profile cases. He liked the publicity for his agency and himself. The widespread national attention given the Crater Lake case in the first few weeks might have seemed a public relations coup—if he could solve it. The Director gave special instructions to agents in this teletype message of July 23rd, titled "URGENT."

> AUTHORITY GRANTED TO CIRCULARIZE LAW ENFORCEMENT AGENCIES AND ALL SERVICE STATIONS RE CREDIT CARDS IN STATES NAMED... SECOND WORD IN SECOND SENTENCE SHOULD BE QUOTE MURDERER UNQUOTE. IF SERIAL NUMBERS AND ACCURATE DESCRIPTIONS OBTAINED FOR MISSING WATCHES AUTHORITY IS GRANTED FOR CIRCULARIZATION LAW ENFORCEMENT, AGENCIES AND PAWN SHOPS IN SAME STATES. INSTRUCT ALL OFFICES ISSUING THESE

> LETTERS TO ACQUAINT ALL EMPLOYEES
> WITH IMPORTANCE OF IMMEDIATE ACTION
> ON CALLS RECEIVED AS RESULT OF LETTERS.
> YOU ARE INSTRUCTED TO GIVE THIS CASE
> ADEQUATE AND CONTINUOUS INVESTIGATIVE
> ATTENTION, UTILIZING EVERY RESOURCE TO
> EFFECT IMMEDIATE SOLUTION, INCLUDING
> ASSIGNMENT OF ADEQUATE PERSONNEL...
>
> KEEP BUREAU FULLY ADVISED OF ALL
> DEVELOPMENTS.
>
> HOOVER
>
> *FBI file Vol.1, p. 21*

Within a few months, Hoover's interest had waned. It was clearly going to be a tough case and there were distractions. The 1952 presidential election was in full swing. Hoover always had a great interest in elected presidents and the attorneys general they appointed.[25] One week after the Crater Lake murders, bank robber Gerhard Arthur Puff was apprehended after many months on the run. During the sting, Puff shot and killed Special Agent Joseph Brock in a New York City hotel lobby. This also brought a lot of media attention on the bureau and distracted Hoover from the murders in distant Oregon.

In fairness to the Director, as the years went by and the chances of solving the Crater Lake murders became increasingly remote, Hoover checked in on the case sporadically. In 1961, he wrote a letter to Charles Culhane's widow, Irene, explaining he could not give her a letter of clearance from the case. Eight pages from the end of the file in 1967, Hoover's name appears one last time, regarding fingerprint comparisons for Kenneth Moore and John Wesley Cole. It was the bureau's Hail Mary. Their last, best chance to solve the case. Clearly

---

25 The Federal Bureau of Investigation is one branch of the Department of Justice. The FBI Director reports to the Attorney General.

Hoover saw the possibility, if the fingerprint comparison was positive, but it was not. The four latent prints, Moore's and Cole's, turned out negative.

In a case this complicated and important, there are several lenses through which one might see it. Looking at it based on the FBI file and their attempt to solve it—the effort, failures, and plain bad luck—is the most illuminating because it explains why the case remains unsolved. It is also the most interesting way to look at the Crater Lake murders because the FBI was the source of so much information. There is no other agency that could have put as much effort into it. In the end, one cannot help but wonder if a smaller, local agency might have done more with less; worked the case closer geographically and spoke with people in the area of the crime. Hindsight shows us that that might have been the only way to discover the perpetrators in their lifetime.

A Sudden, New Lead

In the investigation's early stages, the FBI file indicated they might be able to solve the case quickly—in the dashing, modern fashion of the bureau's famous cases of the '50s. Their best chance for that kind of outcome rested on ballistics and fingerprint testing. To find a .32 or 7.65mm slug exactly like the one that killed Albert Jones, Q3. Or matching a fingerprint from either the two credit cards at the scene or the two quarters from a phone booth. A positive result for any of these could lead to the perpetrators, but not if they disposed of the murder weapon or handled the credit cards carefully before tossing them.

By 1957, the Portland Field Office had Special Agent in Charge Milnes take over for Poster. By this time, they had ceased working the case full time. To the public, justice had been served when Jack

Santo was executed in 1955 for another murder, but the bureau knew better.

The case appeared stalled completely by 1957 when a report two hundred pages from the end suggests they got a tip from someone on or near the Klamath Reservation that might lead to the perpetrators.

> ... The Portland office requests Bureau authority to circulate by word of mouth to some 25 Indians in the Klamath and Crater Lake area that the Bureau will pay $1000 for information leading to the identity of the subjects. Portland states it is the opinion of individuals in law enforcement and private industry familiar in Indian customs that the murder of the captioned victims in Crater Lake National Park was committed by Indians.

> *FBI file Vol. 7, p. 55*
> *September 28, 1957*

One wonders what prompted the report, and the reward offer. The bureau language did not reflect their usual swagger. Rather, the phrase "familiar in Indian customs" makes them sound out of their depth. After this late arriving insight, it's not surprising the reward offer did not motivate anyone to come forward. It would be another nine years before they would revisit this theory, but by then it would be too late. In September 1957, they were as close as they would ever be to catching the men most likely responsible for the deaths of Jones and Culhane—who were at that time alive and well.

The L.E.

The key to finding the perpetrators lies in a centuries old Principle of Occam's Razor or the law of parsimony. It's pretty simple.

No Clues, No Suspects, No Activity

The most accurate explanation of a thing or event is made with the fewest assumptions.

Another definition is closer to this story and its conclusions.

Between any two hypotheses predicting the same outcome, the simpler, more logical explanation is closer to the truth.

Contemporary law enforcement jargon condenses Occam to an acronym, The L.E.—the likely explanation.

This double homicide is a perfect crime. It went unpunished and the perpetrators were never found—in their lifetime. The mystery is enlarged by the scope of the investigation: so many agencies working untold man hours without ever naming a suspect. It is only in hindsight—one may step back and see the totality of the case—that a likely explanation presents itself.

The answer to who killed Jones and Culhane exists within the FBI file. It's not in the beginning, when the investigation had the most momentum and push. Neither is the solution to this case in the middle of the file, when Jack Santo got everyone's attention and held it for years. The answer to who killed Jones and Culhane is at the farthest edge of the FBI investigation—right before they quit.

It's not the critic who counts; not the man who points out how the strong man stumbles or where the doer of deeds could have done them better. The credit belongs to the man who is actually in the arena... because there is no effort without errors and shortcomings...

Theodore Roosevelt

No Clues, No Suspects, No Activity

Section One of this book was culled entirely from the FBI's official file of the Crater Lake murders. It provides the vast majority of what is known about the case, filled in fractionally by the Oregon State Police file—2137 pages versus 85. To be clear, this narrative could not exist but for the release of the FBI file. Even though that came almost three years after our Freedom of Information Act request, it was a raft of information never previously shared. Also, the file provides a good look into how the bureau attempted to solve the case and the effort they put into it.

With the benefit of hindsight, it is very easy to cherry pick the places where they performed their mission and, in a few other places, where they did not. To understand how Jones and Culhane died and who did it, it's important to look at everything and, where possible, try to see it in a new light that may reveal answers to those questions. This glare does not always make the bureau look pretty or smart. Nevertheless, we do it to understand what happened and give more meaning to the lives of the victims. Whenever this new information makes the bureau appear to come up short of their best intentions, it's good to balance that criticism. As Teddy Roosevelt wanted his detractors to understand, it's a lot easier to criticize the bullfighter than to walk into the ring and fight the bull.

Section Two: New Information

The split fir underneath which Albert Jones and Charles Culhane were executed.

7 | The Actual Crime Scene

> The corpse at the scene of a brutal homicide can often tell those investigating the death many things. The forensic evidence left behind on the corpse, often times becomes the silent witness against those who commit the most heinous of crimes.
>
> *Mike Byrd/Miami-Dade Police Department*
> *"The Corpse as a Scene"*

Out of respect for Albert Jones and Charles Culhane, we need to reconsider the circumstances of their deaths to understand them more accurately. Knowing exactly what happened in the woods that day points more directly toward the perpetrator, which serves the victims. Many details that follow are difficult to write about because they describe two good men at their worst and last moment. The case remains unsolved partly because of a reluctance to look unflinchingly at the original scene for clues about how the men died.

The men's bodies were discovered in the woods by seventeen-year-old Rex Ash, a farm boy from Missouri who spent his summers at Crater Lake and eventually moved permanently to Klamath Falls. He described what happened that day to *Medford Mail Tribune* reporter Dani Dodge in 2002.

"We were working west from the highway, all spread out about 20 feet apart. I thought, 'Oh, Lordy! There they are.' It was really hot and they had started to bloat. I'd never seen a dead body like that." Ash yelled out for the other searchers.

"It was a bunch of kids and everyone was gathering around to see what was happening. We might have destroyed some of the evidence. We didn't touch anything, but tore up the terrain quite a bit."

A photograph of the searchers was printed in the local paper the following day. It shows the search crew that found the bodies, including Ash. They are lined up in two rows like a team photo, but it's not a trophy shot. It's serious. Two attempt to smile. Most of them look a little spooked.

Tied to a Tree

Examining the first state of the bodies is a study in terror and violence. It's hard to look at, but knowing exactly how they died is valuable because it says something about the men who killed them.

In the chaos, the executives were tied up. They were vulnerable and couldn't move. If both men had their hands tied behind them, it would explain why the bullet paths were so alike: neither victim presented a moving target, so each shot was placed carefully for maximum effect. The result speaks to that effectiveness. After being shot, the victims were left momentarily tied up while their shoes were removed.

That the victims may have been tied to a tree during their execution explains almost everything about the bodies in their original state,

The search group that located Jones and Culhane in the woods under the big split fir. Rex Ash (standing, far right) found them. He lived in Klamath Falls the rest of his life and was friends with Alan Eberlein. John Owings (bottom, right) took a photograph of the bodies. One member of the crew brought a camera and photographed the scene. Another searcher recalled it.

"He stepped over [Jones and Culhane] and around them and got in their faces practically. He was going to sell them [the photos] to a crime magazine and make a fortune, but the FBI took them away."

The images on the film were never seen again, but they probably depicted the murder scene in its original state.
Courtesy: Klamath Falls Herald and News

but it's a problem too. During their autopsies, the Medical Examiner did not see marks on either victim's wrists.

This crime was committed in a hurry, so they were tied up, shot, then cut loose in a short amount of time. Is it possible that wrist bindings would not leave a mark on a person who died two days before and were only tied for a minute or two? Both executives were wearing long sleeve dress shirts.[26] It is an extremely unpleasant hypothetical. The medical term describing skin wounds and elasticity

---

26 Culhane appears to wear cufflinks, too.

from binding and ligature is *vitality*. There's nothing in the available literature that quite matches the circumstances of the Crater Lake case. Many aspects of the scene are consistent with the men having been tied to a tree for a short time, but nothing in either autopsy confirms or refutes it.

Another detail of the scene that suggests the victims may have been tied up is the almost identical proximity of a jackpine to each—to their immediate right and even with their waist.

The nearness of each victim to a tree was not lost on investigators, whether they saw the original scene or not. Both the Oregon State Police and FBI mentioned the twin lodgepole pines, as well as the robbers' likely intention to tie them to the trees.

Had the scene been investigated with the bodies in their original position, next to and on top of the jackpines, it might have elicited other questions related to the victims being tied to the trees:

- How does one acquire this unique skill—knowing how to tie a human to a tree?
- In what sort of profession is one required to tie up people or animals?
- Were there any local suspects who committed a crime that involved tying their victim's hands?

These questions find their most complete answer in three suspects who, coincidentally, all knew each other.

What the Condition of the Bodies Says About the Shooter

Markings on the brass shell casings indicated they were ejected from the same .32 or 7.65mm semi-automatic handgun. Jones and

The Actual Crime Scene

Culhane were each shot through the neck. The bullet paths were almost identical, though in opposite directions. Both shots were contact type, point blank. Given the similarity of the injuries using the same firearm, it looks like one man shot both victims.

Observations from the original scene and both autopsies yield several clues about the killer.

- The robbers kicked and beat both men severely before shooting each in the neck. Given the violence done to them, there was an element of anger, even rage. The killer, and perhaps his accomplice too, was an angry individual who may have a history of violent crime.
- If the perpetrators bound both victim's hands behind them for a short time then cut the bindings before running away. Besides the gun, at least one of them had a knife.
- The killer did not hesitate to use a gun when he had to, demonstrating a level of familiarity. He was comfortable around firearms and may have used them in the commission of other crimes.
- The killer was extremely careful where he shot both victims. He knew that severing each victim's brain stem would immobilize and, eventually, kill them. He'd likely killed this way before—either a person or animal.
- After being shot, both victims had their shoes removed. Culhane's brown Florsheims were never found. One of the offenders found the fancy wingtips desirable footwear. Like the shoe's owner, the thief was likely middle-aged too.

8 | Persons of Interest and Big Personalities

The Punk Theory

The murders at Crater Lake were the biggest story in the Klamath Basin in eighty years—since the Modoc War in the early 1870s. Everybody in those parts heard about the murders, including a former sheriff who thought he knew who did it. Lloyd Low had served the citizens of Klamath County for twenty-four years, retiring in 1948. As a young man, he served in the First World War with the Army cavalry in Germany. Returning from overseas in 1919, he homesteaded near Tule Lake on the same land the Modoc refused to leave and fought over. He kept the ranch all his life. Before being elected Sheriff in 1924, his father, Charles Low, preceded him in the position.

Comfortable speaking his mind, Lloyd Low expressed his opinion about the Crater Lake case to Wallace Myers of the *Herald and News.* The reporter had already penned several accounts picked up by the wire services and splashed across front pages nationwide. Readers remained curious about the mysterious disappearance and violent double homicide. The FBI was tight-lipped as the investigation began, and after Monday's autopsy findings, there was no new information.

Casting around for any new angle, Myers must have thought Low could provide some valuable insight and a good quote or two. On July 24th, Myers brought the former Sheriff to the scene along with the current Sheriff, Red Britton, and Circuit Judge David Vandenburg. Imagine having all these high-ranking public officials following a reporter to a crime scene today. It would not happen. Besides showing how times have changed, it also demonstrates the level of intense interest in this case, especially by the people closest to it. All except Low had been present the day the bodies were found. Myers described what happened when they arrived at the big split fir.

> Typical of other visitors to the scene, Vandenberg, Britton and Low theorized on how the crime was actually committed as they stepped gingerly about the tragic area. To aid them in making their deductions, the writer assumed prone positions on the exact spots the murdered men's bodies were discovered.
>
> ***Wallace Myers***
> **Klamath Falls Herald and News** *July 25, 1952*

All the theorizing resulted in a good story for Myers two days later under the headline "Ex-Sheriff Lloyd Low Holds Crater Theory."

> My first thought on this case is that the job was done by some young punks… Say between 17 and 22 years old.
>
> ***Lloyd Low with Wallace Myers***
> **Klamath Falls Herald and News** *July 26, 1952*

His theory that a youth gang was able to pull off this carefully executed double homicide without getting caught or found out later is not terribly persuasive. The former sheriff sounds a little cranky, at first. Later in the piece, he talks about the overlook and murder scene with detail and clarity.

> They were probably driving up the road and saw Culhane and Jones standing there looking out over the canyon. The boys figured it would be a good stickup. They saw the men's car had California tags and probably figured the men would have pretty good piece of money with them, being from out of state and on a trip... I think the boys decided the one driving the car would stay with the car while the rest of them did the stickup. They jumped out, threw a gun on the two men and hustled them across the road into the woods... They took the two men way back in the woods until they figured they couldn't be heard from the road. That's another thing that points to young punks. Experienced crooks wouldn't have taken those men over 75 or 100 feet from the road. They would have gone just far enough that they couldn't be seen from the road...
>
> I don't think they really meant to kill the men. I think they gagged them and intended to tie them to those two little jackpines...
>
> Now the autopsy showed this fellow Jones had a fractured skull and some bruises in the groin. Of course we know both the men actually died from a bullet to the head. Seems Jones probably got the skull fracture and groin bruises when he put up a fight. He might have figured those tight gags were going to strangle he and his buddy anyway and when he saw his chance, he jumped the robbers. He was a big, strong man and probably figured he had a good chance. I imagine the shooting started during the scuffle with Jones.

Persons of Interest and Big Personalities

Lloyd Low's account sounds like it was written down verbatim by Myers and reads like a stream-of-consciousness. It is visual and accurate in many details which Low could only have guessed at, but the FBI file confirms.

Besides the commission of the murders and by whom, Low thought he knew what happened.

> After the shooting, I guess they ran back to the road figuring to move that other car (Culhane and Jone's) [*sic*] but when they got to the edge of the woods they saw Eberlein and Jack Vaughn had arrived. Somehow, they managed to get back in their own car and got out of there.

> **Lloyd Low with Wallace Myers**
> **Klamath Falls Herald and News *July 26, 1952***

This description suggests the killers returned to the road sometime after the Eberleins (and Vaughn) arrived at the overlook—then became aware of their truck and presence beside the Pontiac. It is an evocative visual. Lloyd's theory lacks, however, when he suggests the killers returned to the overlook to fetch their vehicle in the aftermath of the crime. According to Low, two youthful killers and a driver all kept quiet about this explosive, famous crime forever after. Also, he casts doubt on the likelihood that experienced "crooks" would bother taking their hostages so far into the woods. Perhaps Low walked in from the overlook with the other men that afternoon, which can seem like a long way; but from the roadside directly above, walking briskly and downhill all the way, it only takes a couple minutes. It's not as far as Low makes it sound, but he'd only been there once. Plus, he was almost sixty-four years old at the time so it may have seemed farther than it was.

Still, seventy years hence, there's something refreshing about a law enforcement official who visits a complex crime scene and pens a 1500-word essay the following day about how it all went down—unafraid to call it the way he saw it. Lloyd Low was cut from a cloth they don't manufacture anymore—a no-nonsense, Western-style lawman who said whatever he thought.

Unfortunately, his judgment failed him in one area. Lloyd Low knew the person who most likely committed the Crater Lake murders. He was instrumental in sending this individual to state prison in 1934 for a crime with striking similarities: a brutal robbery, assault, and threat of murder before tying up two male victims—just a few miles from the overlook. In the intervening eighteen years, Lloyd Low apparently forgot about it—and the man responsible.

To be fair, several other county officials had dealings many years before with the man responsible for the murders; none of them had any suspicions about him in this case either.

Before Low's story ended, he provided corroboration for Frank Eberlein's description of the bodies' original position. Myers probably told Low how the men were found.

> When Jones made his break, it looks like Culhane had already been set down with his back to one of the trees. I imagine Jones jumped when the little punks were getting ready to tie Culhane to the tree. Culhane looks like he was shot sitting down and it looks like Jones was shot while he was probably squatting or stooping. When you hit a man in the groin, he will naturally stoop.

> **Lloyd Low with Wallace Myers**
> **Klamath Falls Herald and News** *July 26, 1952*

After visiting the scene and penning the article about it for the local paper, Lloyd Low enjoyed his retirement for another eleven years before he died in 1963.

The Man with the Missing Finger

A Portland man named Lincoln Linse asserted in 1969 that he was an eyewitness to the kidnapping of Jones and Culhane. The *Medford Tribune*, among others, ran a story on this, and the Oregon State Police were compelled to investigate. Corporal George Winterfield authored the report. It was the first official document to bear Linse's name.

In it, Linse said it was not the first time he'd told his story to law enforcement. According to him, he tried to tell the FBI the same story in 1952, but was ignored. Seventeen years later, he decided to tell it again. This time, people were listening.

According to Linse, while a twenty-four-year-old student at the University of Oregon, he spent the summer of 1952 working for park concessionaire R.W. Price at Crater Lake Lodge. Linse said he was driving an old Chevrolet truck from Klamath Falls delivering goods to Crater Lake Lodge on July 19th. According to the OSP report, while Linse was driving west on Highway 62 along Annie Creek Canyon, he saw a 1936 black Pontiac sedan parked "some distance… from where the bodies were found." As he was driving past the scene, Linse told Winterfield, he saw "4 male individuals on the roadway." Shortly after, Linse said he heard two shots or "reports" while driving.

With its heavy payload of canned goods, the delivery truck motored slowly up the hill. Pulling hard, Linse geared down where the grade steepened at the edge of the caldera. Suddenly, from the direction of the kidnapping he had observed a few minutes before, the 1936 black Pontiac came up fast and pulled beside him. Inside of it, two men "glared" in his direction while they drove in a reckless manner on the winding, two-lane road.

After returning to work, Linse said he saw the men in the lobby at Crater Lake Lodge. The younger of the two again glared in his direction.

146

Linse picks up his story the following morning. He was leaving the lodge to make another supply run to Klamath Falls when the black Pontiac attempted twice to block his way. Fortunately, he got around them and continued down the mountain.

Linse's last interaction with his harassers occurred during a fuel stop at the pump by the Park Headquarters. The black Pontiac had followed him and pulled over nearby. The two passengers resumed their intimidating behavior and continued to "glare in his direction." During this last interaction, Linse noticed for the first time several distinctive physical characteristics about them. The older one had a tattoo of a nude female on his left forearm. This same man wore a beaded belt with the name "RALPH" on it. Most memorably, this older man was missing a finger on his left hand.[27]

Before he left the gas station that day, Linse noted the Pontiac's out-of-state license plate and wrote it with his finger in the dust coating his dashboard. When, a few days later, Linse heard about the murders in the park, he went back to his vehicle to find the license number, but it had been erased. Another lodge employee had driven the truck and wiped the dash clean. Despite writing it down and driving the truck that day, he could not recall the numbers. Whatever state the license plate originated from was not included in the report.

Besides the information Linse shared with Oregon State Police in 1969, he had a theory about the murders that he shared with Corporal Winterfield and was related in the report. Linse said he had read many newspaper accounts about the murders of Al Jones and Charles Culhane over the years. He had a hunch that the perpetrators "were not strangers to the Crater Lake area." He also stated that the black 1936 Pontiac central to his account was uncommon in 1952. Given the unusual make and model, Linse thought the FBI "with little effort should be able to come up with the vehicle."

---

27 Curiously, Lincoln Linse is also missing part of a finger.

Persons of Interest and Big Personalities

After taking the report from Linse, George Winterfield contacted FBI Special Agent Ron Sherk of the Portland Field Office who said he would see if Linse's "information was of any value." Sherk was present on July 21, 1952, the day Jones and Culhane were found in the woods. There is no corresponding report generated by SA Sherk or any other agent in the FBI file concerning Linse's claims. Winterfield's report is the last item in the sixty-five page Oregon State Police file concerning the case.

Over the years, Linse has continued to share his story. He recounted it for Cheryl Ousey in 2001 when she was preparing her thesis. For the fiftieth anniversary in 2002, the Associated Press retold Linse's story with the headline "Man Says He's Witness to 50-Year-Old Murder." Since then, Linse's account has not changed but has gotten somewhat richer in detail.

In 2013, after retiring from a career in finance and accounting, Lincoln Linse met reporter Ian Parker and this author when we were putting together a TV story about the Crater Lake murders set to run during sweeps and near the crime's anniversary. Inside his neatly kept ranch-style house on the hill between Beaverton and Portland, Linse shared many more details than are contained in Winterfield's OSP report. In fact, there were too many to include in our TV story, or in these pages. It was an extremely full account and difficult to ignore.

After the interview, Ian Parker and I debated whether or not to include him in our piece. Ordinarily, we would need at least two reliable sources agreeing on facts to report them in a story for broadcast. Because this was a feature story and sweeps piece, we decided to include him because his account was interesting and colorful. We never said he was an eyewitness, but he did. Viewers could decide for themselves whether or not Lincoln Linse was telling the truth. After the story aired, many viewer comments concerned Lincoln Linse and his account. In fact, most accepted it at face value, suggesting authorities should be looking for a fingerless man named Ralph with a nude woman tattooed on his forearm.

Linse has support for his claims. He and Alan Eberlein have become acquainted over the years. Regarding Linse, Eberlein told me that "there may be something to it." Given Alan's support, it's worth breaking down.

Linse claimed he witnessed the kidnapping in progress when he saw "two scruffy guys walking with two businessmen" before they all disappeared in the woods. This would describe the beginning of the kidnapping and forced march. In the report, it's not clear if the incident he witnessed was at the overlook or somewhere else on the road. In either case, could the killers have performed a kidnapping, two killings, and then return to their car in time to catch up to Linse on Rim Drive?

For the sake of argument, let's say the offenders drove their 1936 Pontiac as fast up the hill as we drive it today, and that it took them the same twenty-five minutes to reach the lodge from the overlook. Could they catch up with Linse? Adding thirty minutes for the crime whose inception Linse claimed to witness, plus another twenty-five minutes driving from the overlook to the lodge, they would arrive there in fifty-five minutes—that's five minutes behind Linse if he took twice as long to get there. Linse claimed the killers overtook his truck on the road, which would be even sooner. By these distances and estimated times, the killers could not have caught up to him— but this is not calculus, so it isn't impossible—just extremely unlikely.

What about the rest of Linse's story? First, wouldn't the killers have felt compelled to leave the park, rather than drive further into it? Given the killer stood inches away from each victim when the gun went off, he likely had blood on his clothes. Also, they had all the items stolen from the victims in their car. Riding around with all this incriminating evidence in their possession would be dangerous, and pretty stupid. Second, why would they seek attention after successfully getting away with murder? Given a choice between following Linse, and risking getting caught red-handed, or returning to Jones' Pontiac to steal its contents on their way out, the latter seems a more reasonable motivation.

At the intersection of OR 62 and the bottom of Rim Drive, the perpetrators would have had to guess which direction Linse was driving that day. How did they know he was going to the lodge?

Linse's version of events assumes that they saw him as he witnessed the kidnapping. In those fraught few seconds, Linse recalled one of the victims holding up his hand with the thumb and forefinger extended—signaling to Linse that someone had a gun. That would mean everybody—the robbers, the victims, and Linse—were all looking at each other at the same moment in time.

As the FBI was building their case, how could they have failed to make a report with an eyewitness able to identify the perpetrators' clothing, tattoos, and vehicle? The FBI file names forty-six of the one hundred twenty-four park employees who were interviewed with "negative result," including fifty-seven employed by Crater Lake Lodge. At least one of these lists of names should have included Linse, but they do not. His name does not appear anywhere in the FBI file.

There is an account from another man, Paul Herron, a maintenance worker at the Lodge who took a bus from Klamath Falls to work on July 19th. Peering out the window, Herron claimed he saw the green Pontiac at the overlook when he was riding by at 3:15 pm that day. As an observation, it's not particularly helpful. What it demonstrates is that the bureau took the time to interview him and generate a report about it. It stands to reason that, if the FBI recorded Herron merely seeing Jones' Pontiac, they would have taken the time to write a report with a man who claimed to witness the kidnapping in progress and could identify the killers.

Linse's story is hard to put down. After spending a few hours with him in 2013, Ian Parker and I found him charming, intelligent, and persuasive. He convinced me that day—before our FOIA request was granted and a lot of other information presented itself.

Given the passage of time and lack of any new evidence, Linse's account continues to stand out. For anyone new to the story—reading or writing about it—it draws you into his world. If true, it is frightening to imagine Linse witnessing the abduction and his later encountering two dangerous killers.

It's easy to challenge Linse's account. It does not seem possible Ralph could have caught up to Linse in the first place; and if he couldn't catch him on the road, the later encounters couldn't have happened either. Linse said he told the FBI the whole story in 1952, but there's no record of it when there should be.

By sharing this humdinger of a story that puts himself at the center, Linse has the same effect on this case as did Jack Santo. Each in their own way becomes a distraction from what really happened and knowing who did it.

According to Lincoln Leonard Linse's obituary, he "died in his sleep on March 12, 2023 after a long battle with prostate cancer." There is no mention of the Crater Lake case or his involvement in it. He was ninety-five years old.

The Sly Old Hermit

In the first few weeks after the murders, public interest was acute. There was a killer on the loose, possibly two. The feds cast a net into every western state searching for information that might lead to a suspect. They caught a few straightaway—real bad men with another thing in common. None were in the park on July 19th.

The first suspect who caught everyone's attention was a local man living not far from Crater Lake. George Dunkin had a reputation as a loner who despised authority. It turned out he had a mean streak too—as deep as the remote canyon he inhabited. West of the park, twenty miles as the crow flies, is a gorge carved by Elk Creek. In it and away from civilization, Dunkin made a life for himself prospecting and living off the land. Winters in the valley were especially rugged. Today, we'd call him a survivalist. In newspaper accounts, he was described as a "fugitive mountaineer" and a "sly, old hermit." Locals said Dunkin had been living there since the 1930s. In 1952, Dunkin was sixty-seven years old and weighed one hundred twenty pounds—essentially a little old man.

Dunkin began to attract a lot of attention in early 1952 which, if you are a hermit, is never a good sign. It began when he saw several game wardens watching his movements outside his cabin. It turned out his suspicions were real. The Forest Service had been tipped off that Dunkin was shooting wild game out of season. The next time he saw them, Dunkin discharged his rifle above their heads. That is where all his troubles began. The wardens quickly retreated and left Dunkin alone, but only temporarily.

Shooting at federal employees has a way of attracting the law. Oregon State Police Trooper Phil Dowd was called out to arrest Dunkin on the evening of July 24, 1952. There aren't instructions in the OSP handbook about how to sneak up on hermits. Arresting any poacher is a dangerous business. It's hard to believe, but Dowd went out there all by himself. From the woods by his cabin, Dunkin got the jump on Dowd as soon as he got out of his vehicle. George fired once—with his deer rifle. Dowd was struck in the chest and died right there in the woods. After killing him, Dunkin knew he wouldn't be left alone for long, so he packed up and escaped into the canyon. After what happened to Trooper Dowd, OSP wisely decided to give George some space. George Dunkin was left alone in the wilderness. For months, he remained hidden. State and federal authorities kept a close watch, hoping George might reappear.

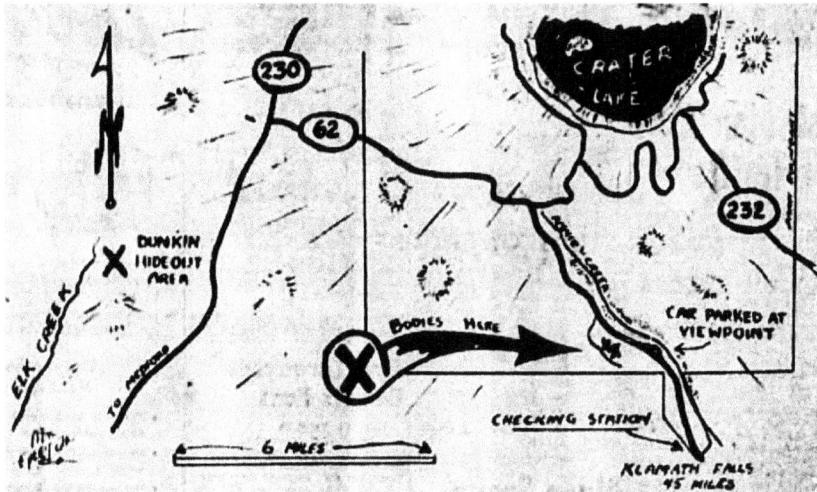

Map from *Klamath Falls Herald and News* **on July 25, 1952 appears with a story about George Dunkin.**

Dunkin's escape made an interesting sub-heading in the stories about the murders at Crater Lake. In this hell and gone corner of the state, three murders in five days was a rare occurrence. There was a problem trying to pin the Crater Lake murders on George. It didn't add up. He had neither the means, the motive, nor the opportunity. At the risk of putting too fine a point on it, hermits don't drive around robbing strangers, stealing their watches, then committing random homicides.

George didn't walk into Crater Park either. The remote river canyon where he lived was more than twenty miles away. Too far for someone without access to a car. Besides, all the terrain in between was too rugged. Though George must have been one tough old buzzard, he was sixty-seven. There was no way he could cover all those miles then walk back to kill the Trooper five days later.

That didn't mean George Dunkin wasn't dangerous and a threat to anyone who might stumble onto him in the woods where he was hiding. He had to be captured.

Trooper Russel Maw was assigned the case. Maw must have been comfortable living in the woods. For weeks, he watched and waited in a cabin owned by Dunkin's nephew near where they believed the old man was hiding. Wisely ditching his trooper's uniform, Maw dressed like a mountain man and eventually was able to approach Dunkin in a most unlikely place to make an arrest: the middle of nowhere. Dunkin was taken into custody without a fuss, though he was armed—still in possession of the 30-30 rifle he used to shoot Dowd.

He spoke softly when he described the night he shot the Trooper. "It was dark. I didn't aim. I shot in his direction."

If that's true, both shooter and victim shared a moment of mutual astonishment, which turned badly for both of them, but mostly the trooper.

After living alone in a tiny cabin above an isolated canyon for twenty years, George Dunkin spent the rest of his life confined to a cell at Oregon State Prison in Salem. His nephew collected the reward.

Monday's Mysterious Caller

On Monday July 21st, a long distance call was placed at 1:15 p.m. from Medford to the garage at Fort Klamath. It was only a few hours after Al Jones and Charles Culhane's bodies were discovered. The caller and the story he offered that afternoon quickly aroused the attention of the state police.

In 1952, long distance calls were not all connected instantly, particularly in rural areas. Some had to be physically connected, placing wires into a switchboard. The switchboard operator that afternoon was Phyllis Haas. If a long distance call had to be put through as this one did, she asked callers for their name and address, in case they were disconnected. The caller identified himself as "J.D. Harney" and his address was "536 Plum Street" in Medford. Haas promised to call him back as soon as the line was clear, which she effected in the next few minutes. Around 1:35, she called back Harney and connected him with Myrtle Wimer at the Fort Klamath Garage.

Harney indicated to Wimer that a 1951 Pontiac would soon be towed to the garage and that he would like to take possession of it for his friend Albert Jones, who was laid up in a local hospital.

Medford Train Station

When Myrtle inquired which hospital, Harney seemed unsure. She reminded him that Medford had two hospitals, Community and Sacred Heart. Harney then indicated it was the second she had mentioned, Sacred Heart.

Myrtle sensed something wasn't right about the caller. She had heard about the missing men and the abandoned Pontiac; everyone in Fort Klamath had by then. Her understanding was that the car was still somewhere up the road in the direction of the park, so she told Harney that the Park Service currently had possession of the Pontiac.

Still peddling the myth that Jones was alive, Harney said he would inform Jones of all the information Wimer had shared and that as soon as Jones was released, he and Harney would pick up the car. Then Harney hung up. The call lasted one minute and fifty-two seconds. Myrtle Wimer immediately called the Klamath County Sheriff's Office which, in turn, contacted the FBI.

Given the timing and seeming insider knowledge of the caller, the FBI looked into it immediately. They began with the switchboard operator who, it turned out, had had a memorable conversation with Mr. Harney who had behaved rather badly in their short exchange. When she described calling him back after clearing the line, she said,

"He would like to take my head off."

The man who called himself "J. D. Harney" was what police today call "a person of interest"—someone who might have greater knowledge of the crime. It might be the murderer himself. Though he spoke fewer than two minutes, the information he offered indicated a deeper knowledge. The call was traced by Pacific Telephone and Telegraph Company to the phone booth outside the Medford Train Station.

Within a fairly short time, the telephone in the booth was disassembled. Several parts were kept for fingerprint evidence, including the top four quarters; two of them yielded impressions that were entered into evidence.

Before that, Medford Police Sergeant Lyle Perkins and Lieutenant Charles Champlin were dispatched and went straight to the station, just three blocks from police headquarters. Looking for anyone who might have seen or heard anything unusual at the phone booth, they immediately got a hit. Baggage handler Al Yoakum said he noticed a man in the phone booth during the time of the call. He remembered him because the caller had been inside it "a considerable time."

Yoakum noticed two other details. He wore a distinctive yellow sport shirt and had a receding hairline.

When Yoakum got off work, he went with detectives to several local bars looking for Harney. They also visited a haberdasher looking for the shirt. Neither venture was successful.

The FBI looked everywhere for J.D. Harney. They found out that, indeed, Plum Street in Medford does exist. The problem was the address. There is no 536. The bureau contacted seven residents whose address numbers were closest and interviewed each without result. The mail carrier, Chester Silliman, was interviewed. He believed he'd seen a letter addressed to 536 Plum Street recently, but returned it to the post office. An agent from the Portland Field Office tried to find this letter at the Dead Letter Office on NW Hoyt in downtown Portland—to no avail.

Partial palmprint lifted from the handset in the phone booth. This episode at the train station provoked an intense investigation in the days following the murders. Nothing came of it.
FBI file photo

In July 1952, J.D. Harney might have seemed like a good lead and someone who might break the case only a few days after it began. Seventy years later, he belongs more in the category with Jack Santo and Lincoln Linse: a distraction taking away valuable time and effort from finding the real killer.

There are several ways the mysterious caller might

have known the details he shared with Myrtle Wimer without ever having met Albert Jones, let alone shot him in the woods. The *Herald and News* published a story in their edition on Monday that he may have read before he got to the phone booth. In that story, as reported by Wallace Myers, Jones and Culhane were still missing, which sounds like the material Harney used for his yarn. It is also possible that one of the men involved with the search on Saturday or Sunday told someone about the missing executives and that information reached Harney's ear.

The main problem with Harney—and the reason he doesn't fit the bill as the actual killer—is the complete fallibility of his scheme: Trying to steal the Pontiac would only lead authorities to him. Anyone smart enough to pull off a perfect crime like the Crater Lake murders would not return to the scene the day the bodies were found and attempt to steal the victim's car..

Not surprisingly, fingerprints lifted from the phone booth handset and twenty-five cent pieces extracted from the coin slot were of no evidentiary value when the FBI compared them with several potential suspects in the late '60s, one of whom, by his own admission, participated in the murders.

Skippy Gets a Lift

"The fairest picture the whole Earth affords," Mark Twain once hyperbolized about Lake Tahoe.

Where Eastbound Highway 50 meets the top of the Tahoe Basin is one of the best vantage points from which to view the lake, appreciated by hundreds of motorists every day. In just a few miles, the highway becomes a treacherous two-lane road perilously snaking through a granite fairyland of scrubby pines clinging to a cliff a thousand feet above the "blue, blue lake in the sky."

Persons of Interest and Big Personalities

When long haul trucker John Lovelace came up over the pass on July 23, 1952, he could not have failed to notice the azure depths of Lake Tahoe spread out before him. After that, he negotiated the cliffside curves without a problem. The trip was going pretty smoothly that evening, with him admiring the scenery, bound for Utah, with a load of goods for Sears Roebuck.

When he came to the shoreline of the lake, Lovelace got onto Highway 89 East. Just before reaching Nevada, Lovelace had to slam on his brakes to avoid hitting a man standing by himself in the middle of the road outside Stateline. After the big truck came to a stop, the man jumped inside the cab—uninvited. William "Bill" Russell sidled across the big bench seat until he was face to face with Lovelace.

Russell was a sight—with green eyes set in a sunbaked face. Tall and thin, one hundred fifty pounds barely covered his six foot, two inch frame. Equally distinctive, the forefinger on his left hand was scarred, disfigured by a snakebite wound. Russell wore his shirt open and his sleeves rolled up to display numerous tattoos, including the image of Mighty Mouse on his right arm. The ink, piercing eyes, and tanned, chiseled features surely made an impression on the driver as the two sat together in the middle of the road. According to his police statement several days later, what most caught Lovelace's attention was a revolver hanging from Russell's belt, a .45 Colt Frontier with a ten-inch barrel.

Russell wasted no time taking control of the situation. He threatened Lovelace and ordered him to drive on. As if nothing had happened, Russell pulled out a matchbook, separated a match, and casually struck it one-handed to light a cigarette. He drew deeply, but the smoke did not calm him. Russell demanded Lovelace's wallet. Short of cash and afraid Russell might shoot him, Lovelace offered to redeem a personal check. Russell thought his hostage lacked the proper motivation.

"I don't want to have to do to you what I did to those two men in Crater Lake. You heard about those two men in Oregon? Well, here sits the boy who done it!"

The FBI file described what happened next.

"Russell... relieved Lovelace of a small amount of money and a wristwatch."

At some point, Russell told Lovelace he was hitchhiking home to Minnesota, which was not true. Russell was from Ponca City, Oklahoma. The truth was that Russell didn't really have a plan or destination. He was out of money, down on his luck, and desperate to change his situation. He rode with Lovelace past Stateline and down the other side of the Tahoe Basin. A short ways into the endless bland expanse of Nevada near Sparks, Russell demanded money again. Coincidentally, Lovelace and his family resided in Sparks. Given the unpredictable nature and appearance of his unwelcome rider, Lovelace omitted sharing this personal information. Yearning for home, his ordeal was not over.

Lovelace cashed a check at Porky's Cafe for $35.73 hoping this might satisfy Russell and send him on his way. Something about Sparks did not appeal to the bandit, which is not hard to believe. He demanded that Lovelace drive thirty miles east to Fernley. Finally satisfied with his surroundings in Fernley, the highwayman jumped out of the truck cab and disappeared.

Footloose and flush with cash, Bill Russell walked a while until he found a place to stay. By this time, he had concealed his Colt in a white bag. Russell informed a motel clerk he was hitchhiking to Oklahoma. Despite having just scared the wits out of John Lovelace, Russell had not lost his sense of humor. In the lobby of a long-forgotten, fleabag motel, Russell signed the register "Skippy O'Neal." Bill Russell decided to lay low in Fernley where he remained the next two days.

Russell had been on the run since May. He had gone AWOL from Amarillo Air Force Base in Texas where the young private found military life too restrictive. Eight weeks later, he was hopping trains and hitchhiking to find work. On the way he acquired the Colt. When the money ran out, he began robbing victims at gunpoint.

Not unlike Sparks, no one stays long in Fernley, if they don't have to. By the time Deputy Sheriff Stanley Tower arrived to apprehend him, Skippy had, uh, departed.

Russell hitchhiked as far as Elko and stayed the night in another motel; this one was conveniently located across from a snooker parlor. On this next leg of his adventure, Russell did not rob or terrorize anyone and chose to use his real name at the motel. The following day, he set out hitchhiking again—this time to Salt Lake City and beyond. Initially, he caught three rides east—all without incident. The fourth car to pick him up that day was driven by Arnold Shadis. Something in Russell changed during this fourth ride. Skippy the Road Bandit was back. The file indicates Shadis got pretty much the same treatment as Lovelace: robbed at gunpoint then made to drive Russell to his next destination.

> ... a short distance from Duchesne, Utah, he told SHADIS to pull off on a side road and that he pulled the .45 Model Colt Frontier Revolver from his belt to force SHADIS to do so. He said he intended to force SHADIS from the vehicle and take same but that he changed his mind when SHADIS told him that he would got [*sic*] him some money.

> *FBI File Vol. 2 p. 159*

Arnold Shadis cashed a check for thirty dollars, handed it over, and Russell disappeared once again. With his new grubstake, he looked for lodging and got a room at the Duchesne Hotel. In an effort to outsmart the police, Russell used a new alias at sign in. One sure to throw authorities off his track. He was no longer the fun-loving, long barrel revolver-toting bandit formerly known as Skippy O'Neil. In Duchesne, Russell chose a new name for himself, "Jerry O'Neil."

While Russell was busy inventing aliases and finding himself a room, Shadis drove directly to the police department and told them about his nerve-rattling drive through the desert to Duchesne. Roadblocks were established. Police checked all the hotels; there were only a few. It did not take long to find a man matching Bill Russell's description. Men with Mighty Mouse tattoos tended to stick out in Duchesne, Utah. Still do.

The hotel clerk took the police upstairs, but Russell's room was empty—except for his white bag. In it, Sheriff Arzy Mitchell found all of Bill Russell's worldly possessions. What does a man carry with him on a cross-country crime spree? The Colt was in the bag, so was Russell's immunization register card. He'd gotten his tetanus shot that February. Also in the bag were some nail clippers, two plaid sport shirts, and a social security card. This made identification easy and, with the big revolver taken as evidence, the snakebitten drifter had been defanged. But where had he gone?

William Russell spent his last hours attending a local carnival. Even after traumatizing several victims that week, he was out enjoying himself. It's easy to imagine him drawing unwanted attention. Lighting a cigarette one-handed is not the sort of parlor trick that Duchesne's mostly Mormon citizenry appreciates. Whatever Bill's mindset, it would be changing shortly.

The FBI's Salt Lake City Field Office was made aware and agents immediately headed east a hundred miles to the carnival. With the help of Russell's unique physical characteristics and Sheriff Mitchell, they had no trouble finding him. While some believe body art imbues its wearers with the power of the images, this was not so in

Bill Russell's case. Mighty Mouse did not save the day despite his nearness to Bill.

The FBI was feeling good about having captured Russell, and the case against him in the Crater Lake murders seemed compelling at first. Word quickly got into the papers. It was Russell's bragging to Lovelace that made everybody think of him as a suspect. Plus, he looked the part. But, to some agents, it seemed too good to be true. How could a lone hitchhiker pull off the entire job at Crater? Further complicating the case was Russell's Colt. It was the wrong caliber.

Most problematic in connecting Bill Russell to Crater was that he had an unassailable alibi. The epilogue to the crime spree should have been a last bit of punctuation that capped off his desperate, desert odyssey. Unfortunately, it was the dullest part of the whole dumb caper.

On the evening of the day Jones and Culhane both went missing, the tattooed desperado from Ponca City had dinner with his aunt and uncle in Sacramento, California. After dinner, they attended a movie. Good news for Russell, it gave him an unassailable alibi in the Crater Lake murders. But too bad for Skippy, his relatives didn't realize their nephew was in a bad way and buy him a bus ticket straight to Oklahoma. It would have saved everybody a lot of trouble.

Frank Eberlein's Tip

When Al Jones and Charles Culhane left Specialized Service the day they died, Frank Eberlein was the last familiar face they would ever see. It's understandable that the case was personal to him. Outside the victims' families, he was as attached as anyone to it. Albert Jones was his friend.

His nearness to the crime was both emotional and physical. He actually witnessed the original scene, which had to be difficult. Alan

Persons of Interest and Big Personalities

Eberlein said his father didn't like to talk about what he saw in the woods that day. His reticence did not extend to his interactions with law enforcement, however, and he assisted investigators any way he could. Frank Eberlein spoke numerous times with the FBI, answering all their questions. The FBI file reports a lot of information derived from Frank Eberlein. It shows up mostly in a seventy-seven-page document that rounds up all the information gathered by the bureau in the first month.[28]

After cooperating in every possible way and seeing the investigation stall, Eberlein grew frustrated. During his interviews with the FBI and OSP, he realized they were not working the case together; rather, each was trying to solve it for themselves. Alan recalled it many years later.

> He'd talk to one agency, like the State Police, and they wouldn't know something he'd spoken with the FBI about. Each had their piece of turf and it caused a lack of communication.

Interview with Alan Eberlein
March 31, 2020

Eberlein wanted to know who killed his friend. He wanted the case solved. This deep desire to see justice for his friend led him into areas of speculation outside the case that law enforcement was working.

An acquaintance shared a story with him that, to Frank, sounded like an extremely good lead. It was a few years after the murders—a time when the FBI was scuffling, running out of leads and unable to solve the case.

Out of the blue, Frank got a tip from a work acquaintance named George Brown. His veracity, at the time, was not ironclad. Alan

---

28 FBI file, Vol. I pps. 242-317

recalled his father mentioning that Brown had a bit of a drinking problem. Nevertheless, Frank found him credible enough to share a story with Sheriff Britton that Brown had told him.

George Brown was working a highway construction job just outside Crater Lake National Park shortly after the murders. It was Friday. Payday. Eager to start the weekend, workers lined up for their week's wages. Brown noticed something odd with one of the crewmen standing near him in line. As Eberlein described it:

> George was working construction around Prospect, a highway project, and the contractor had a son who was worthless but on the payroll nonetheless. The kid never had any money and then one morning he showed up and he had money and a new wristwatch. He quit and drew his pay and left. Everybody wondered where he got the money and where he got the watch. George Brown thought the kid had to be implicated. My dad told Red [Sheriff Red Britton]. Red said, "These guys [the Santos Gang] that they thought did it were going to be executed. They didn't bring this up because they didn't want anything to delay the execution of the Santos Gang." This was always the one missing piece that bothered dad.

> *Alan Eberlein*
> *Interview with Cheryl Ousey, 2001*

Frank Eberlein was correct about one thing. There is no mention of George Brown or his account in any reports—which strongly suggests Brown was never interviewed in the first place—and that's too bad because the story of the crew boss' son deserved attention. He had a fat wallet and a new-looking gold watch, then suddenly quit and disappeared—without an explanation. Working outside in the area of the murders might have given this guy the opportunity to get familiar with the overlook and the woods beside it. A crucial prerequisite for whoever brought Jones and Culhane there.

After Frank told Red Britton the story, the sheriff shared something that Frank had long suspected. Britton told him the FBI thought they already had their man and weren't interested in confusing the case. The man to which Sheriff Britton was referring was almost certainly John R. Santos, also known as Jack Santo—notorious road bandit and serial killer. Naturally, the FBI liked him to the exclusion of other suspects. He was made to order.

Jack Santo showed up on the FBI's doorstep like an anonymous gift, but not a bouquet of flowers. More like a rattlesnake in a box—with a gift card attached drawn with scenes of cash, carjackings, and inert bodies hidden in the woods.

Jack Santo and His Mountain Mob

In 1955, Special Agent Patterson prepared the bureau's second Summary Report about the case. It was the most comprehensive document on the Crater Lake murders since a report filed in 1952. Six pages of the seventy-seven-page report contain a list: one hundred ninety-five names under the heading "Suspects Eliminated." However insignificant it appears on the page, it represents the sum of the bureau's effort to find the killer or killers—the big roundup of every person they considered even briefly in the case. One hundred ninety-five is quite a large number in any investigation. It demonstrates the scope and effort put into the case for three years running. It also shows the futility in trying to find a good suspect. The vast majority of names on this list appear only once. Some receive slightly longer treatment: a description of the crime that brought them to the bureau's attention and the reason for the suspect's elimination. A few criminals had their misdeeds thoroughly described, resulting in the period dramas of George Dunkin, Bill Russell, and the mysterious J.D. Harney.

The suspect who got the most attention by far was Jack Santo. He was the subject of dozens of reports. His thirteen criminal associates generated quite a few reports, as well. Like the Crater Lake murders, Santo is largely forgotten now. But he was notorious in his day— as well known as any crime figure in America the year before his execution—and for good reason.

You could not avert your gaze from the leader of the Mountain Mob. Six foot two and stocky, Big Jack paid a lot of attention to his appearance. In every courtroom photograph (and there are many), his thick wavy hair was combed and his pencil-thin mustache neatly trimmed—sort of a Hollywood lumberjack.

He first gained notoriety after the strangulation death of a well-to-do widow, Mabel Monahan. She was a retired Vaudeville performer living alone in a quiet Burbank ranch house. On the evening of March 9, 1953, she answered a knock at the door. Standing just outside, a petite blond woman said she was having car trouble and asked to use the phone. Before Monahan could answer, Barbara Graham pushed her way inside followed by Jack, Emmett "The Weasel" Perkins, Baxter Shorter (a specialist in blowing safes, or box man), and John True—a rugged, soldier-of-fortune type in the Santo mold.

They had broken into Mabel's house looking for cash skimmed from gambling tables in Vegas and Palm Springs. Why would a slightly disabled old lady keep that kind of money inside her home, especially unprotected loot? The way Jack heard it from Perkins— who heard it from a third party even less reliable—her former son-in-law was mobster and casino owner Luther "Tutor" Scherer. She was keeping the skimmings locked up in her bedroom closet. Over one hundred thousand dollars and nothing between those fat wads of cash and Big Jack except an over-the-hill showgirl and a safe small enough to blow with a cherry bomb.

Big Jack, Emmett Perkins, and Barbara "Bloody Babs" Graham during a break in the Mabel Monahan trial in Los Angeles. Bab's sad life was made into a classic film noir movie *I Want to Live!* Susan Hayward won an Academy Award for her portrayal, which questioned the ethics surrounding capital punishment. Graham, Santo, and Perkins were executed for this crime at San Quentin on June 3, 1955. Courtesy: Los Angeles Public Library Photo Collection

Unfortunately, like most of Jack's work at the end of his career, the Monahan job was based on bad information and was poorly executed. There was no skimmed casino money in Monahan's house, or even a wall safe. Jack insisted there was. When she could not satisfy this impossible demand and began pleading for her life, they tied a pillowcase around her head.[29] When the dirty work was done, they left almost empty handed—even though the old dowager had $15,000 worth of jewelry in a purse hanging in her closet.

Two days later, Monahan's body was found by her gardener. A few days after that, information began trickling in to the District Attorney who had the box man, Baxter Shorter, brought in for

---

29 Barbara Graham received the death penalty for killing Monahan, which she denied. Any of the other robbers that day was capable of murder, particularly Emmett Perkins.

questioning. It only took a little squeezing before Shorter named Santo and the other accomplices.

In perhaps the best example of Jack's cunning, persuasive style, he talked his way out of being charged or arrested for this crime—convincing detectives that his involvement was "just a big misunderstanding." They let him go.

Within a few days, Jack got to Shorter and took him for a ride. His mother testified that the last time she saw her son he was climbing into the backseat of Santo's car. No one ever saw Baxter Shorter alive again—or dead, for that matter. His body was never found.

Underestimating Santo's ruthlessness, the LAPD had inadvertently set up the box man. Now their stool pigeon would never sing again. Eventually word got around and everybody who knew anything about the Monahan job clammed up—which was smart. You'd have to be crazy to rat on Jack Santo. Even behind bars, he was a big, swinging dick. If he couldn't do the job himself, Jack knew who to call.

Before his execution at San Quentin two years later, Santo would be tried and convicted in two other capital murder cases. In three separate trials, juries found he participated in six murders, not including Shorter.

Jack had a flair for publicity. For weeks, the Monahan trial generated breathless headlines and juicy details. Jack zeroed in on the *Los Angeles Times* as the best vehicle to make his case in the court of public opinion. Santo began spinning tales of a self-styled Mountain Man Mobster with his own criminal syndicate. The enigmatic backstory he provided featured his days doing honest work in the Sierra gold fields—leaving out how he "high-graded" and cheated other miners in a later failed business venture. He liked to talk about his military service and that he was always guided by a code of ethics, honor, and honesty, fighting the good fight, etc. etc. There is no record that John Santos or Jack Santo ever served in the military during the years he might have been eligible. In fact, most of what is known about Jack's life indicates that he screwed people over every chance he got—from wives and lovers to complete strangers and everyone in between. But that was not the narrative he shared with the *Times*.

The source of his undoing, according to Santo, were less principled associates, professional misunderstandings, or plain bad luck. He got the last part right. His luck officially ran out in Burbank, California.

The first robbery/murder involving Santo occurred in 1951 in Nevada City. At the time, Jack's criminal enterprise was centered there, in the Sierra foothills. It involved the owner of a mining operation whom Jack thought was holding a lot of cash hidden in a safe—the same scenario as the Monahan case, but two years earlier. Sadly for the mine owner, this botched robbery would also end tragically.

The operation was planned by Santo, though he did not participate. He was afraid he might be recognized by the mine owner with whom he'd had some dealings. Without much planning and carried out in a manner that was literally scattershot, three masked men showed up one night at the doorstep of Folsom goldmine operator Edmund Hansen. The thieves believed Hansen had a safe full of cash and valuables and, like the Burbank job, they brought a box man to blow it up with nitroglycerine, or "juice." When Hansen first saw the men in their disguises, he screamed and ran out the back, but not before being shot several times. He was subdued and brought inside.

The first hitch in the caper came when the robbers could not locate Hansen's safe because, like Mabel, he did not own one. Undeterred by his wife's pleading, the robbers undressed and tortured Edmund in front of her, lighting matches around his groin area. When they realized the big score Santo promised would not be forthcoming, they walked out of the Hansen house, got into a waiting getaway car, and left. Remarkably, Hansen survived and was taken to the hospital.

Doctors were cautiously optimistic despite not being able to remove all the bullets lodged inside the old 49er. After a few days, he was able to speak to police. Unfortunately, both he and his wife were too traumatized to give accurate descriptions of the intruders. Another setback was Hansen's health, which turned out worse than originally diagnosed. The day his doctors predicted he would be able to testify at a trial, Hansen sat up in his hospital bed to give a statement. Before he could speak, he fell back into his pillow and died.

It took a while, but eventually the Nevada County Sheriff got wind of the Santo gang's involvement in the Hansen murder. Though he was not present that night, several co-defendants named Santo as having planned the attempted robbery. His girlfriend and common-law wife, Harriet Henson, drove the getaway car.

Like any self-respecting gangster mol confined to a jail cell, Harriet confirmed all of Jack's alibis. She was more than just a good sport. This rough and ready gal was in deep with Jack and his nefarious dealings—at least the five murders he committed in the Sierra foothills. She was not part of the Monahan job, except to testify that Jack was with her on the date in question—a complete lie.

Harriet Henson grew up in hard times and fell in with hard people. One account describes Henson's formative years in Montana as marked by poverty, abuse, and a sexual assault. Harriet Henson might have perceived Santo as rescuing her from a worse situation.

During the Monahan Trial in Los Angeles, she was a witness for the defense. The print media showed no mercy and described her as a "mountain wildcat," which sounds pretty sexy, until you see her photographs. She looks more like a frail librarian. In the Hansen Trial, she was deemed an accessory and got away with time served.

If only she'd quit Jack after the Hansen job, but she didn't. The next big ripoff masterminded by her boyfriend got Harriet a life sentence[30]—remanded to California Institute for Women in Corona—for another bungled robbery, the most deadly one yet.

---

30 She served seven years then was released from California Institute for Women in 1961. She returned

Persons of Interest and Big Personalities

Behind her horn-rimmed glasses was a murderess who participated directly in the deaths of five people, including three children. No one alive knew Jack Santo and the extent of his criminal enterprise better than she.
Courtesy: LAPL Photo Collection

The crime that most drew the FBI's attention to Santo occurred between the Hansen and Monahan jobs, just two hundred miles south and ten weeks after the murder of Jones and Culhane in Crater Park. One of the most brutal, senseless mass murders in California history occurred in 1952 in Chester, a remote and idyllic logging town, nestled in the middle of the Sierras. Several mills cut and trimmed the raw lumber, employing much of the male population at a competitive wage. The little timber town was prosperous, big enough to support two grocery stores. One of these was operated by Gard Young, a well-liked and respected Mormon.[31] The grocer lived by many of that faith's hard-working principles. He eschewed strong drink, was honest to a fault, and did his best to serve the community. Besides providing fresh groceries to his neighbors, Young also was willing to cash the local lumbermen's payday checks every Friday. This was because there were no banks in Chester. The nearest was a Bank of America branch in Westwood, fourteen miles away, which was where the estimable grocer did his banking.

---

to her old waitressing job in Auburn.
31 The grocer was related to the religion's modern founder, Brigham Young.

Persons of Interest and Big Personalities

Considerably less well thought of in the Chester community was a down-on-his-luck house painter, Larry Shea. When he wasn't working, which was most of the time, Shea enjoyed deer hunting and trout fishing. He also occasionally drank to excess. These avocations brought him into the orbit of Jack Santo. Just as Jack had a reputation with the ladies in the Mother Lode—men enjoyed his company, as well—but not for the same reason. Jack Santo knew areas of the northern Sierras as well as any hunting guide. He always got his buck, legally or not. He was an expert horseman, gun collector, and fisherman. In other words, what they used to call "a man's man." Shea was more average in abilities and appearance. Naturally, he gravitated toward his good-looking friend—a little too closely. Jack once sold Shea a stolen car. For some reason this did not cause a rift in their friendship and Shea played happy host at his Chester cabin to Jack and his friends whenever he was in the neighborhood.

Santo was always on the lookout for business opportunities to fit his skill set and aversion to real work—in other words, easy money. During one of his visits, Shea mentioned a local grocer doing very good business and also operating as the local bank. It was common knowledge that Gard Young did his banking on Thursday. He took the cash in stacks of twenties, which was the denomination local loggers preferred when signing over their week's wages. Santo knew a good thing when he heard it. He would have liked it even better if he'd known that Young's withdrawals regularly exceeded $7,000. That's eighty thousand bucks today, a considerable amount.

On Thursday October 2nd, Jack drove up from his home in Grass Valley for the long weekend. He planned on staying with the Sheas and brought along a couple of friends to join the party—his girlfriend, Harriet Henson, and Emmet Perkins. The latter had acquired a nickname that he probably didn't enjoy, "Weasel." It stuck because of Perkins' beady eyes and big ears. He really did resemble a weasel—a rodent, at any rate.

Persons of Interest and Big Personalities

Shortly after arriving, the trio decided to drive to Westwood, where they parked and waited at the curb just in sight of the Bank of America. They drove a green four-door Oldsmobile with a cream top. In his typical freewheeling fashion, Santo had borrowed it that day from another girlfriend in Grass Valley, Bernadine "Bernie" Pearney.

With a physical description of the grocer and his car, eventually the Santo Gang recognized Gard Young entering the bank. After doing his business inside, Young made one more stop in Westwood. A couple blocks down the street, he pulled over, walked around his big Chrysler sedan, and opened the rear door. Four small children hopped out and excitedly walked from the curb into an ice cream parlor.

Inside the green Olds, they realized four small children were traveling with the man they intended to carjack and rob. It's one thing to hold up a middle-aged man, but to do it in the presence of four small children is problematic. Children may not understand the nature of an interaction between grown-ups, but they can describe what they see. This might have presented a large enough complication to call off the job that day, but Jack was not discouraged—not while he was standing on the verge of a big score. He had established a pattern of making bad decisions in the moment that compounded themselves. All were motivated by greed and financial desperation. What set him apart from common criminals who share this behavior was his callous disregard for human life. Jack Santo did not care who got hurt or even killed as long as he got what he wanted.

When the group emerged from the ice cream shop, the four children carried their cones across the sidewalk into the backseat, careful not to spill. Three were Young's daughters: Sondra was just three years old, Jean was seven, and Judy was six. The fourth child was a neighbor boy named Michael Saille who was four years old. When Young drove away and steered the big Chrysler in the direction of home, he did not know he was being watched. Neither did anyone in Westwood notice the two-tone Oldsmobile that pulled out shortly after.

For a few miles, Gard Young drove west on Highway 36 back to Chester, still unaware of the danger moving swiftly in his direction. Carrying seven wrapped bundles of twenty-dollar bills in thousand dollar stacks inside your jacket pocket has a way of sharpening one's senses. It is possible Mr. Young may have seen what was coming.

What happened next is not well understood because the participants did not agree in their court statements. Santo's and Perkins' testimony each served themselves. Harriet Henson went out of her way to favor her boyfriend, Jack. A few horrible details are not in dispute, however.

Everyone in Young's vehicle was bludgeoned repeatedly until none showed any sign of life. All five were placed in the trunk of the vehicle, which was driven into a thicket. After leaving the scene, Santo, Perkins, and Henson returned to Larry Shea's cabin with seven thousand dollars in twenty-dollar denominations.

Jack's taste for high living became the instrument of his undoing. After having returned to the Sheas, Santo sent Perkins and Henson back to Grass Valley in the Oldsmobile to establish an alibi. With a drink in one hand and a telephone in the other, Santo wasted no time making a long distance call to girlfriend number two, Bernie Pearney, requesting her companionship for the weekend. She was crazy about Jack, even if she had to share him with Harriet. Bernie Pearney knew she was his favorite, though. She was a looker too, and a girl who liked to party. Before they got off the phone, she was making plans to take the bus to Chester that afternoon.

Fresh from beating to death four small children and an innocent grocery man, Jack was feeling so good about his situation, he decided to take Bernie on a spending spree in The Biggest Little City in the World—Reno, Nevada.

Jack and Bernie had a ball. At a popular Western Wear emporium, the clerk recalled the comely Pearney. The blonde-haired, suntanned beauty was described at trial and in the papers as resembling a "rodeo queen." The store clerk also remembered Jack peeling several twenties off a thick roll in payment for the fancy new duds. Later that night, Jack got so loaded he tossed an ice bucket through the window of their motel love nest. Perhaps the crazy antics weren't just meant to impress his girlfriend, but intended to establish an alibi for his whereabouts the day of the murders. Like all of Jack's cockamamie plans, it did not work out. Shea's phone records put Jack in Chester during the time in question.

His big binge with Bernie was uncovered by, of all people, the wife of a Sierra County deputy sheriff, Fern Watters, with whom Bernie was acquainted. Plumas County Sheriff Mel Schooler described how it happened.

"Mrs. Watters' suspicions were aroused when she talked to Bernie, and Bernie told her she hadn't worked all week and that she had just been on a weekend spending spree with 'the bigshot,' Jack Santo."

Schooler added, "Bernie boasted about it, because she figured she had taken Santo away from Harriet. Bernie had a whole bunch of new clothes—blouse, skirt, and $500 in her purse. She said Santo won a lot of money in Reno."

When authorities followed up on Jack's success at the gambling tables that weekend, he hadn't won a hand.

At trial, searchers described what they found in the car just off the road and partially hidden in the brush. The trunk of the Chrysler was not shut. Opening it, they were met with a gruesome sight. Five lifeless bodies were stuffed into the compartment, "stacked like cord wood." Rescuers began to remove the bodies one by one. In the process someone heard a faint cry emanating from inside the trunk. Little Sondra, the youngest of the group, clung to life with a bloody, fractured skull. She was rushed to the hospital.

The little girl who clung to life next to her deceased siblings and father eventually lived. After having recovered from an indescribable trauma, the state and her mother thought Sondra Young well enough to testify. From the witness box, the little girl who was now five years old, stood up and pointed at Santo.

"That's the man who hurt my Daddy."

In a life of low points, this was Jack's nadir. The jury found Santo and Perkins both guilty and sentenced each to death. Older residents of Chester and Chico who remember this terrible episode still refer to it as The Chester Massacre.

After being found out, Santo was unmoved. Most people would not enjoy being on trial for the murder of three children and their father. But Jack wasn't like most people. He lacked a conscience. During the court proceedings, he was carefree—smiling at the audience, reading the newspaper during testimony, and yawning when the proceedings bored him. He had apparently lost interest. Can you blame him? He was already on Death Row for killing Mabel. How many times can you execute a man, even one as bad as Jack Santo?

Jack gave a rambling interview to the *Oakland Tribune* about Chester in June 1954. The subject was Harriet Henson and her involvement in the quadruple homicide. Had she been there at all? Most court watchers found it hard to believe any woman would participate in a brutal mass murder involving children; for that reason, she got a lighter sentence. When speaking of it, Jack again put himself in the best possible light. Though he once extinguished a cigarette on her thigh while he had her tied up, for the press he affected a chivalrous attitude toward his ex.

"The girl is not guilty. She simply wasn't there. I warned her the story she gave out would get her involved, and she has only herself to blame."

In other words, a complete lie.

For her part in the murders, Henson was sentenced to life in prison. After seven years, she was released from the California

Institute for Women in 1961. She was thirty-eight years old. She returned to her old waitressing job, picking up shifts at Lou La Bonte's in Auburn, trying to put her life back together. After that, she disappeared from the record, which is unfortunate for this narrative. Perhaps no one else besides Jack Santo had a larger story to tell about his criminal exploits than the girlfriend, Harriet Henson. If anyone knew his darkest secrets, it was she. But that story died with her.

Santo and the FBI

During the Chester trial, the FBI downplayed their interest in the Santo Gang and only occasionally spoke to the media about Jack in connection to the murders at Crater Lake. One newspaper article in 1953 ran a headline summing up the bureau's reticence.

FBI Mum on Santo Link to Crater Lake Killings

> The FBI today refused to confirm or deny the possibility it is checking to determine if convicted murderers Jack Santo and Emmett Perkins may have been involved in the slaying of the General Motors executives in Crater Lake National Park in 1952... FBI Special Agent in Charge William M. Whelan of the San Francisco office said, "We are conducting an intensive investigation to solve the murders at Crater Lake. In the course of the investigation we are talking to many people. We have nothing to say at this time regarding Santo or Perkins."
>
> ***Bill Fiset***
> **Oakland Tribune** *December 1, 1953*

Though Jack claimed he was innocent in the whole matter and they had no evidence connecting him, the bureau was not satisfied. If the FBI couldn't get Jack to admit to doing the Crater Lake murders, they should be able to shake loose someone from his inner circle who could put Jack at Crater on July 19th. So they started asking. Unlike the three prior trials that featured several members of the so-called Mountain Mob rolling over on Jack for lighter sentences, not a single one put Jack at Crater Lake, including Barbara Graham. The most cooperation they could find was Santo's host in Chester, Larry Shea.

After being implicated in the massacre, Shea was persuaded by the prosecutor to make a deal and testify against his old hunting partner. While he was in a cooperative frame of mind, agents on the Crater Lake case paid him a visit. Had Shea ever heard Jack mention anything about two murders up north in July that year?

Shea offered agents a tidbit. After pheasant hunting in the uplands near Woodland, California, Shea recalled Jack saying something during a night of heavy drinking.

> Someday the FBI will really work me over, but good, for a job that happened up in Oregon.
>
> **Jack Santo to Lawrence Shea**
> **FBI File Vol. 6, p.61**

The FBI seemed to finally be getting somewhere. Shea was clear about so many details; that's why this item turns up in the file. The only problem was that, according to Shea, Jack made that drunken admission in 1951—more than a year before the incident at Crater Lake.

Regardless of Shea's inability to provide a tangible lead, the FBI still liked Santo—a lot. Santo had a family connection to Crater Lake. He was born in Medford, the gateway to Crater Lake. Jack still had family there who ran a gem shop on Main Street with Jack's given name on the sign, Santos. It may be assumed they played down their kinship with their son and brother, the child murderer.

Jack had visited Medford as recently as October 1951. His primary reason for that trip was not to see his family but to commit a burglary with two pals from the old neighborhood, the Bauer Brothers. It looked promising. They had a local policeman working for them on the inside, which is not surprising. Jack had a habit of keeping close any law enforcement friends and frequently used them in his alibis. His cop friend let him know that the Medford Police were on to him and that ended it. Jack returned to Grass Valley empty-handed.

Besides having visited the region less than a year before, Santo drew the FBI's attention in other ways. The first was obvious: the sheer number of violent crimes he'd recently committed. Another was his nonchalance about human suffering, which the Chester case made obvious. The FBI file summed up Jack's potential to have done the murders at Crater Lake this way.

> The murders committed by this gang have been brutal and the modus operandi used is similar to the MO which was apparently used in this case. There is no specific evidence linking SANTO and his associates with the murders in this case; however, the similarity of operation during the same general period along with the fact that they are entirely familiar with and have operated in this area make them the most logical suspects in the case to date.

> *FBI file Vol. V p.158 6/14/54*
> *SA Stuart J. Cameron*

Before they were done, the bureau tried to get information about Crater from Perkins, Harriet, Barbara, and all the members of the Mountain Mob past and present. The bureau interviewed two ex-wives, several ex-girlfriends, non-criminal associates, and a former cellmate. Given the sample size, it's not surprising that there was an array of opinions and recollections.

All painted Santo as larger than life. His hunting partners, of which he had many, considered him a gifted outdoorsman—with questionable ethics. Jack frequently invited them to hunt out of season, sizing up each man's comfort level while breaking game laws. He figured that if a man could be talked into poaching deer, he might be talked into more serious and lucrative criminal pursuits. All Santo's drinking buddies said he could hold vast quantities of liquor. Whether he was sitting in a duck blind or behind the bar

Jack Santo looking nervously around the courtroom in Los Angeles during the Mabel Monahan trial. He was found guilty and sentenced to death. At the time, many believed he committed the Crater Lake murders though no evidence ever connected him despite the FBI's best efforts.

Courtesy: LAPL Photo Collection

pouring drinks, Jack Santo was always in charge. He had the kind of big personality towards which other men gravitate. Not all his friends thought so highly; several admitted they were afraid of him.

The multitude of women who knew Jack described him like some rare form of alpine catnip, a rusticated lover with an insatiable sexual appetite who knew how to treat a lady. Like his male friends, a few women deviated from the narrative of irresistible masculinity. They described a tendency to treat them with cruelty to the point of sadism. According to a few anecdotes, it sounds like Jack also performed the functions of a pimp—selling at least one girlfriend for sex.

Persons of Interest and Big Personalities

It's no wonder he's the subject of two true crime novels, *Decathlon of Death*[32] by Jack Leslie (1979) and *A Massacre of Innocents* (2016) by Loren Abbey and Pamela Zibura. The first is a roundup of Jack's criminal career while *Massacre...* concentrates on the Chester case. He's also portrayed in the classic film noir, *I Want to Live!* (1958) for which Susan Hayward won the Best Actress Oscar playing Barbara Graham. In the movie's setup, police follow her to their hideout in El Monte, a dumpy little walkup above an auto shop. Jack and "The Weasel" are laying low there to avoid police after the Monahan job. At the same moment police break down the door, Jack slugs Barbara in the mouth. It is the first appearance of Jack's character in the film. (He appears again later in a courtroom sequence.) Graham is the film's subject and they focus on her last few months awaiting execution on death row. Jack's criminal exploits and personal life could easily carry a film too. Perhaps better than Barbara.

In spite of the bureau's effort to link Jack to Crater, he wasn't having it. He was happy talking at length about anything else, though. His favorite subject of discourse was himself—rambling on about how loyal and principled he was. There was no need for concision or accuracy. Jack was just killing time until it ran out.

Jack's high profile continued to attract attention from newspaper writers the rest of his life. Inside his cell on Death Row, he kept up his charm campaign with the *Oakland Tribune*. Editors assigned the Trib's top reporter Bill Fiset to pay Jack a visit.

Driving from the Tribune Building past Bay Meadows Racetrack and the adjacent marsh, the old highway veered west. At the Chevron Refinery, the San Rafael Bridge connected Point Richmond to San Quentin Prison on the Marin side. The whole trip took Fiset half an hour—from downtown Oakland to SQ driving toward Mt Tamalpais all the way—a very pleasant drive.

32 It tells the story of San Francisco *Examiner* reporter Ed Montgomery, who followed Santo's California trials and wrote sympathetically about the charges against and prison treatment of Barbara Graham. Their relationship was depicted in the movie.

Persons of Interest and Big Personalities

For some time now, the newspapers had played Jack like a slot machine that often paid out in great copy and headlines, but Jack got something out of it too. He craved the attention. When Fiset pulled the handle this day, Jack came up crazy eights, again. He was slowly going mad; prison psychologists noticed it too. The next day in the *Tribune*, his rantings were quoted extensively.

"If you want to write about all this, all I ask is that you tell the truth. I don't want a word in the paper in my favor, if it's a lie.... You can't have associations like I have and not know things, but at this point I'm not about to open up at all.... If I wanted to save my bacon back in Los Angeles I could. There are people shaking in their shoes wondering if I'm going to open up, but I won't, believe me. I'm not a paid policeman."

After this bit of nonsense, Fiset asked Jack point blank about the murders at Crater Lake. He denied them. Moreover, Jack said the FBI knew he wasn't involved, which was actually true by that point. Then he added,

"But they could take me up there and hold a trial and get a conviction the way things are going."

Poor Jack. After you kill three children, a crippled widow, two honest men, and a box man, you cannot catch a break.

Besides failing to get any of Jack's cronies to inform on him, the FBI had other problems. The murders of Jones and Culhane didn't look like Jack's other jobs. There was no premeditation in the Crater Lake case. In the Monahan case, Chester Massacre, and Hansen job, Santo planned for weeks ahead of time to make big scores, in the thousands of dollars. Though he planned badly in all these jobs, they were organized—not spur-of-the-moment for the random contents of two wallets.

By far the biggest problem for the FBI was, try as they might, on the day of the Crater Lake murders, they couldn't put Jack any nearer Crater Lake than the Sierra foothills—300 miles away.

Persons of Interest and Big Personalities

Jack's alibi for the Crater case was a simple paper trail. He had receipts for payments made around Grass Valley and Auburn the day before and day of Jones and Culhane's disappearance. After having the contents of his residence searched for evidence in the other killings, two bills turned up. One was dated Friday, July 18th—payment to his doctor in Grass Valley. What blew the bureau's case out of the water was a check for five dollars—payment for tires Jack bought on credit in Auburn. The check was dated July 19, 1952.

Enough time had passed that no one at these businesses remembered Jack paying in person, but it didn't matter. The receipts established his whereabouts less than twenty-four hours before and on the day of the murders—more than eight hours distant by car.

Santo created alibis for himself in other crimes, like having a girlfriend lie about his whereabouts. But in this case, the receipts were pretty unassailable. The FBI thought so anyway.

> Investigation... reflects JACK ALBERT SANTO cashed a $5 check on 7/18/52 at Auburn and another $5 check dated the same date at Grass Valley. Investigation Auburn also reflects that payment made 7/19/52, which is pertinent date for purchases of automobile tires previously ordered by Santo.
>
> *FBI File, vol. 5 p. 186*
> *SA Wm. Tower Sept. 3, 1954*

One other way to connect Santo to Crater were the six automobiles he had access to around July 19, 1952. Rangers recorded more than four hundred automobiles in the park that day. None were Jack's. There were many ways for the bureau to try to connect Jack to the murders in Crater Park: vengeful ex-associates, jealous girlfriends, a bunch of automobiles he might have driven, his egotistical love of recognition causing him to be seen there and remembered later.

Though he had more loose ends than an old army blanket, none of the threads reached as far as Crater Lake.

Despite the bureau's inability to connect Jack, everyone else with an interest in the case had and continues to have Jack front and center. His name appears prominently in every update, newspaper, and magazine story up to the most recent—a very good piece in the *Alta* by Julian Smith in 2021. He is an eight-hundred-pound gorilla, unavoidable—and that's the problem. After all these years, he still casts a shadow long enough to convince earnest investigators that he must have done it. But they haven't seen page 186 of Volume 5 in the FBI file.

One person who was probably aware of Jack's lack of opportunity to participate in the killings continued to believe he was involved. After conducting her own investigation in 2002, Catherine Simms was emphatic that Jack Santo killed her grandfather, Albert Jones. She wrote about it in a research paper that year.

> Perhaps we may never prove beyond a doubt that Jack Santo and his gang were responsible for these murders but at this time we are convinced that they were somehow involved.
>
> *Catherine Simms*
> *Two Men Cruelly Gagged...*

Former L.A. Police Chief Jack Donahoe conducted his own investigation into Santo to try to connect him in the Crater Lake case. Donahoe appreciated a good mystery. He'd been a captain in the department during the Black Dahlia murder in 1947. He was still chief when Jack was charged in the Monahan case. Donahoe apparently believed he could connect Jack to Crater and went north to the Beaver State to do some sleuthing on his own.

Persons of Interest and Big Personalities

If Donahoe could crack the case, it would burnish his credentials, but not have reflected so well on the FBI or its director. Whatever Donahoe thought he had on Santo was never explained. Or could Donahoe have realized, like the bureau, that Jack was somewhere else when it all went down in the woods beside Annie Creek Canyon?

Before his execution in 1955, Jack offered the most outrageous explanation for his whereabouts on July 19, 1952. He sensed correctly that the FBI had nothing to go on. However, while he still had their attention, Jack decided to poke the bear one last time, spinning another tall tale—a big, fat Western-style lie—starring Jack, of course.

The way Jack tells it, he and Harriet (whom he could count on to corroborate any story he invented) went fishing on July 19th in an area of the Sierras he called Little Tell Creek—about an hour from his home. There was a big thunderstorm that afternoon, but not before he and his girl pulled seventy-five trout from the productive little stream. (Over the limit, a violation of California fish and game regulations—poke, poke). Quite a catch, which they shared at a fish fry with friends later that evening.

The FBI looked into these details. The weather in the vicinity was clear all day. No thunderstorms were reported. Their friends did not recall ever seeing them, let alone enjoying a fish fry with them. Where is Little Tell Creek? It surely must have some terrific fishing. Of the hundreds of Sierra waterways teeming with hungry trout, none are named Little Tell Creek. There isn't a Little Tell Creek anywhere in California. Not that Jack cared. He could have said he was sailfishing in Baja with the governor.

Jack Albert Santo died inhaling cyanide inside the gas chamber at San Quentin on June 3, 1955. Two other executions were similarly carried out that day, those of Emmett Perkins and Barbara Graham.

9 | Finding the Murder Scene Today

A few days after the murders, a local reporter walked onto the scene with a few county officials to gauge their reaction and write a story about it. After Wallace Myers filed his piece in the Klamath Falls *Herald and News* the following day, nothing has been recorded in that exact location; not in newspapers, TV, or park records. It is referred to, but without specificity. Though it's hard to believe, the murder scene had been forgotten about, which seems slightly disrespectful to the deceased. Where was the exact location that Al Jones and Charles Culhane were taken, then gagged and murdered? Could this place, if it were found, still hold clues about what happened here? Not physical clues, obviously, but might the location say something about the crime and who did it?

For our report in 2013, producer Ian Parker and I went with Crater Lake Park Historian Stephen Mark, looking for and hoping to find the tree and murder scene. Though he may know more about Crater Lake and its history than any person alive, Mark could not find the tree and neither could we. It was disappointing and a little hard to believe. The case is mentioned on the park's website. One would think this location would have enough notoriety to draw a few curiosity-seekers. That is not the case.

Though its exact location was lost to time, that did not mean it didn't still exist out in the woods somewhere and might even be rediscovered. It would be difficult, though. Directions to it in the reports vary—with different distances and routes.

Former Sheriff Lloyd Low was pretty clear about the place where Jones and Culhane were killed. He said it was a quarter of a mile from the road. However, a searcher said it was one eighth of a mile from the road while OSP Trooper Bergmann said it was "approximately ¼ mile south of Highway 62…" The FBI teletype from July 25th gives a third estimation, "CRIME SCENE THREE QUARTERS MILE DISTANT FROM AUTO…" Despite the all-caps emphasis, it is the least accurate. The problem is that none of the men estimating the distance walked in the exact same way. They all had a slightly different experience getting there. Understandably, their accounts do not quite agree.

Besides the confusion about the distance to the scene, its direction from the overlook also got mixed up. The FBI file said it was "northwest," which would put it on the other side of Annie Creek Canyon.

Shortly after the murders, park authorities drew an official map of the two scenes. They put the Pontiac more than a mile south of the overlook (see Photos). This only leant to the confusion.

Despite the contradictions, there was enough information that one might separate the accurate information from the bad. According to the three reports, it was near Powerline Road, one quarter to three quarters of a mile from the overlook. Viewing this area on a map or in a satellite view, it is fairly large—too large to locate one tree or group of trees.

Finding the murder scene within it seemed almost impossible, but I wanted to try because that's what you do when you're inside the rabbit hole, looking around and liking it.

The most difficult step is the first. To begin, I used a computer application related to the one I used to reorganize the FBI file. In Google Earth, satellite photos are combined to give a complete view of virtually any place on Earth. Even sitting at a desk inside the Scarborough Public Library in Maine with a snowstorm blowing outside, one may pull up an image looking straight down on the woods between the overlook and Powerline Road in the middle of summer, and see it like a hawk flying above the treetops. In addition to this amazing capability, one may zoom around three-dimensionally, see the relative heights of the trees and measure distances between points. Looking at it this way, the woods become decipherable— even if the location of the murder scene could be anywhere within it.

Another powerful tool was the ability to measure distances in the app. For example, with a mouse click one could measure in feet the distance of the Pontiac to anywhere on the screen.

Besides the advantages of technology, several seventy-year-old photographs contained a great deal of information because, like Google Earth, they were not subject to human error. These old pictures revealed something constant about the place because trees do not move. They may fall down, get eaten by bugs, or be destroyed by a forest fire but they stay in the same exact spot and grow taller as long as they're alive.

Three photos from that day show the surrounding woods, as well as several big trees near the bodies. Two are official Oregon State Police photos shared with me by Cheryl Ousey in her 2001 thesis. The third is a much rarer image that belongs to the park. Stephen Mark gave it to me when we met in 2013 (see Photos). Putting Mark's photo alongside the two OSP photos, the trees could be compared.

Finding the Murder Scene Today

At the time of the murders there were five large conifers very near the scene. Each was two or three times wider than a telephone pole—of medium age and large compared to the other trees. Were they still there? Several fire events had burned over areas in the vicinity since 1952, but none reached the area of the old south gate entrance. Except for new construction, disease control, or to remove hazards near campgrounds or roads, there's very little tree cutting in Crater Lake National Park.[33] It was likely the trees in the three photos were still standing.

From the photographs, one could use the average height of the men in the photos to estimate the width of the tree trunks nearest them. Likewise, the trees' distance and direction from one another could be approximated. Another significant detail: Two trees looked bigger than the other three. The five trees formed an irregular pattern—with the two largest trees conveniently in front. What appeared to be the largest tree was, coincidentally, the one underneath which Jones and Culhane died.

There was a possible sixth reference point: a large patch of bare ground between the two largest, forward-most trees. But trees may have grown over this area in the intervening years.

All this data taken together could be used to hand draw a map of the grouping. Not exactly science, but it was a start. Even with the six data points, the woods were too large and varied to locate the five trees in it. More information would be necessary.

Inside Agent Willard Linehan's report for the FBI, he recorded a seemingly small factoid about the scene which, seventy years hence, stood out.

> The bodies were located two-thirds of a mile northwest of the place where victims' car was found and they were approximately 190 feet southeast of a

---

33 Commercial logging is allowed in many other national forests.

rough powerline road which parallels the highway at
that point.

FBI file Vol. 1, p. 244

This is a tricky passage. For instance, the distance between the
Pontiac and the murder scene was incorrect; it put the latter on the
wrong side of Powerline Road. The relative direction is southwest,
not northwest. What stands out, however, is the distance of the
scene from Powerline Road: one hundred ninety feet. There is no
explanation how Linehan arrived at this number, but it sounds like
he and another agent walked it off with surveyor's tape. Another
aspect of this old calculation was that it might be easily plugged into
Google Earth, so I did.

Suddenly, the area of the search narrowed considerably. Instead
of a square mile of woodland, it became a line, one hundred ninety
feet distant and parallel to Powerline Road. Given the estimates of
the distance from the highway being between one-quarter and two-
thirds of a mile, this made the line in the woods about a quarter of
a mile long. If the scene really was one hundred ninety feet from
Powerline Road, this popsicle stick-shaped area contained it.

What about orientation? In which direction was the scene facing?
Or similarly, where was the highway (or Powerline Road) in relation
to the scene as photographed? Just as the several estimates of distance
disagreed, so were all the compass directions different. They might all
be wrong but what if one were correct? I tried them all. One stood
out.

Trooper Bergmann wrote that Charles Culhane's feet pointed
"due north." Bergmann regularly drove up and down Oregon Route
62. He'd observed this area on a highway map before—not just on
the day of the murders. Calling it "due north" had a certitude about
it, like the FBI measurement from Powerline Road. If Bergmann's

directions were off by ninety degrees or more, this exact spot would remain like a piece in a jigsaw puzzle dumped from the box. But if one knew in which direction the camera was pointed in the several existing crime scene photographs (based on Charles Culhane's feet pointing north) then one would know the direction the trees faced. Their specific configuration would be fixed and easier to find. At least a few pieces began to fit.

I liked Bergmann. There was a confidence in his report that stood out from the others. Reading between the lines, one sensed his professionalism and that he wouldn't report anything he wasn't sure about. After spending hours looking for this special configuration of two large north-facing trees, I thought I found the group I'd been looking for. There was nothing special about the place. It was as unremarkable as any other five trees in these woods: just a stand of fir, lodgepole, and ponderosa pine in the middle of the forest. In front of the two largest trees lay a bare patch of dirt.

If one drew a stick figure on the satellite image at the base of the big tree where Charles Culhane lay in the crime scene photos, the little figure pointed straight up—due north.

There was another puzzle piece that might fit and, if it did, provide a complete picture. I drew a line from underneath the biggest tree straight back to the nearest point of Powerline Road, being careful to place it between the trees. As soon as I clicked, the distance appeared. One hundred ninety-one feet. Nearly perfect. Another piece fit.

Confident that this was the murder scene, other measurements could be made. The distance between where the Pontiac was found at the overlook and the murder scene was almost exactly one-third of a mile. Also, the nearest point on the road—one-quarter mile distant—was across from the turnaround up the hill, not the diagonally-aligned overlook.

Even though the place I found was the scene of a horrible double murder, it would be dishonest to say I was not thrilled. It was satisfying and, in the moment, sort of a revelation. For so many years, this place was a complete mystery to anyone who wondered where it was.

For several hours, I could not take my eyes off it. I could zoom around the app and see the entire woods, highway, and canyon in 3D. Better than ever, I was able to visualize the crime. It was clear now in my head. From the overlook to the turnaround—then straight down the hill to the split fir. And that's when it hit me. What happened: the struggle and violence and fear. To see this patch of dirt where Jones and Culhane were beat down and killed—for nothing. Two good men were gone forever, taken from their families and left to die in these plain, lousy woods. Thinking about it made me agitated and tense. It was time to call it a night.

The Split Fir and Two New Discoveries

It didn't take long before I felt a pull in the direction of the overlook. I needed to see it for myself. Anyone who backpacks, hikes, or climbs in the woods and mountains knows locating specific places in the middle of nowhere can be elusive. It's not like finding the new Thai place on Burnside, but I felt confident I could locate the scene, walking in from the road. The only issue was it was the middle of winter and Crater Lake is one of the snowiest places in Oregon.

In early March, I called Union Creek Resort. The resort was Albert Jones' destination the day he was murdered. It did not seem completely appropriate that I should stay there, whilst trying to find the place where he died, but curiosity outweighed propriety. I could not drive all the way out there and miss the resort. It was central to the story.

I booked cabin twelve for later that week and it was a good thing I did. In just a few days Governor Kate Brown would shut down almost every commercial establishment in Oregon for the Pandemic. She advised Oregonians to stay inside for the time being and most did. I walked across Sandy Boulevard at rush hour that week—one of Portland's busiest intersections—stopping in the middle to look both ways. There were no automobiles driving in either direction for half a mile. It was a weird world that seemed to stop moving.

Thursday and Friday were my days off then. Thursday morning, I found myself driving south on Highway 97 in the direction of Crater Lake National Park. There was almost no traffic on the highway that day, either. Even in March, there's usually a regular stream of cars if the weather's clear, which it was. But Highway 58 all the way to 197 was practically empty. Everyone was staying home at Governor Brown's direction. I could not. I had to see this place, if I could find it. It took six hours—from Happy Valley to Union Creek, Oregon. Under clear skies and an open road all the way, it was an easy drive. I felt a little guilty for enjoying the views of Diamond Peak and Odell Lake; the same scenery Charles Culhane saw on his second to last day. But it was so pretty with snow in the mountains. A few hours later, I was in Union Creek.

Driving down the dirt road to the resort, there was a small glow at the end of it. The adjacent woods were completely dark, penetrated only by my headlights. Twisting a squeaky doorknob, I let myself into cabin twelve: an unpretentious log cabin with a queen bed, bathroom, and tiny galley kitchen. Someone had turned on the wall heater for me, which seemed odd because the resort looked deserted.

The little room smelled like a sawmill. The little glow I'd seen emanated from a lamp on the bedside table. Except for the highway sign, it was the only light in the whole resort.

Unpacking my briefcase and laptop, I wanted to go over the satellite map one more time and compare it to two sections of the snowy road I'd just driven through. I quickly discovered that WiFi and cell phone service do not intrude on the peace in Union Creek,

Oregon. Disconnected from the rest of the world, I only had the starlight through the window to keep me company—and a short whisky, cheese, and crackers. Then I lay down and pictured the map in my head. The wheels started turning, but in the wrong direction, away from sleep.

During the day, it's easy to keep your mind on task, driving and planning. When it's dark out with your head resting on a pillow, pictures and scenes that had been kept to the side find their way forward. Jones and Culhane laid out under the tree. That crappy patch of woods. The Pontiac door swung open. I went over it for hours until the stars disappeared and the sky turned light gray. The curse of insomnia had sabotaged me—as usual, the night before something big. I may have slept an hour.

Rolling out of bed and parting the curtain, the sky between the trees was a brilliant bright blue. The sunlight pierced the woods at a low angle, illuminating little patches of snow.

When waking up is painful, coffee is good. I was glad to see a tiny coffeemaker perched above the sink. After a few minutes of percolating, two small caffeinated cups dripped into the pot. Adding sugar and powdered creamer, it was satisfying inside the snug cabin, and just in time. My mind was still bothered. I was in the place Al Jones planned to stay and looked forward to, but never reached. Later, I would see the same forest view he saw before his eyes shut forever. A decent night's sleep would have kept the dark thoughts away. I busied myself getting ready.

Driving from Union Creek Resort to the overlook took thirty minutes or so. In that time, three cars passed me going the opposite direction. The new south gate entrance, located just off Highway 62, was open, but it looked unmanned and there were no cars there. I knew I would be alone today—wherever I went.

Driving past it, the overlook was difficult to see under six feet of snow. Of course, there was no place to park. High snowbanks on both sides discouraged a U-turn, but there was no traffic either. I wheeled the jeep around in the middle of the highway and headed back up the road.

The nearest pullout was more than a mile uphill on the canyon side. There was evidence in the snow that a few people had gotten out and walked around. On the other side of the highway, the snowbank had a little lip at the top where marks indicated someone had scrambled over it.

I threw my old Tubbs snowshoes, poles, and backpack next to the car. Tightening the binding around my boots took more pulling than usual. Then I was off. The snowshoes made a gentle clacking sound, dangling from the toe clips. It was the only sound out there that morning.

I had the canyon on my left side and the highway to my right, and every few minutes a car passed by. In the woods and elevated six feet above the road, I could see the drivers and passengers clearly, but they never noticed me standing there in my hunting jacket.

At one point, I could see down the cliff face to the waters of Annie Creek, a silvery thread between the willows and shallow snowpack. I listened to the faint trickle at the bottom of the abyss then realized I was standing alone on the edge of a cliff. Carefully, I placed my steps and pole plants along the ledge until it widened and I was back in the woods.

A few minutes later, I recognized the wide, treeless area next to the highway. It was the overlook covered in six feet of snow. Walking heavily into the middle, I unshouldered my pack and rechecked my gear: Cameras, flashlight, two cheese sandwiches I made the day before, a blanket, and two big waters. I also carried a compass, my phone, and a map, which I probably didn't even need. I knew this specific area by heart now. I could see it and the murder scene just through the woods with my eyes closed.

On my phone, I'd plotted the latitude and longitude of it. I saw the little blue pulse indicating where I was now standing at the overlook.

Finding the Murder Scene Today

A short ways south and west of it, a compass symbol indicated the murder scene. To orient myself, I turned my body directly towards it, then looked up at the sun. It was just off my left shoulder—as high as it would get today. It was already noon.

On the snowbank above the highway, I removed my snowshoes and cradled them in my arms then slid on my butt. Walking across the desolate highway, my boots had left a path of snowy footprints that quickly melted and disappeared into the warm blacktop.

The snowbank on the opposite side was slightly too high to see over. I threw the gear on top of it. To get myself up, I plunged both hands and feet into the side of the snowbank, as deep as I could, searching for any hold to support my weight. But the snow was soft and the harder I scraped, the more fell under me. Each time, I wound up standing on the highway looking around, afraid of being run over by the nonexistent traffic. The effort was tiring. I worried a little that this adventure might end before it started. Eventually, the effort created a 45° indentation that allowed just enough purchase, in two quick steps, to bound up and get my torso flat with the top. After flopping around a bit, I got my feet under me. Brushing off the snow, I collected my gear, adjusted the pack and pole straps, and took off again—with the sun still to my left.

In many ways, navigating in snowshoes is easier than walking the same ground in summer. Snowshoeing is a greater exertion and slower, but the line is direct—without obstacles to step over or around. I attempted to move in a straight line to the scene as fast as possible, timing myself. I moved quickly, but the traverse across the hill had to be regularly corrected to keep tracking west. It would have been easier to go straight down the incline, but that would lead away from the scene.

Breathing hard to maintain the pace, I stopped slightly east of my destination. My stopwatch indicated this energetic push took almost ten minutes to go a third of a mile. This did not seem possible, but the course corrections slowed me down.

Finding the Murder Scene Today

I checked my phone, which flashed the message "No Service." The map application had not updated since leaving the overlook, so it would not help either. I stuffed the phone back into my jacket and took a look around. Except for the snowshoe trail I created, there were no other signs out here—not even a paw print.

I walked a short distance over the tops of buried little conifers, bent slightly and looking forlorn. Now I stood in the middle of a narrow, treeless line that went straight through the woods. It took a few moments to realize I had stumbled across Powerline Road. This was... something. At least I knew where I was. This seemed like a good time to take a break. The cheese sandwich I'd made the day before tasted like an old dog treat. Fortunately, I had a lot of water to wash it down. I pulled the phone from my pocket and tried it again.

Reopening the map application, to my complete surprise, a pulsing blue dot mimicked my movements along the road. Beside it, the compass symbol hovered benignly over the spot where Al Jones and Charles Culhane had died. I could not believe my lousy cell phone navigation app was working again. The phone indicated I had "No Service"—yet there it was! My position relative to the scene. I immediately began walking in that direction.

The scene was one hundred ninety feet through the woods in a line from the road. Picturing a surveyor's tape stretched out between the trees, I followed it and found myself standing in a small clearing.

Awkwardly, I maneuvered my snowshoes around and, for the first time, saw something I recognized. It was the little configuration of trees I knew from the photograph that Stephen Mark gave me—except now the ground was white.

Staring at the tree that Jones and Culhane had died under, I noticed that it was split down the middle. You couldn't miss it, though I had until this moment. The big trunk divided into two medium-size trees that reached into the sky, slightly off center. Looking at Stephen's photo, I realized the old image faintly indicated that the trunk was split. I'd looked at this picture a hundred times, but never noticed it before. Neither had I read any description in the files about the character of the tree the men were found underneath. This significant clue as to where exactly the men died was a revelation. Another indication that this was the tree in the crime scene photos was its unusual width in satellite images of the five trees in the woods. It was not round like all the trees near it. Rather, the tree appeared oddly wide. The trunk splitting into two medium size trees explained the anomaly that gave it a specific signature viewed from above.

If this was the tree, it should have a blaze mark carved somewhere on it. I circled slowly in the snow, not sure if I should look up or down. What would a seventy-year-old blaze mark look like? I stepped cautiously around the split fir, like in a cemetery. But there were no grave markers underfoot, just the snowpack and the circle I was inscribing in it.

And there it was. Chest high. A greenish, vertical scar and perfect rectangle—eighteen inches long and three inches wide. It looked like a square-ish scab that had healed over. Instead of scar tissue, green tree sap filled the cut. On top of the sap, a resident of these lonely woods had left a footprint.

The tree scar made eight data points total: the bare ground north of the split fir, five trees all lined up, the blaze mark, and the split fir in Stephen's photo. Once again, the puzzle pieces fit. I tried to take it all in and the surrounding area. It was not much to look at. Mostly medium size or smaller evergreens and even more spindly ones struggling to get a foothold.

It was depressing to think that this unappealing patch of woods was the last thing Albert Jones and Charles Culhane saw before they died. They deserved a lot better. I did not know them personally, but I respect the lives they led and regretted their end. They were enjoying themselves: En route to a weekend fishing trip and tour of one of the prettiest places on Earth. Then in a heartbeat their worlds turned upside down. Finally finding the scene was not as satisfying as I hoped it would be. There was no fullness in it—just a lonely, empty feeling.

This place was so odd. Not more than a quarter mile from a busy highway. The hum of cars was audible through the trees, but next to the split fir, it was desolate and removed. It was not like standing in the woods near a campground or walking a quarter mile from the trailhead. There you might expect to see another hiker or camper. Here by Powerline Road, you were all alone—yet almost within shouting distance of the road.

Glancing over my shoulder, the sun had slipped lower than I realized. I'd lost track of time. It was getting colder, too. I needed to get out of there. Then I remembered one last theory that needed testing. Was the quarter mile route straight uphill to the highway easier and faster? I checked the map and shuffled off. I did not look back.

The blaze mark carved into the split fir on July 21, 1952 in order to allow investigators to return and look for evidence in a featureless patch of woods.

All uphill, the line went straight into the incline. It was much easier to negotiate than the sideways trek from the overlook. In a few minutes, a clearing appeared through the trees. Another minute and I was six feet above the blacktop again. The paved turnaround uphill from the overlook was just to my right. Quick stepping through the open sections, the ascent took less than five minutes.

I couldn't believe how quickly I'd covered it. I thought about going back. Even in the waning light, it would only take a few minutes. The snowshoe trail I made marked the way, so there was no getting lost. Mostly, I was interested to see the woods and follow the route I believed was the one Jones and Culhane took with their killers, stepping just a few feet above their last footfalls.

But I didn't go. I'd had enough—gotten as close as I could or wanted to get this day. Now I needed to create some distance.

Driving back to Portland, the physical exertion of the trek released a few welcome endorphins and the insomnia cloud finally broke. Driving up the highway, my mind wandered—not to the dark places, but areas that looked somewhat brighter. I began to wonder if the name of the man who pushed Jones and Culhane into the woods existed somewhere in the record. There were so many names—mostly one, Jack Santo—but, based on the file, Jack was out. What if there was another name inside the law enforcement records? Someone who had been ignored for some reason, yet that person was actually involved?

Something else stood out. Something many others mentioned who walked in and stood next to the split fir in 1952. The FBI, OSP, and the sheriff all conjectured at some point that the killers had prior knowledge of this area. How else could they have arrived at the ideal location to perpetrate a robbery? And if they knew about this place beforehand, it stands to reason that the killers lived nearby.

What else did the facts of this murder say about the men who did it?

Elements of the Crime and What It Says About the Perpetrators

It was a busy Saturday inside Crater Lake National Park. The perpetrators abducted the victims while cars drove by on Highway 62. *They were extremely comfortable in the location. They knew the highway and traffic flow. They took temporary ownership of the place to get Jones and Culhane into their car and move them up the road.*

Jones and Culhane were taken from the overlook to the woods one quarter of a mile off the main highway. The perpetrators knew the forest where they took Jones and Culhane was not visited by tourists, even on a busy Saturday in July. They could not have found this place by accident. The perpetrators lived locally and either their work, recreation, or both gave them some familiarity with the woods by the overlook.

The Crater Lake murders remain a "perfect" crime. The perpetrators were not reckless. They demonstrated a lot of composure and some experience. Though it may have been the first and last time they killed anyone, the crime's efficiency showed one or both assailants had committed a similar, prior offense.

No one ever informed on the perpetrators during their lifetime. If anyone else knew about the murders, they kept quiet about it—out of fear, respect, a business obligation, or a family tie. They had an exceptionally tight social network.

The offenders stole an expensive pair of wingtip dress shoes. This was not desirable footwear for younger people in 1952. The perpetrator who took the shoes was middle-aged like their owner, Charles Culhane.

The FBI conducted an exhaustive investigation tracing vehicles in the park on July 19th—without result. Since the offenders drove a car into and out of the park that day, they either owned or had access to a vehicle that was not traced to them.

The offenders were ready to tie Jones and Culhane each to a tree. Because the plan was to tie up the victims, they had experience doing it—most likely, tying up and untying farm and ranch stock. They worked as ranchers, trappers, or cowboys.

The offenders had a .32/7.65mm pistol and used it when they felt they had no other choice. They were comfortable around firearms and had used them before, possibly in a prior criminal act.

Despite a thorough investigation, the perpetrators were never suspected in their lifetime for the murders of Jones and Culhane. *The perpetrators were able to effectively disappear.*

The victims' wounds were nearly identical, and unusual. The similarity in the two shots that killed Jones and Culhane, and their placement and efficacy, indicate the shooter had killed this way before, probably an animal or ranch stock. The killer had experience as a rancher, hunter, trapper, or cowboy.

A hand drawing based on the five trees at the murder scene and their relative positions. The sideways "M" represents Powerline Road.

Section Three: Kenneth "Coyote" Moore

Date: 7/25/67

Transmit the following in _____
(Type in plaintext or code)

Via _____ AIRTEL _____ AIR MAIL
(Priority)

- -

TO: DIRECTOR, FBI (70-18550)
           ATTENTION FBI IDENTIFICATION DIVISION
           LATENT FINGERPRINT SECTION

FROM: SAC, PORTLAND (70-759) (P)

SUBJECT: UNSUB;
           CHARLES PATRICK CULHANE;
           ALBERT MARSTON JONES - VICTIMS
           CGR - MURDER
           OO: Portland

           Re Bureau letter to Portland, 8/27/52 concerning the
submission of latent prints in captioned matter.

           On 7/24/67, Captain [   ] Oregon State
Police advised that he had been furnished the names of two
suspects in instant matter and suggested that records at the
Identification Bureau be searched for fingerprints and thereafter
that such prints be compared with latent prints previously
submitted to the Bureau in this matter. The identity of the
individuals are as follows:

b6
b7C   KENNETH MOORE, aka Ky Moore, FBI No. 376 241;

           JOHN WESLEY COLE who lived in the vicinity of Chiloquin,
           Oregon.

           According to Captain [   ] both of these individuals
were Indians and were both found frozen to death in Klamath
County on 3/28/62. Captain [   ] stated he had no further
description for these individuals.

           70-18550 - 493

3-Bureau
2-Portland
RES:jld
(5)

REC. 5

JUL 26 1967

Approved: _____   Sent _____ M _____ Per
           Special Agent in Charge

10 | The Best Suspect Is the Only Suspect

More than seventy years after Albert Jones and Charles Culhane were cruelly shot down for a few hundred bucks, the most accurate narrative and best suspect does not seem sufficiently interesting to fit Oregon's greatest unsolved homicide. No suspect could be as enigmatic or cruel as Jack Santo. Likewise, what actually happened by the overlook does not measure up to Lincoln Linse's thrilling account of his several risky encounters with the killers. Linse's story was amazing. Everyone's favorite suspect, Big Jack was a sociopathic serial killer—and a child killer to boot. These are the narratives everyone writing about this case put forward, true or not. Anyone interested in knowing what really happened by the overlook that day, and who did it, will have to settle for a little less drama.

Solving a case that's been misunderstood for so long requires a complete reboot. Let's start with what we know. All the details in the FBI file, large and small, tell a fact-based story which directly and indirectly describe the perpetrators. Who fits with what is known about the case?

Ultimately, there is only one individual with all the singular qualities the perpetrator possessed on the day of the murders. He was smart enough to pull it off—with help. He was mean enough to mistreat and kill two innocent men for the contents of their wallets. He lived near enough the scene of the murders to know the traffic patterns and, most crucially, the desolate patch of woods where he took the victims. He had a consistent criminal history including an assault where the victims were tied up. Because of the culture and place where this suspect resided, everyone he knew would keep quiet about it—even if they heard about his involvement in the murders. Last but not least, the best suspect in the case admitted to committing the murders on at least one occasion.

Initially, Kenneth Moore was only a minor player in the story, like George Dunkin. Moore's name popped up only twice in the FBI file, and that was in the last few pages regarding a negative fingerprint comparison. In her 2001 thesis, Cheryl Ousey mentioned Moore and found two documents about him that no longer exist. One was a fragment of a 1967 OSP report about Moore's 1934 assault and conviction. The other was a memorandum about the circumstances of Moore's death—the coda to this story.

In her conclusion, Ousey made the case that Jack Santo had done the Crater Lake murders. Alice Simms, after her own investigation, agreed with Ousey (or perhaps it was the other way around) that Santo killed her grandfather. Alan Eberlein was aware of Kenneth Moore during our first conversations, but had not considered him much. When the author began this project in November 2019, Moore was barely on the radar, destined for anonymity.

From here to the end of this book, the narrative concerns only Moore—an evidence-based examination of him and the world he lived in.

An Admission of Guilt

Only two men admitted to the killings under the split fir. One was Bill Russell, but his alibi for July 19, 1952 was quickly confirmed. He could not have been in Crater Park that day, according to his aunt and uncle who were with him in Sacramento.

There was another confessor, however—not nearly so dumb as Bill. This other man's confession was first revealed to a member of the Marion County Sheriff's Department and eventually found its way to the Oregon State Police.

According to OSP, a man named Kenneth Moore quietly confided in his friend, Oscar Arrell—who he believed would never divulge the awful secret—that he, Moore, had been present during the killings. Other than sharing it with his wife, Arrell kept that confidence until December 9, 1966 when, in the last few hours before Arrell died, he reminded his wife one final time about Moore's confession and asked her to contact the sheriff.

This extraordinary story eventually moved up the chain of command—county to state to federal investigators. Yet, the FBI did not include a reference to it anywhere in their file. It is apparent, however, that the bureau was aware of it, based on other documents in the last few pages of the file. Everything we know about Oscar Arrell's deathbed confession is contained in Marion County and Oregon State Police reports.

Though they arrived late in the investigation, the two men named in the deathbed confession instantly became the two best suspects in the case and, other than Jack Santo, the only suspects seriously investigated by the bureau and Oregon State Police. Unlike Santo, they were never eliminated.

According to the Marion County Sheriff and Oscar Arrell's wife, the second man to confess to the Crater Lake murders lived just a few miles from Crater Lake National Park in Chiloquin. Kenneth Moore went by two nicknames, "Coyote" or just plain "Ki." Ki Moore had an extensive criminal history, including one offense very similar to the murders at Crater Lake—a robbery/assault in 1934 where he and an accomplice bound two men after beating and robbing them. For that, he went to Oregon State Prison for forty months.

Only a fool would claim to have done these murders, if it wasn't true. Bill Russell did it to scare a truck driver he intended to rob; and he was dumb—dangerous but dumb. In Ki Moore's case, there was nothing to be gained by confessing. Given his prior criminal history, if word got out, he could land in jail, guilty or not. It would have been foolish to risk that. That is why his confession to a single person whom he trusted has the ring of truth to it.

Moore's Secret and Oscar "Whitey" Arrell

Oscar "Whitey" Arrell maintained Moore's confidence for fourteen years, until a few hours before he died—when he reminded his wife about the secret he swore to keep. He knew and she knew that this information was explosive—and that it came too late. At that time, Kenneth Moore had been dead for almost five years.

The story of Oscar Arrell appears in the Oregon State Police record on page fifty-two. It jumps off the page. It is Marion County Sheriff Thomas Bachelder's firsthand account with Arrell's widow, Hazel, in Silverton. Dated August 26, 1967, it is the single most important document in thousands of pages concerning the Crater Lake murders. Fifteen years after the murders and almost five years after he died, this is the tip that finally brought Kenneth Moore to the attention of the FBI. There is no mention of Sheriff Bachelder, Oscar Arrell, or his deathbed revelation anywhere in the FBI file, however. Though tainted by a racist stereotype, the OSP account provides almost all the information—including the fact that Moore said he had an accomplice that day, John Wesley Cole.

JONES, ALBERT MARSTON - Victim
CULHANE, CHARLES PATRICK - Victim

> On July 24, 1967, Sheriff Thomas Bachelder and Sergeant S. Davidson, Marion County, called at this headquarters and informed they had received information from an unidentified individual to the effect that two subjects identified only as Ki Moore, an Indian formerly residing in Chiloquin, and a half breed Indian, John Cole, also a former resident of Chiloquin, were the subjects responsible for the murder of the two referred to victims.

> *Capt. R.G. Howard (OSP)*
> *MURDER (Supplemental Information), p.1*

Oscar Arrell's deathbed confession is described as well.

> We were later informed that the information received was supplied by Mrs. Oscar Lawrence Arrell, the widow of Oscar Lawrence Arrell, who formerly resided in Chiloquin. The information as to the identity of the informant is to be kept confidential. Mrs. Arrell stated her husband, now deceased, had informed her that Kenneth Moore told him he had been responsible for the duel [*sic*] murders.

> *Capt. R.G. Howard (OSP)*
> *MURDER (Supplemental Information), p.2*

The Marion County Sheriff indicates Hazel Arrell knew about Moore's connection for several years before her husband died. Also, she gives the reason why no one ever said anything about Kenneth

Moore. His name and his actions that day in July became the most closely held secret ever in these parts. Those unfortunate enough to know it made sure not to tell or ever talk about it.

> Hazel Arrell acknowledged that her late husband did have information that Ky [*sic*] Moore had committed this crime. She stated that approximately 3 years ago she and her deceased husband had been to Chilquin [*sic*] and that they had passed near the crime scene. It was at that time that her husband told her that "Ky Moore" had told him that he, Moore, had been involved in the crime. Mrs. Arrell said that she asked her husband why he had never made this information known. He had replied "That's one of those things that nobody talks about," and cautioned her not to reveal this information to anyone.

Hazel Arrell knew Kenneth Moore and had a low opinion of him.

> Mrs. Arrell said that she had lived in Chilquin [*sic*] for many years and was also quite well acquainted with the Indians, including Coyote Moore, who she described as no good.
>
> Due to the fact that no mention had been made of John Wesley Cole, Mrs. Arrell was asked if she knew this subject and she reported that she did.
>
> Mrs. Arrell was asked if she knew of any other persons who might have knowledge of the crime and said that both suspects had families who might know.

> *Officer's Report 7-26-67*
> *Thomas E. Bachelder, Sheriff*

We only know a little about the life of Oscar Lawrence Arrell. According to the 1940 census, he was born June 27, 1894 in Minnesota. He was drafted in 1917 and served in World War I. His grave marker, which includes Hazel, is at Willamette National

The Best Suspect is the Only Suspect

Cemetery outside Portland, Oregon. On Christmas Day 1925, his first wife Lucille Weeks ingested strychnine (an ingredient in rat poison) and was pronounced dead at the Agency Hospital on the Klamath Indian Reservation, as it was then called. In the allotment case to determine her estate, Weeks' sad life was described by Oscar. Though she was only 32 when she died, her three children had all predeceased her—her son with Oscar died at birth.

By the time of the 1940 census snapshot, Oscar Arrell was living outside Chiloquin in Beatty with his second wife, Katherine. Curiously, in this document Arrell is identified as "Indian" though in the inquiry into his first wife's death he testified that he "has no Indian blood."

A crucial element in the story about Moore and Cole is that Arrell didn't invent it the day he died. He'd shared it earlier with at least one other person—Hazel, his wife. It was something they carried with them—a burden perhaps, from which Oscar sought release in his last few minutes on Earth.

Given how crucial Arrell and his wife's statements are to the case, it's fair to ask if either of them might have been lying. John Wesley Cole's grandson and his wife believe Arrell might have been at the overlook that day, committed the murders, and pinned it on Moore and Cole. Let's say that's true. This presumes that Oscar Arrell got away with murder—since no one ever suspected him. Why, in your last few breaths, insist your wife remind the Sheriff about it and risk being found out later? Also Arrell never admitted to doing it, like Moore. He only said he knew who did it.[34]

Almost fifteen years after the murders, Hazel Arrell seemed to possess more information about the Crater Lake case than anyone ever had before. Investigators asked if she knew anyone else who

---

34 Arrell was not a model citizen, either. He was charged with burglarizing a home in Chiloquin in May of 1926, which was a bad month for him. Three days earlier, he had been caught dismantling a car on the reservation and was charged with larceny.

could corroborate her allegation. She offered several names. They were all men who had a close past association with Moore and "might have some knowledge of the crime." Bachelder lists the men and their information this way.

I Lee Hatcher- Chiloquin, Oregon
II Jim Chipman- " " (runs rooming house)
III Paul Wampler- Chiloquin, Oregon (cattleman)

INFORMATION MURDER INVESTIGATION, Page 3
Marion County Sheriff Thomas E. Bachelder, 7/26/67

Eighteen days after Mrs. Arrell reported this, several people connected to this inquiry were brought in for interviews.

Wednesday September 13, 1967

On September 13, 1967, Special Agent Bill Gray of the FBI's Portland office and Oregon State Police Trooper Bill Christiansen drove to Chiloquin to meet the surviving relatives of Kenneth Moore and John Wesley Cole—Moore's brother and Cole's son. Besides them, there were five other people who came in. Two were former friends whom Hazel Arrell had mentioned in her statement. There was also the widow of a third friend. An ex-Sheriff was invited. A fifth friend of Moore and Cole's, who was not invited, elected to come in anyway. All seven interviews were conducted between 8:50 a.m. and eleven that morning.

Alvie Youngblood was the first interview subject. He had been the Klamath County Sheriff's resident deputy in Chiloquin for many years, living there with his wife, a tribal member. Youngblood got right to the point about the two men he'd known since 1931. According to the OSP report:

The Best Suspect is the Only Suspect

"He knew Moore and Cole and believed the former was capable of murder." Youngblood did not believe John Wesley Cole was involved.

One half hour after Youngblood sat down, Bess Wampler (left) came in. She was the widow of Paul Wampler who was a good friend of Moore's, according to Hazel Arrell. Bess' late husband was described as a cattleman, which he was, but he is best remembered for the logging company he started and is still operated by his family today, Paul & Robert Wampler Logging Inc.

Born in Indiana in 1897, Wampler moved to the Klamath Basin in 1903. For most of the rest of his life, he resided in the same small towns, Fort Klamath and Chiloquin, where Kenneth Moore grew up and lived out his life.

According to their obituaries, Wampler first met his wife riding horseback down the street in Fort Klamath. Paul died in 1988 and Bess four years later. They are buried in Fort Klamath Cemetery. During his life, Paul was a financially successful person and respected in the community. He had an enthusiasm for life. He was a hunting guide and horse packer,[35] but his passion was logging, specifically horse logging.

He was also described as a friend and drinking partner of Ki Moore. Their association indicates something interesting about Ken-

---

35 *The Klamath News* September 11, 1925

neth Moore. He socialized with seemingly upright citizens like Paul Wampler who had no criminal record. Or perhaps their friendship says more about Wampler, who may have chosen his friends without discrimination. It is possible Wampler employed Kenneth Moore in his logging operation or on his ranch, and that they worked together at some time in their lives.

Before Bess Docia Briscoe married Paul Wampler (below), she made her way to the Klamath Basin via the Oregon Trail. After marrying, she and Paul lived in logging camps for ten years.

Bess Wampler also knew Kenneth Moore. When asked about him and his possible connection to two murders in Crater Lake in 1952, Bess recalled something her husband told her around that time. She said her late husband "had stated at the time of the murders that Kenneth Moore was capable of doing something like that."

You can make a lot or a little out of Bess Wampler's information. Only a little was related in the report. Reading between the lines, when her husband made that statement to her, he wasn't talking about a stranger. The person he considered capable of committing a double murder was a man he had grown up around and knew well. It is also possible that Wampler knew more than he was saying, but chose not to share the whole dangerous truth with his wife.

The Best Suspect is the Only Suspect

Paul Wampler believed Moore was capable of committing murder. What compelled him to share this extraordinary notion with his wife? A man who's insecure in his marriage might say it to impress his spouse—that he runs around with dangerous people and isn't afraid of them. But what if Paul wasn't trying to impress his wife, and instead was trying to keep her safe by warning her about Moore?

Or did Bess Wampler hear the fuller version of the story, like Hazel Arrell? That Moore did the killings by the overlook and she should never speak about it. Fifteen years later, while being interviewed, did she decide to stop short of a full disclosure? Who could blame her? Until then, no one with knowledge of Moore's potential involvement would touch this story with a ten foot pole. It was radioactive. That's why the feds were there that day. Admitting her husband told her Moore did the Crater Lake murders could set in motion serious trouble. It would necessitate more interviews, under oath, using Bess' disclosure as leverage to gain further information. Any unguarded admission by Bess could help launch a federal investigation with her testimony at the center. What small town widow wants that?

Curiously, of the small subset of people to speak about Moore's possible involvement in the Crater Lake murders, both were widows, Bess Wampler and Hazel Arrell. It seems that before any insider would speak about the case, the source of that knowledge had to die.

In the record of her interview, Bess Wampler's statement merits just four sentences in the report. Without any other description regarding her recollection, Paul Wampler's words from 1952 hang suspended—not a very sturdy peg from which to hang a big case. But those few words are informative, nonetheless. It strongly suggests that Moore was living in the area at the time of the murders. Paul would not bother alerting his wife if he knew Moore was someplace else the day of the murders. It also demonstrates that Paul Wampler thought Moore had means, motive, and opportunity, which would be very difficult to prove seventy years later.

The Best Suspect is the Only Suspect

Bess Wampler's interview shows that at least four people who knew Ki Moore suspected he might be involved in the murders of Al Jones and Charles Culhane—add to that list Sheriff Youngblood and an OSP Trooper at the scene in 1952. More than any other suspect by far, there is so much suspicion cast on Moore and his involvement in the murders that there is really no one else to consider—except the man Moore said was with him that day, John Wesley Cole.

Immediately after Bess Wampler departed the interview room, two men chose to speak to investigators together. Lee Hatcher and Nick Rossi had both been frequent drinking partners of Moore, but neither "heard anyone mention anything about a murder."

Rossi went further.

"If someone locally had done it, someone in Chiloquin would have heard about it before now."

That statement had already been discredited twice that morning. Since they were all interviewed separately, Rossi was likely unaware of Bess Wampler's disclosure and the former Sheriff's suspicions. What's odd about Rossi is that he wasn't invited to participate. Rossi was not on Hazel Arrell's list of people who might have knowledge of the crime. He volunteered to be interviewed, but it is not clear why. Apparently, he thought he knew enough to speak with investigators, though he had nothing material to share, except to say that neither he nor anyone else he knew had ever heard anything about the murders or Moore's possible involvement in them. Another apparent falsehood in Rossi's statements is the suggestion that no one had ever heard of the murders of Jones and Culhane. It was a big story fifteen years earlier that took place only a few miles from Chiloquin. Suggesting no one had ever heard of it before sounds deceptive. Of the seven people interviewed that morning, Nick Rossi worked the hardest selling Moore and Cole's innocence.

In his interview at 10:10 a.m., Kenneth Moore's brother, Leonard, stated he was his brother's only living relative. He said he never heard

Kenneth mention anything about a murder and never knew him to own a pistol despite the fact that Moore was previously convicted for using a .38 pistol in a 1934 robbery/assault. Leonard Moore admitted his brother owned several firearms—both rifles. Before he died, Ki Moore owned a .22 Hornet and a 30-30 for deer hunting.

No one said anything negative about John Wesley Cole, including his son who was the last person interviewed that morning at 10:50 a.m. According to Edward Cole, his father "was a friend to almost everyone on the reservation." As for firearms, Edward remembered his father had rifles and shotguns, but never a pistol.

One other man, Jim Chipman, was another friend of Moore's. He ran a rooming house in Chiloquin. Chipman said he had heard nothing about the murders in relation to Moore and Cole. His interview merited one sentence in the report.

Judging by OSP's record of the interviews, neither Agent Gray nor Trooper Christiansen had much confidence in the discovery that day. Perhaps they had run into a wall. Nevertheless, it was the best and last opportunity they would ever have. The entire session concluded by 11 a.m. and only took a little over two hours. No follow-up interviews were scheduled.

Flying almost completely under the radar that day was Lee Hatcher. It would seem that he let Nick Rossi do the talking; in fact, the report does not record any direct statement from Hatcher. All these years later, only a few people recall "Pops" Hatcher. He was described in 2022 as a guy who "liked to party" and was well-liked.

Another would-be person of interest whom no one was aware of that day was "Pops" Hatcher's stepson, who called himself Lee Hatcher, but whose given name was Harold Nathan Hicks. "Pops" did not mention him. No one did. In fact, his name has never been brought up in connection to this case, but it perhaps should have been, particularly given Hicks' violent past.

Like many of his contemporaries in Chiloquin at the time, Harold Nathan Hicks went by several other names or aliases. One was Harold

Hatcher, but he was known most prominently as "Lee Hatcher." In the late 1940s and '50s, he was a talented rodeo cowboy competing in all the big events around Oregon and Northern California using Lee Hatcher as his rodeo name. His best event was saddle bronc riding, a dangerous contest where physical injuries were common. Hatcher was accomplished, placing regularly and winning.[36] There is no record of Hatcher participating in roping events, though they are a big part of any rodeo.

John Wesley Cole's grandson, Robert, got to know the rodeo cowboy Lee Hatcher, pretty well—eventually marrying into the family. Robert called him "Harold Hatcher" and described his father-in-law's reputation.

"He was a guy you didn't mess with."

Over thirty months and many hours of interviews, Robert shared a lot of helpful background information about several people in this book, including his grandfather. He never went so far as to suggest he knew who had done the Crater Lake murders. In September of 2022, I was wrapping up this story, vetting it with all the sources. I came back to Robert Cole for any corrections he might have to the sections concerning himself and his grandfather, John Wesley Cole. During the last minute of what I thought was our last conversation and just before saying goodbye, he brought up the subject of "Harold Hicks," whom I only knew as Lee Hatcher and Harold Hatcher.

"You should probably take a look at him." Less than a minute later, we said goodbye and hung up.

For a few moments, I sat on the couch and wondered what I had just heard. Looking at the notes I'd scribbled. I did not know what Robert Cole was talking about. We'd already talked about Lee Hatcher, the skilled rodeo cowboy and prickly father-in-law that Robert sometimes called Harold Hatcher. Who was Harold Hicks? A search of his name produced this item on page three of the *Herald and News* dated March 25, 1962.

---

36 *News-Review* Roseburg, Oregon September 5, 1950 p.2

Woman Shot Five Times Accidentally

Verna Hicks, 24, of Chiloquin was in serious condition in Klamath Valley Hospital with five bullet wounds in her left side inflicted "accidentally" by her husband, Harold Hicks, 38, in an early morning shooting Saturday in Chiloquin.

According to Chiloquin Police Chief, Harold Sliger, the Hicks were playing cards in the James C. Wright home in Chiloquin when the .22 caliber automatic pistol Hicks was "fooling around with" went off five times wounding Mrs. Hicks. Officials were called to the scene at 12:20 a.m. and she was transported to Klamath Falls by Chiloquin ambulance.

Hicks was quizzed by Sliger, the district attorney's office, and State Police Officer Dwayne Down and released pending further investigation.

Officers said there were other guests in the home at the time. Three of the Hicks' children and four of the Wright children were asleep in an adjoining room.

Mrs. Hicks was in surgery Saturday for removal of the bullets and was listed as "fair" by the hospital.

This seemed significant enough that I telephoned Robert Cole one more time a few days later. I asked him if he had heard of the shooting. He said he had but was overseas when it happened and did not remember anything else about it. When I asked if his wife was one of the children sleeping in the adjoining room, he said he did not know. Neither was he interested in discussing Harold Nathan Hicks in connection to the Crater Lake murders. Why did he suggest, in our last conversation, that I should look him up? He did not elaborate. Our conversation ended shortly after. We have not spoken since.

For shooting his wife five times at close range, Harold Nathan Hicks was charged with assault with a dangerous weapon. Hicks pled down the charge to simple assault and was sentenced to one year in state prison.

Eight years before shooting his wife, Lee Hatcher was actively rodeo-ing, and about twenty-eight years old when the Crater Lake murders occurred. His stepfather, "Pops" Hatcher, was a close associate of Kenneth Moore's. Any greater connection between the crime and Lee Hatcher/Harold Hicks would be speculation. In fact, that is what his daughter once told me while rejecting my theory about Moore and Cole.

"My dad had a reputation here. Had he been a suspect in these murders, they would have said the same thing about him as they did Kenneth Moore because they (law enforcement) were naturally suspicious people. My dad and Kenneth Moore were men of action. They were people who didn't use a lot of words. They used actions. They weren't going to say anything. They were gonna do it.... So them saying that about Kenneth Moore does not hold water. They would have said it about others."

Gray and Christiansen met a similar resistance to their inquiries in 1967. They may have realized there was no way anyone who knew Moore and Cole was going to give them up. Even though Bess Wampler said her husband had suspected Moore, Special Agent Bill Gray must have realized the ship had sailed in regard to finding an actual witness or any evidence strong enough to reopen the case. Perhaps that's why there is no record of the interviews in the FBI file. Fifteen years after the murders, the less said about it, the better. Also, it avoided a paper trail that suggested the real killers had gotten away.

Despite avoiding disclosing anything in their interagency reports about it, the bureau must have believed there was a strong possibility Moore and Cole were involved, or someone near them. In 1968, the bureau offered a $1000 reward for information about the Crater Lake case and circulated it on the reservation. The amount was not so great as to draw attention, but was unusual that it came sixteen years after the incident. The bureau had not given up. No one came forward with information and the reward was never claimed.

Les "Swede" Harroun was another member of law enforcement who was deeply suspicious of Moore and Cole, and had been for a long time. He was present the day Jones and Culhane were found in the woods. Then a private with OSP working out of the same office in Klamath Falls with Lawrence Bergmann, he never forgot what happened.

Like so much information regarding Kenneth Moore and John Wesley Cole, Harroun's suspicions were revealed posthumously. After he passed away, the trooper's wife, Ruth Harroun, told a reporter in 2002 that her husband "suspected them (Cole and Moore) from the beginning because they were outlaws, and around at that time."

Les "Swede" Harroun (far right) pictured with Asst. Director of the Park Service, Thomas J. Allen and Ranger John Wosky (middle) at the scene on July 21, 1952

224

Echo Across the Marsh

On December 28, 1933, Moore and an accomplice named Silas Barclay went to rob a trapper's cabin on Klamath Marsh belonging to Jimmy Fink who had left for the day. Barclay and Moore must have believed they had the place to themselves and, apparently, did not think the chimney smoke was odd before they broke in around nine o'clock that night. It is hard to say who was more surprised when the cabin door swung open. Inside, they found two men seated by the fire, a father and his son, Herman and Cecil Seaman. That is when the trouble started. The attackers wasted no time taking control, brandishing a thirty-eight revolver.

Like the Crater Lake murders, this robbery did not go as planned, yet was carried out with extreme violence and the threat of death. According to charging documents, the victims feared for their lives. The Seamans were threatened at the point of a .38 revolver then beaten with a blackjack. Fortunately, they had the good sense not to fight back. After tying them to a bed frame, Moore and Barclay stole thirty-seven dollars, twelve coyote hides, two skunk hides, a muskrat hide, several traps, and four firearms of unknown make or caliber.

Eventually, the Seamans freed themselves and notified the Sheriff—providing good descriptions of Moore and Barclay and their car. It took one day to find them. They were brought in and, after a court appearance, bail was set at $10,000.

An Oregon State Police Memorandum contained this passage comparing the Crater Lake murders to the Seamans' assault.

> Kenneth Moore is identified... with aliases of Coyote Moore and Ki Moore. He is the same as SO Klamath County #904 arrested 12/28/33 on charge of assault and robbery. It is noted on the fingerprint card

submitted by the SO Klamath County under date of 1/5/34 that Moore bound and robbed two trappers. It is worthy to note in the homicide referred to, both subjects were gagged prior to being shot.

Capt. R.G. Howard (OSP) 6/25/67
MURDER (Supplemental Information), p.2

Here's how the D.A. described the crime.

... acting together and being armed with dangerous weapons respectively a .38 caliber revolver and a black-jack did commit and assault Herman Seaman and Cecil Seaman with intent if resisted to kill or wound...

District Attorney Dayton Van Vactor
December 30, 1933

The Klamath County Parole Board gave a "history of the crime."

This individual, together with SILAS BARCLAY went to cabin occupied by father and son and there tied the father and son to a bed and robbed them of some money, hides and traps. It took the father and son six hours to release themselves. Kenneth Moore and Silas Barclay are classified as bad men in this locality.

District Attorney Dayton Van Vactor
Sheriff Lloyd Low
Report After Sentencing to Penitentiary

In the charging document, Moore was asked to explain why he did it. There is one word typed in the space provided.

Broke.

In January 1934, Moore and Barclay[37] both pleaded guilty. Moore landed in prison for his longest stretch by far, he was sentenced to five years. Barclay received the same.

The charging papers and several pages of documents associated with the assault remained in the possession of Klamath County for eighty-six years before anyone looked at them again. Though it's only a few pages total, it is more information about Kenneth Moore than exists anywhere else. There's nothing earth-shattering here, just some information about his parents (both were Klamath Indians) and marital status. He was separated from his wife at the time. She'd moved to Northern California. He was short on cash as already mentioned. What is interesting is that he didn't contest the charges. He was completely resigned to his judicial fate. Given all the bad luck he'd had in his life to that point, this

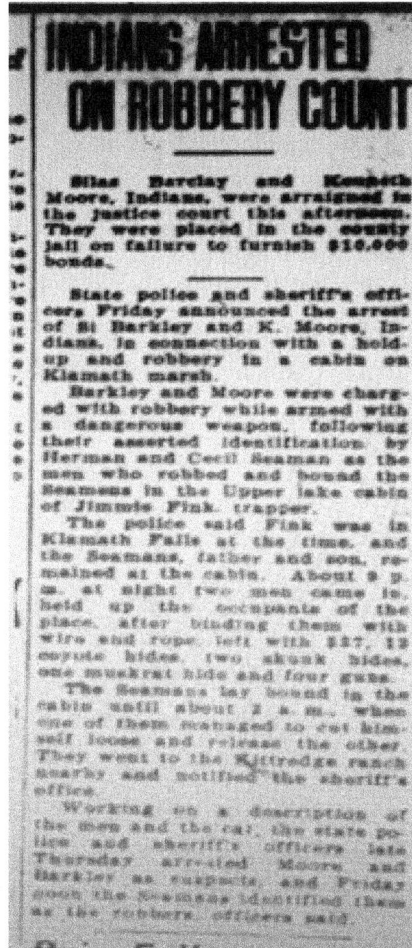

---

37 Before getting caught robbing Jimmy Fink's cabin, Silas Barclay was already a famous outlaw in the territory, having broken out of several jails and earning the nickname "Slippery Silas." When locked up in a tiny jail in Copco California in 1925, he climbed down from the top story of the courthouse using a dozen blankets braided together! It was his third escape from a local jail. A few days later, he was re-arrested and returned to Chiloquin. In a little jail like Chiloquin, guards and inmates eat together, or used to. While they were all having dinner that night, Barclay made a dash for the door. Once outside, he hopped on a "pinto tied to a hitching post" and got away again.

outcome seemed almost inevitable. It's just fortunate it didn't turn out worse; at least, nobody got killed. This time.

There are several significant similarities between the Seamans' robbery/assault and the Crater Lake murders, which is why OSP made reference to them.

- Both were robberies where the victims were beaten.
- The Seamans were both tied to a bed frame. Jones and Culhane were about to be tied up, each to a tree.
- A gun was used to intimidate the victims.
- A car was used to arrive and depart from the scene.
- Two men, Moore and Barclay, worked together to rob the Seamans. Moore said he and one other man, John Wesley Cole, did the murders in Crater Park.
- The general area of Klamath Marsh where Moore and Barclay robbed the Seamans is twenty-five miles, as the crow flies, from the overlook.

There is one very large dissimilarity between the two crimes. Kenneth Moore and Silas Barclay were caught assaulting the Seamans in 1934 and did long prison stretches for it. No one was ever apprehended for killing Jones and Culhane in 1952.

Keeping Moore's Secret

When his name finally appeared in a Marion County Sheriff's report in 1967, Moore had been dead almost five years. Shouldn't someone have realized his connection sooner?

In 1952, the FBI compiled a short list of "hoodlums on the reservation who have previous criminal records and could be considered suspects in this case." From that brief description,

Kenneth Moore should have come to the FBI's attention at that time, but he did not make the cut. Eighteen years was sufficiently long for the Seamans' assault to have faded from memory and Moore with it.

Even after Moore became known to the bureau, in 1968 they offered a $1000 reward to anyone on the reservation with information about the Crater Lake murders. Nothing happened. Besides the passage of time and the tribes' disinclination to help the feds, how else was Moore able to avoid being named in the case?

The Klamath Indian Reservation is a large piece of land. Until the Klamath Termination Act in 1954, the tribe (as well as its Modoc and Yahooskin members) shared approximately 1.5 million acres. If a person needed to hide out, he could do that there. Moore kept a very low profile in his last years. A relative of his said he lived in a trailer on her family's ranch and worked there to pay his rent. Living in these circumstances anywhere in the West at that time, a ranch hand could easily avoid the law. Doing that on the Klamath Reservation would be even deeper cover.

Five years after he died, it came to light that several friends suspected his involvement at Crater. To another, Moore admitted he did it. But no one ever said anything—until Hazel Arrell called the sheriff in 1967. What were they all afraid of and why did they keep secret *the thing that nobody talked about*?

The full weight of the Justice Department's most powerful investigative instrument, the FBI, would come down like a hammer on anyone involved in a case like this. One need only fast forward twenty years for an example of how the FBI and courts reacted to Native Americans killing white men. At the Wounded Knee Occupation in 1973, two FBI agents were shot and killed on the Pine Ridge Reservation during a raid to arrest and question members of the American Indian Movement. Even though the FBI instigated the initial encounter and trespassed without a search warrant, when the shooting started and two agents were killed, it prompted an all-out legal war against the Oglala Sioux that lasted for years. The FBI and U.S. Marshals arrested and jailed tribal members who had nothing to do with the shooting, ransacked and burned houses of suspects, ridiculed members for their religious beliefs, and harassed the Oglala Sioux people generally (see Matthiessen *In the Spirit of Crazy Horse*).

In the case of *United States of America v Leonard Peltier*, the defendant was found guilty in two counts of first degree murder and sentenced to two consecutive life sentences.

While Moore and his accomplice did not kill an FBI agent, they did kill two members of the white establishment. Given the circumstances, it would have been hard to make a case for leniency. Federal prosecutors would have been expected to charge the defendants to the fullest extent. In this case, that would be the death penalty—legal in Oregon at the time (and today).

That they were able to keep their involvement hidden from law enforcement for fifteen years is as remarkable as the crime itself. In hindsight, it demonstrates a sense of self-preservation and discipline to maintain the shroud of collective secrecy.

Finally, harboring a murderer or two might be the lesser of two evils. Another reason the few who knew felt compelled to keep quiet about Moore was self-preservation. He had three assaults and a rape attempt on his record in the not so distant past. Snitch on a guy like that and you're asking for trouble—particularly when suspicious deaths of Native people were not uncommon, yet often went uninvestigated.

Moore's History: Family and Criminal

Outside of two random newspaper stories and a relatives' recollection of him, all that is known about the life of Kenneth Moore is based on information derived from the Oregon Department of Corrections, the Klamath County Sheriff's Department, and census data snapshots. Each is a one-sided glimpse into the middle years of Moore's life, which include several details about his growing up years. According to charging documents, Kenneth Moore was born in Fort Klamath, Oregon on November 22, 1905.[38] On that day both parents, William and Mary, were forty-two years old and resided in Chiloquin. They were both members of the Klamath Tribe. Kenneth's education ended in the eighth grade. The record shows he had his first brush with the law when he was 17 years old, on April 30, 1923. He was fined $50 for driving under the influence of alcohol.

Census records for 1910, 1920, 1930, and 1940 elaborate somewhat on his family situation. His father William remarried a woman named Lucinda Moore who was ten years his junior. Living with them in 1910 and 1920 were Moore's siblings Elliot, Quimby, and Theodore. Elliot and Quimby were seven and four years older than Kenneth. Theodore was three years younger than Kenneth, and he would have his own difficulty keeping out of trouble—doing four years in Salem for robbing a Chiloquin liquor store.[39] They all lived together through 1920. By 1930, Kenneth had moved out. In 1940, three years after being released from prison, he was living with his family again. Among Moore's family members, his brother is the most interesting, based on census data. In 1930, Theodore described his occupation as "trapper" and reported that he had earned $900 from it the previous year. To give some context to this, in all the census records from that period in Chiloquin, $900 was the most I could find for income from trapping. This occupation was not uncommon among the several hundred people listed. Then as now, most people claim less than they actually make—particularly when they barter and trade. Though this amount equals about $10,000 today, Theodore's claimed income in 1930 indicates he was an

---

38 More likely, he was born in Klamath Agency Hospital
39 *The Evening Herald* Monday January 30, 1939

extremely accomplished trapper. It's logical to assume his brother Kenneth was also an experienced trapper because he stole pelts and traps (along with several firearms) in his 1933 assault and robbery of the Seamans. Kenneth Moore's father, William, listed his occupation in the census as "innkeeper."

According to charging papers in Klamath County, by 1934 Kenneth Moore had earned a "bad reputation." His rap sheet indicates that from early adulthood until he was thirty-four years old, alcohol and intoxication led to most of his confrontations with the sheriff. This is more complicated than it sounds. Even before Prohibition, Native people could be jailed for simple possession.

The State of Oregon ratified the Eighteenth Amendment to the Constitution in 1919 which criminalized "possession of liquor." This was the charge when Moore was twenty years old and had his second brush with the law. He spent three months in county lockup and was fined two hundred dollars—the equivalent of about seven thousand dollars today. Thus began Moore's lengthy, complicated, and racially biased involvement with law enforcement.

Fourteen months later, Moore was again caught with liquor. This time, Moore was charged federally and released to U.S. Marshals. His subsequent incarceration, if any, was not recorded. Six months after that, he was charged with attempted rape, but released. A few days after his twenty-third birthday in 1928, he committed his first assault and battery and was found guilty. His sentence was not listed. Ten months later, he violated the Drug Act and went to federal prison at McNeil Island in Washington State for a year and a day. When he was released on July 11, 1930, Moore was twenty-four years old. He spent the next New Year's Eve at the reservation's Agency Hospital after being charged with disorderly conduct and being fined twenty dollars. Five months later, he was picked up again for violating the Prohibition Act. This time, he was taken by the U.S. Marshals to Portland and spent six months in Multnomah County Jail.

Comparing Ki and Big Jack

For two men from disparate backgrounds, Ki Moore and Jack Santo had a lot in common. Most obviously, they lived much of their lives in the same geographic region—within a few hundred miles of each other—Klamath Falls, Oregon and Grass Valley, California.

Both men had a problem with alcohol that affected their ability to get a job and keep it. Moore got in quite a bit more trouble when his drinking got out of hand because of his status as a Native American, while Jack had his own share of violent, alcohol-fueled episodes but, because he was white, avoided the law for these.

When the money ran out, Jack Santo and Kenneth Moore occasionally committed crimes to alleviate their financial stress. This underlies all the capital murder cases involving Santo and Moore's involvement in the Crater Lake case. Lack of income motivated this mayhem and murder.

When engaged in honest work, both men preferred working outdoors.

Moore and Santo were both middle-aged at the time of the Crater Lake case. In 1952, Moore was forty-six; Santo was fifty-two.

Each had a dangerous reputation and might be described as a Western outlaw. Both did lengthy stints in prison—Moore in Salem and Santo at San Quentin.

Both men behaved violently toward women. Jack was described as having physically abused Harriet Henson; Moore was charged once with rape.

How the men differed is, perhaps, more telling. Jack Santo promoted himself during and after his trials, cultivating a reputation as the "Leader of the Mountain Mob." He enjoyed the notoriety. In his previous life, Santo was a medium-size fish in a small pond. He transformed into a much larger fish after the Monahan Trial and being confined to Death Row. In contrast, Kenneth Moore, after his prison release in 1937, was a minnow swimming in the weeds until he disappeared completely in the years after.

Based on photographs of each, both men appeared handsome in their youth and early middle age. It is safe to assume they were also popular with the opposite sex. In Santo's case this was particularly true. Santo was enigmatic and popular with women who went for his rough, mountain man persona. He was also known to fraternize with prostitutes, including Barbara Graham. Santo married three times. Nothing in Moore's history suggests he was so keen about the opposite sex. Moore had a wife when in his 20s.

Moore's and Santo's family histories were also quite a bit different. Santo's ancestors on his father's side emigrated from Southern Europe to the United States. Kenneth Moore's mother and father were listed on his charging document as "Klamath Indian." His ancestors resided in the Klamath Basin for thousands of years.

The main difference between the men as suspects in the Crater Lake case was that Santo could not have killed Jones and Culhane. He was in the Sierra foothills the day of the murders. Ki Moore had no such alibi.

Connecting Moore to Crater

The story of Ki Moore's admission to Oscar Arrell—that he murdered Jones and Culhane—has a strong whiff of truth about it.

Does Moore's admission mean he did it?

There is no direct evidence that puts Ki Moore at the scene on July 19, 1952. He was never found in possession of the murder weapon or any object stolen from the scene. Neither was any car Moore had access to among the four-hundred-plus vehicles traced by the FBI. Nothing puts Moore there that day except his own words, repeated by another. Also, the suspicion of several people who knew him well.

The Best Suspect is the Only Suspect

What if you threw out Oscar Arrell's deathbed confession? Would Moore still be a good suspect?

What is so special about Moore, besides his admission, is that unlike every other name in the FBI and OSP files, nothing eliminates him. In fact, everything we know about the killer's profile fits Kenneth Moore, which it must if he did it.

- Motive: money problems. Moore had them.
- Means: Moore knew how to drive and had access to automobiles. He used a car to commit a previous robbery/assault in 1934.
- Opportunity: according to at least one of his friends, Paul Wampler, Moore was living in the area on the day of the murders.
- Consistent prior criminal history: the Seamans' assault was very similar.
- A history of violent behavior up to and including the time of the Crater Lake murders.
- Knowledge of the overlook and adjacent woods: Moore grew up in the immediate area of Crater Lake National Park, specifically Chiloquin and Fort Klamath. His brother indicated that Kenneth Moore hunted the local woods and likely trapped game there too.
- Ability to disappear: There is no record of Kenneth Moore's address in July 1952. The only information about his whereabouts is secondhand—that he lived in a trailer on a ranch near the reservation.
- Anyone who was aware of Moore's likely involvement in the murders was compelled to keep it a secret. Moore had a small social circle that did not include any blabbermouths.
- Killer or killers were middle age: Who would find a pair of wingtips such desirable footwear as to untie them from a

dead man's feet and carry them away? An older person might consider an expensive pair of Florsheim shoes worth keeping. Moore was well into middle age in 1952—forty-six years old. The accomplice he named was older; John Wesley Cole, was seventy-two.

- Comfortable tying a man to a tree: Moore had a previous conviction where he tied two men to a bed. He also worked as a ranch hand.

A False Narrative

The most popular understanding of any complicated event is shaped by the culture in power at the time when they describe or write about it. Winners write history. The story that two GM executives were robbed and killed in Crater Lake National Park by serial killer Jack Santo was forwarded by the FBI and accepted by the media. More accurately, the bureau never admitted Jack could not have done it. They left him out there and newspaper stories kept the myth afloat. Jack served a purpose—in a way, he was used.

The Santo-based explanation to the murders raises more questions than answers. For instance, how did Santo know the woods by the overlook were vacant? There was no reason to believe Santo had ever been there before. Medford is seventy miles away and Jack left there in his youth. Why was he suddenly doing a random carjacking for small change in Oregon when all his known robberies were in California, planned ahead of time to rip off victims for thousands of dollars? What was Jack doing tying victims to trees? He'd never done that before. Why did Jack's criminal associates protect him at Crater Lake when they rolled over in every other case against him? How could Jack have done the murders by the overlook if he was in Grass Valley, California that day? This narrative with Big Jack at the center, tantalizing as it is, concealed the truth of what happened and who did it.

When you insert Ki Moore for Jack, the events of July 19th make sense. It goes like this:

> The Crater Lake murders involve four people: Albert Jones, Charles Culhane, Kenneth Moore and, according to Moore, John Wesley Cole. Moore and Cole attempted to rob Jones and Culhane beside Highway 62 at the Annie Creek Canyon Overlook inside Crater Lake National Park. The victims were then driven a short distance up the road. From there, they were taken across the highway to a remote section of the woods. Jones and Culhane were assaulted and gagged. When Moore and Cole attempted to tie each of them to a tree, Jones fought back and the crime escalated to murder. The perpetrators got away. The case remains unsolved.

County Officials Who Knew Him

Besides being the subject of a colorful newspaper story shortly after the murders, former Klamath County Sheriff Lloyd Low had figured in Ki Moore's law enforcement dealings eighteen years before. His name appears on Moore's 1934 indictment. During his career, Lloyd Low came into contact with Moore several times as did his father, Charles, the previous sheriff. Their names all appear on court documents—beginning with Moore's first assault conviction.

Lloyd Low wasn't the only county official who had a history with Moore. District Attorney Dayton Van Vactor prosecuted Kenneth Moore in the Seaman case. He was also present in the woods on July 19th after searchers discovered Jones and Culhane.

Though the former Sheriff recognized the significance of the jackpines, realizing Jones and Culhane were going to be tied to them, neither he nor the D.A. made the connection with Moore's 1934 assault and tying his victims to a bed frame.

Moore is not the only killer who waited many years to reoffend, causing his criminal instincts to be forgotten about. Likewise, Low and Van Vactor are not the only law enforcement professionals with short memories. In the small town of Luneburg, Germany in 1989, by the time authorities suspected and apprehended Kurt-Werner Wichman in the disappearance of Birgit Meier, nineteen years had elapsed since his last interactions with law enforcement. This gap in criminal conduct allowed Wichman to reoffend and temporarily avoid suspicion. It is possible Wichman may have committed additional crimes in the intervening years of which authorities were not aware.

While Moore drew some attention for his violent behavior after the 1934 assault conviction that landed him in prison in Salem, it was mostly fodder for the local newspapers. Despite participating in two stabbings and being the only person present when one man shot and killed another by the side of the road, Moore was not charged in any of those episodes.

Moore's Prison Stretch

Moore's rap sheet was two pages long with many offenses, large and small; among them were three assaults and a rape charge. His last offense was the assault of the Seamans. After pleading guilty, the court sentenced Moore to five years of which he served three years and four months. When he arrived in Salem on May 29, 1934, the state took his mugshot. He wore a pretty hard expression that day. There was a directness about it. He looked straight into the camera, and revealed something about himself. It's dangerous to attribute personality traits based on a picture. However, it is safe to say that the man in this picture is not the type of guy you would mess with. Forty months later, in his release photo, a veil had come down. Taken September 29,

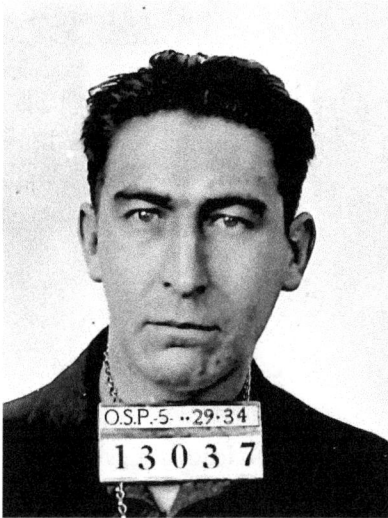

Two of the only four pictures known to exist of Kenneth Moore, taken in Oregon State Prison exactly forty months apart.
Courtesy: Oregon Department of Corrections

1937, it shows a man who looks thoroughly middle-aged, subdued, and a little tired. Unlike his picture in 1934, forty months later, Moore was someone you could pass on the street without noticing. There was nothing behind his eyes. He looked dangerous in 1934; four years later, he looked like an accountant. Was some essential part of his spirit removed by the prison experience? Was it the part of Kenneth Moore that landed him there in the first place? Or had he learned to hide it?

Among the documents in his corrections record is a violation while he was in prison for "stalling on the job." It contains a direct quotation from Moore to the yard captain. They are the only words Kenneth Moore is known to have spoken—apparently his reaction to being reprimanded.

"Now, I hope you are satisfied."

Like his mugshots, this quote says something about him. It is sophisticated-sounding and a little condescending. Not what you'd expect from a common criminal, but perhaps Ki Moore was uncommon.

As part of his release program after leaving prison in 1937, Kenneth Moore was given a job by the state building power lines around Klamath County.

Fingerprint Evidence

All together, there were four fingerprint impressions clear enough for comparison, two coins (from the Medford phone booth) and two credit cards (discarded at the murder scene). Neither Jones' Pontiac nor his shoes, which had been removed and left at the scene, yielded any usable prints.

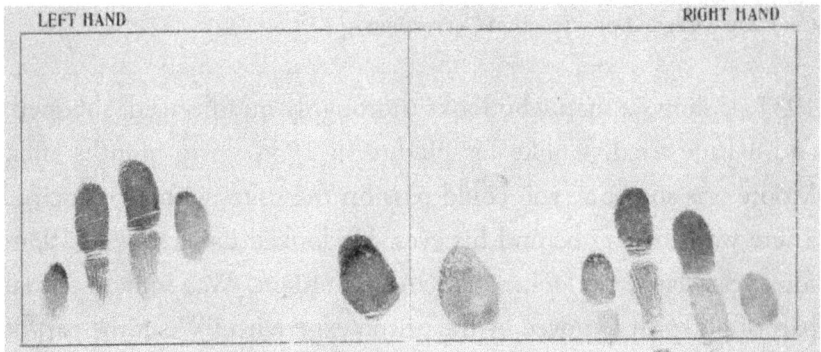

Moore's fingerprint card from 1933.

Very late in the investigation, the fingerprints of five potential suspects were compared to the four impressions without result.

In 1995, Jack Santo, Emmett Perkins, and Barbra Graham had their fingerprint records compared. All were negative. Prior to that in 1967 the bureau compared fingerprint samples of Kenneth Moore and John Wesley Cole.

Kenneth Moore's fingerprints were taken the day he arrived at Oregon State Prison in 1934.

240

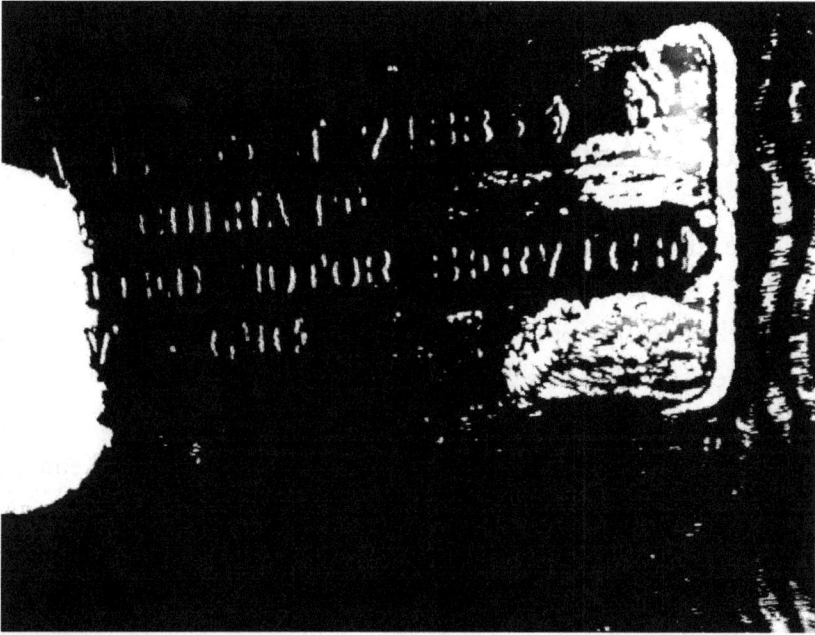

Culhane's gas card, recovered from the murder scene.

Cole's fingerprint sample originated from his arrest in 1935 for overloading a truck and failing to have the required permit and license.

He and two other men were the only drivers found in violation during the operation on May 23, 1935 to check truck drivers and their loads coming through Chiloquin. The three men each paid $13.50 in fines and court fees then were released. Cole is described in the short newspaper item[40] as a "logging truck operator."

Neither Kenneth Moore nor Cole's fingerprints were consistent with the impressions lifted from the credit cards or quarters.

There was never a lot of faith in the fingerprint impressions or that the killer or killers had left them. Culhane's gas cards had been handled by gas station attendants and himself. It was even less likely the killers handled the train station quarters. However, because of the

---

40 The Klamath News May 24, 1935 p.5

dearth of hard evidence in the case, the bureau was forced to consider and compare them anyway.

Named in Another Federal Crime

On the night of March 24, 1938, the Chiloquin Post Office was broken into. Robbers entered through the back door. After they found the safe, they opened it using the combination. A classic inside job. They stole fifty-five hundred dollars in cash. No one was ever charged.

For some reason, investigators immediately suspected Kenneth Moore was involved. Though he appeared to be a changed man in his prison release photo, less than a year later, Kenneth Moore was at the top of law enforcement's list of potential suspects in connection with the post office robbery. Unbeknownst to Moore, his associations and movements post-release were being watched.

June 13, 1939

> ... Information was gained that KENNETH MOORE, alias COYOTE MOORE cased this job and later shared in the proceeds. The informant relates that he has been unable to learn the name of the party actually committing the crime, but that he is an ex-inmate of the Oregon State Penitentiary and was released with Moore; and further, that he and Moore were on friendly terms while serving their sentences.
>
> *Charles P. Fray*
> *letter to George Alexander*

This letter is the last time Moore is mentioned in any law enforcement document until a few days after his death in 1962. Whether or not he had a hand in the robbery, the letter between

Oregon State Prison and post office investigators shows that Moore was on their radar and that his criminal inclinations had probably not changed since leaving state prison.

His potential involvement in a post office heist and an attempt to engage in honest work for the power company were both indications of his personal financial situation.

Reservation Economy During Moore's Lifetime

If Moore was struggling with his finances, he could not blame it on local economic conditions. Renowned for their work ethic, the Klamath Tribe was prosperous and self-sufficient until the middle of the last century when Congress voted to sever their tribal status. Until then, they were one of only two tribes that did not rely on the federal government for support. (The Osage Nation, who possessed lucrative oil and mineral rights in Oklahoma, was the other.) The Klamath Tribes' greatest asset in the first half of the 20th century was the largest stand of ponderosa pine trees in the world, which they owned. Wood from this self-sustaining resource was cut in their sawmills, sold, and shipped throughout the Klamath Basin and beyond. By 1928, just a single mill, the Pine Ridge, produced 250,000 board feet per day, creating an economic tide that lifted the entire reservation. A good paying job could be easily found. The revenue generated an "allocation" for each member as well. These payments supported a good standard of living for the community—about equal to residents living in Klamath Falls. Besides the timber boom, tribal members also used the reservation's ample grazing land to run successful cattle operations.

Eventually, the Klamath Tribe's success was used against them when private timber interests swayed Congress to pass legislation detrimental to them. Congress approved the Klamath Termination Act of 1954, which withdrew aid while simultaneously taking much of their land for federal use. Private timber interests were awarded leases and contracts, while the local national forest was enlarged.

Eliminating the allocations created new and greater financial pressures for individuals and families. Seven years later, Congress decided to legally dissolve the Klamath Tribes entirely—a lethal blow to their self-determination and identity.

The dissolution caused the tribe to lose status and created tension among the members. In exchange for land rights, Klamath, Modoc, and Yahooskin people who chose to leave the tribe were given $43,000 for forty acres of their ancestral land. This created disagreements within families; some desired the payout while others wanted to keep their land. In the end, 72% of the members took the payout. In exchange, they lost control of the forest that had sustained their economy for decades.

In his charging documents in 1934, Kenneth Moore claimed ownership of eighty acres on the reservation. He is not listed as having received any payout.

Little Chicago

Another outstanding condition of reservation life while Kenneth Moore was alive was the prevalence of violent crime in Chiloquin. Though it no longer defines the Klamath Tribes today, it was an inescapable aspect of life on the reservation in the early to mid-twentieth century. The number of violent assaults and murder were documented, real and so numerous, that the local papers started referring to Chiloquin as "Little Chicago." This epidemic of small town crime lasted virtually all of Kenneth Moore's adult life. His many run-ins with the law demonstrate he participated in the scourge of violence; mostly in the years from 1920 to 1934, but his name turns up in newspaper items three times in the 1940s.

2nd Victim of Stabbing Located

A sequel to the stabbing of Kenneth "Coyote" Moore, Klamath Indian found unconscious last Saturday night in Chiloquin was reported by Special Indian Officer John Arkell who moved Stella Kirk to Klamath Valley Hospital early Saturday morning, the 23 year old Indian woman suffering from multiple stab wounds in the body. Both Moore and Stella are said to have been involved in a fracas at the Moore home in Chiloquin but Stella had left the scene Saturday to go to the home of a friend, Nora West, and then to the home of her mother, Loretta Kirk. Arkell said Moore and Stella had been living as man and wife for three or four years and apparently became embroiled in a knifing that sent both to the hospital in critical condition. They were said [*sic*] improving Monday morning. Miss Kirk, daughter of Jesse Lee Kirk, now serving time on a murder charge involving the death of his wife last year, had three deep stab wounds in the thigh area, and a bad cut below the knee.

Arkell said both admitted to fighting at Moore's place at about midnight Friday. Moore said he started for an ax, but Stella grabbed a butcher knife and struck him in the back. They scuffled and Moore gained possession of the knife and worked Stella over.

Klamath Falls Herald and News *March 28, 1949 p.1*

Three years before this horribly violent episode, Moore was a witness to a killing in self-defense between two other men. The three of them had been driving around together after obtaining alcohol—then shooting broke out. It's a crazy story and suggests yet another run-in between Moore and Sheriff Lloyd Low.

The Best Suspect is the Only Suspect

Tice Freed On Self-Defense

Acquitted of a manslaughter charge by a federal court jury at Medford Thursday, Ralph William Tice, 34, Chiloquin Indian testified he shot Eugene Mecum in self-defense and without intent to kill.

"I just meant to stop him," Tice testified, as he related his story of the shooting which occurred August 13 near Chiloquin. Mecum was also a Chiloquin Indian. Tice told how Mecum had become abusive while the two were at the home of Roland Wallupe and were finally ordered out of the house by Wallupe. Mecum had been drinking, he said.

The next morning, Tice rejoined Mecum and Kenneth Moore, the three men driving to the Klamath Indian Agency and later to Fort Klamath where Tice and Mecum went to obtain liquor.

On their way back to Chiloquin, Mecum became more threatening, and they finally stopped near the Paul Hendron home, where Tice and Moore got out of the car.

Tice said he took one of two guns, laying in the back seat with him, as Mecum had been trying to get possession of it during the trip, with the intention of hiding it. Mecum then rushed at him, threatening to kill him, Tice related, and after he called two or three warnings to stop, he fired one shot. After he calmed down, Tice said he went to the Hendron home, told Mrs. Hendron, "I have killed a man and want to turn myself in" and then awaited for the arrival of police officers.

Lloyd L. Low, Klamath county sheriff, Orville Hamilton, acting chief of police of Klamath Falls and John Arkell, Indian service employe [sic], all three testified that Tice had a reputation for being law abiding and orderly while Mecum's reputation was described as "bad".

Klamath Falls Herald and News *December 14, 1945 p.6*

The Best Suspect is the Only Suspect

Like every western town, Chiloquin was rowdier one hundred years ago—and much rougher than today. While some of the stories from that time are apocryphal, a quick scanning of local headlines show that murder and violent crime too often visited this tiny town (the population hovered around 1,000 residents) from the 1920s through the '50s. The violence was often between members of the tribes, which made it worse. One elder described to me in 2021.

"Somebody bothers you, you kill them. Then they don't bother you anymore. It was just people killing people."

Researching Moore's history tells the story of a man who was prone to violence and surrounded by it—a dangerous combination. There is more to it, though. Underneath the criminality and violent behavior, something motivated Moore to do it. It wasn't always money either—his excuse for robbing the Seamans. He committed these acts regularly throughout his life. What drove him? Why did he do it?

11 | The Why

This book started as a straight-up retelling of the FBI file, including especially the many undisclosed details and little stories within it. Nuts and bolts. That is all this book and writer ever aspired to. Then Oscar Arrell and his deathbed admission about Kenneth Moore tipped everything on its side. The new information was messy, but the story looked much clearer. Suddenly and for the first time, there seemed to be one suspect who looked better than all the others—by far. He had means, motive, and opportunity. He had a prior criminal history and history of violence. He had lived in the two towns nearest the murders his entire life; it was likely he knew the area of the woods by the overlook. Finally, he admitted to at least one person that he participated in the murders. If it has webbed feet, feathers, and quacks... the fact that everything seemed to add up was good. The problem was this person and his motivations were well outside my experience, personal and professional.

A white guy from the suburbs (me) could not have less in common with an American Indian who died sixty years ago. I was not a linguist like M.A.R. Barker, a scholar like Robert McNally, or a doctor like Dr. Maria Yellow Horse Brave Heart. I did not know any tribal elder who might speak with me about Moore's involvement. I had never known a single Native American person in my life and had only spoken with a few Native Americans, always for work. Of course, at work, I thought I knew my way around—I've interviewed senators, governors, and ex-presidents. None of that could help me here.

I knew just enough to know what this story needed: an explanation for why Moore did what he did. Yes, it was a botched robbery. Shooting two executives in the head beside the highway in a national park could not have been the original plan. Moore was a robber, not a killer—yet these were violent murders. What motivated him to do it? How did he wind up at the overlook at the exact moment when Al Jones and his boss Charles Culhane pulled up there?

I also knew, or thought I knew, a little bit about his end— Moore's last few years and how he died. One of the last items that surfaces about Moore in the public notice section of the local paper is a guardianship of his estate and referring to him as "a mentally diseased person" when his eighty-acre property was put up for sale.[41] The circumstances of his death are described at the end of this story. His last few hours on Earth define his character too. I began to think I might be able to describe this man with whom I had almost nothing in common.

I started with what I knew about the subject in general. I had been interested in Native American history since college and, after graduating, attended a few anthropology classes at the local community college to learn more about the Native people where I grew up, the Miwok Tribe in Northern California. My wife and I traveled extensively through the Four Corners area in the Southwest studying the tribes there, visiting Anasazi ruins and petroglyph sites.

41 Klamath Falls Herald and News, Friday June 24 1960 p.13

The Why

I photographed them both for pleasure and to study them. Later, after we moved to Oregon, I explored and photographed the caves at Lava Beds National Monument to learn more about Captain Jack and The Modoc War.

My field research was pretty incomplete, though. For instance, the history shared on the markers and signs inside Lava Beds National Monument and Captain Jack's Stronghold was not the tribes' version of events. Internet searches of the subject were similarly one-sided. The old barracks and museum by Kintpuash's grave marker mostly shares the story of the army's presence there. Even if I could process everything I knew, or thought I knew, about the Klamath and Modoc Tribes, it was only half of the story. Initially, I was blissfully unaware of all this. Sometimes, it is helpful not to know what you do not know.

I began with the hope that I might find a living person who knew Kenneth Moore. Though he had no direct family members, children, or grandchildren, he was related to living members of the tribes. Perhaps someone remembered him.

I reached out again to Alan Eberlein. Being non-tribal himself, I wasn't sure if he could help me, but I had nowhere else to start. Within a few hours, Alan put me in touch with the chairman of the Klamath Tribes, Don Gentry. I called Mr. Gentry that day to tell him about my story. I told him I thought Kenneth Moore had killed two GM executives in 1952 and gotten away with it. Then I asked if he could put me in touch with anyone who knew Kenneth Moore. If this sounds a little too transparent, that was partly the intention. Eventually, I would have to vet the book with the Klamath Tribes, so I wanted to be up front from the start. We had a pleasant conversation but, as expected, neither he nor the tribes' public information officer (PIO) could facilitate a meeting with an elder who knew or might remember Moore. To be fair, the tribes' PIO contacted an elder whom she thought might have known Kenneth

Moore, but this person thought a story about the murders of two GM executives in 1952 was "too creepy" and declined the interview.

I was stuck. Though several other tribal elder's names and phone numbers were listed, "enterprising" this story by calling them out of the blue would not be wise. I didn't want to be disrespectful. Tribal elders are not public officials. They are high-status individuals with influence. It would not work to attempt an end-around of tribal leadership. I would need to find another door into the world of Kenneth Moore.

Keane Tupper

I called Alan and told him the tribes would not be able to put me in touch with anyone who knew Kenneth Moore. A little later, he called me back. He knew someone who would speak to me. His name was Keane Tupper.

Keane is a member of the Klamath Tribes. Now in his fifties, he has operated a successful landscaping business in Klamath Falls for many years. One of his accounts includes an industrial property belonging to Alan. Alan warned me that I'd have trouble reaching his friend during business hours, and that during the summer season, he worked almost every day. So I started calling. Usually, I was at work and called between photography assignments at the ABC affiliate in Portland. It took several days of leaving messages before Keane called back. I was driving home late one night when the call rang through. That would be the norm from then on. I rarely spoke with Keane before 9pm, the hour he typically arrived home after work.

Keane is descended from both Klamath and Modoc ancestors—mostly the latter on his father's side. He describes himself as "Indian." His family tree includes two relations of the Basin's most important historical figures: Kientpoos (often spelled Kintpuash, popularly known as Captain Jack) and Chikclikam Lipolkuelatk (aka Scarface Charley). Both figured prominently in the Modoc War of the 1870s. Kientpoos was their leader during the most important battles of the war. Chikclikam Lipolkuelatk also distinguished himself in that conflict and in his life after. Keane was proud of his kinship and believed the Modoc War mattered a great deal still.

No other group in this country must prove their heredity in return for financial compensation—only Native Americans. How great a share one receives is determined by one's lineage, counted in fractions. That is how Keane described it. Keane's father is fifteen-sixteenths Modoc, specifically the Lost River band of that tribe. Growing up, the Tuppers wanted Keane to experience and be influenced by this side of his family as much as possible, which precipitated a move for him early on.

"My grandpa shows up one day at school and says, 'Come on. Get in. We're gonna get a sandwich.' We left Chiloquin and he drove all the way back to Klamath (Falls) where they live.... I went back (to Chiloquin) a couple years later to ride in rodeos and stuff, but not to go back there to stay." Keane and his wife live in Klamath Falls today.

Once we started, Keane and I spoke three or four times a month for most of 2020 and into 2021. Usually, I called him after work and we'd talk for an hour or so. Other times, we spoke for hours at a time. We talked about his upbringing in Chiloquin and after he left, his family, and the tribes. I was interested in hearing about reservation life—to understand the main character in this narrative, Kenneth Moore. I also learned a great deal about Keane's family. The Tuppers are influential in Chiloquin and around the basin. Their horsemanship and rodeo skills are also well known.

Through Keane, I learned that living on the reservation could be difficult in ways that living in the city or suburbs was not. Life had changed a great deal from the economic boom times in the early 20th century. There weren't as many opportunities for work or furthering one's education beyond high school. There was poverty, depression, and occasionally violence between members reminiscent of the post-World War I "Little Chicago" era.

There was a closeness too—a deep, ancestral bond. Even today, on the reservation, it was not unusual for someone to know a neighbor's entire family going back several generations. Their unique, shared history and relatively small number of members made the fabric of the community tight. Families were bound together with the same stuff. Grandparents lived at home with their children and grandchildren and were rarely placed in care facilities. This closeness within families was maintained even after death. When someone passed away, the custom was that only family members transport and bury them. Keane believed this way of life was different from non-tribal people and this distinction was not widely appreciated. I was not aware of it until Keane described it.

Eventually, after many hours of conversation, the stories, places, history, and people Keane spoke about became understandable to me. He did not condescend, which he could have, given my inexperience. But he reminded me that I was not going to master the Native American experience in twenty or thirty hours of conversation. And I didn't, but I got closer to knowing—thanks to Keane's patience.

Around spring 2021, Keane and I lost touch. Work and a family move interfered with my research and Keane's phone stopped ringing through. I did not try his number again until winter of 2022 when I was finishing the second to last draft of this book. Before too long we got back onto the subject of Kenneth Moore and he shared something that, in the moment, I could not believe he had waited to tell me.

Keane said he was related to Kenneth Moore, and in the months since we last spoke, he had reached out to several older relatives. I was a little bewildered that Keane had not mentioned this before. It was consistent with the general avoidance of the subject by every tribal person I spoke with about Moore so it shouldn't have been too surprising. Or perhaps he did mention it before, but I didn't hear him; frequently our cell phone connections were very poor and my recordings of them incomprehensible.

I asked Keane how he was related to Kenneth Moore.

"On my mother's side of the family—the Chiloquin side."

Keane continued speaking about "Ken."

According to Keane's Aunt Betty, Moore lived for many years on a ranch owned by her family and until Moore's death in 1962. This period included the time of the Crater Lake case. Two of his aunts knew him when they were growing up, according to Keane. One described him as "nice to her, but he could be mean too... aggressive when he was drinking."

Betty knew Moore from her childhood through her teenage years. She said Moore lived in a trailer on the property and received room and board in exchange for labor—"working around the ranch, building corrals and fixing fences," according to Keane.

Betty talked about Moore's behavior off the ranch as well, which Keane described.

"Ken mostly kept to himself in the trailer. The people he drank with were the people he drank with.... He'd look up a couple buddies, they would get a bottle and drive around... go drink in the woods, spotlight deer at night. We're one of the only tribes allowed to do that because that's the way we used to do it, traditionally—with fire, not flashlights. It wouldn't be nothing to stay out all night doin' that. But he wasn't fun to drink with. He would get in his car, show up loud, already drunk, just being a jerk. You couldn't make him leave without getting into a fight. He was a bully. He pulled a knife once on an uncle, then the cops pulled up."

This last description of Moore's behavior around alcohol sounds remarkably like his associate, Eugene Mecum, whom Ralph Tice shot and killed in self-defense—with Kenneth Moore present.

What motivated the anger Moore carried around at that time? Keane spoke three words immediately.

"Termination. Anger. Resentment. When that happened... not even being

an Indian anymore, according to the federal government, that was down on Indians.... They got down on themselves.... Be already mad before he started drinking."

I asked Keane where John Wesley Cole fit into the picture.

"I don't know how good a friend he was. The Coles are a good family. They work. Hunting and fishing.... They're good at it. I'm wondering if he (John Wesley Cole) was just driving with the wrong person at the wrong time."

How did Kenneth Moore and the few people who knew or suspected his involvement in the Crater Lake murders keep quiet about it all those years? That is, *the thing that nobody talked about.* Keane described it this way.

"I don't think anybody would ever talk. Some brothers wouldn't know stuff about each other. It's a lot tighter, not sharing information. You don't tell people. They didn't want to know. If you know something and somebody asked about someone you know, (you'd say) I haven't heard nothing about that.... Guys who did it didn't walk around and talk about it. They were pretty good about not opening their mouth. Later on in life, one of them might tell.... It's talking gets people caught in the crossfire, brings the law. White people comin' in. (There is) a mistrust of white people having to be here."

Anthropologists and linguists have studied the subtleties of Klamath and Modoc dialect from native speakers; most recently, these were elders who could recall the language being spoken as children by their elders. When Mabie "Neva" Eggstrom died in 2003, the Klamath Tribe lost the last person fluent in their language. There are no fluent speakers of Modoc alive either. Elements of the language are taught in schools around Chiloquin and Klamath Falls.

The last time I called Keane, the book had not found a publisher and I was living across the country trying to find a job. I trusted that sometime in the next year or two, if this book was published or I published it myself, I might return to The Falls and we could finally meet in person. It was a meeting I very much looked forward to, but things were up in the air.

When you get to know a really remarkable person, it's often for a finite time. And when you say goodbye, if you say goodbye, it isn't always obvious that it's final. The very last word Keane spoke to me was in Modoc—a word he translated as meaning goodbye or later.

"On'cee."[42]

Historical Trauma

In separate conversations regarding the Modoc War, Keane and the tribes' public relations person both described a condition common to American Indians (and First Nations People in Canada) known as *historical trauma*. In the case of the Klamath Tribes, it had several different causes. Generally speaking, the government's effort to wipe out the Modoc Tribe was a major source of trauma. Most if not all of the members who survived the Modoc War and their descendants experienced a deep psychological pain. Also, draining the marshes and redistributing the land underneath to non-tribal persons was a source of much suffering and indignation to Klamath People.

From the way Keane Tupper and other members described historical trauma, it sounded like it was serious and widespread within the tribes. The root causes of it began almost as soon as settlers moved in, so it had been around since the 1800s. This meant that it might have affected Kenneth Moore and caused some of the anger he carried around and inflicted on the many people he victimized in his life. He was described as a bully and a guy who got into fights. He carried a knife and is remembered by Keane as having used it once on Keane's uncle. There is a separate record of Moore being stabbed and

42 Pronounced OWN-chay

another where he and his girlfriend each stabbed the other. That's a lot of violence for one man. In these encounters, alcohol is often referenced. What else, besides alcohol, motivated Moore's violent streak and the anger that drove it?

Understanding historical trauma might explain some of Kenneth Moore's behavior, and possibly his actions on July 19, 1952.

Typing in the keywords, it is not difficult to find authoritative, objective, and Native-based research on historical trauma, as they experience it.

> ... the cumulative emotional and psychological wounding over one's lifetime and from generation to generation following loss of lives, land and vital aspects of culture.
>
> *Dr. Maria Yellow Horse Brave Heart*
> *Historical Trauma Informed Clinical*
> *Intervention Research and Practice, 2014*

How might an individual suffering from historical trauma behave toward others?

> ... Those in the trauma group reported more aggression towards others, but not other types of aggression. Trauma history also significantly predicted severity of all types of aggression, and severity of aggression towards objects/others.
>
> *Rebecca E. Grattan et al*
> *A History of Trauma Is Associated with Aggression...*

Though historical trauma and its effect on Kenneth Moore cannot be proven and does not explain the senseless murders by the overlook, like virtually everything about Kenneth Moore, it is consistent with him having participated. Moore's criminal record demonstrates that he was aggressive and angry in his twenties and thirties. Newspaper records and his family themselves indicate this behavior lasted through his later years, as well.

What could have happened in Kenneth Moore's world to cause him to experience historical trauma? One answer lay in a violent, culture-shattering episode that affected members of his family one generation before he was born.

The Modoc War

For thousands of years, the Modoc and Klamath were one people, residing in the Klamath Basin and further south. Eventually, white settlement forced a geographic split in the 1800s and the separate tribal names took hold. The Klamath occupied the upper area of the basin in Oregon; the Modoc Tribe lived directly south of them, in another large basin, Tule Lake, just inside California. Both tribes share a common language with some difference in dialects. After the split, they were not especially friendly despite a common heritage— like relatives who don't get along very well.

For millennia, there was no Oregon or California. Just a high desert rimmed by jagged, snowy peaks that percolated down into a multitude of huge lakes, rivers, innumerable streams, and miles of unbroken marsh. There was only the land and the tribe, the Marsh People, as some describe them. According to the National Park Service, rock art near Tule Lake at Petroglyph Point dates back more than 6,000 years.

A separate band of Northern Paiute who identified as Yahooskin occupied the high desert and alpine region east of Tule Lake in a range that extended south to the Warner Valley in California. They co-existed fairly peacefully in this unique and beautiful corner of the basin and range for thousands of years because of the abundance the

Petroglyph Point, rock engravings
Photo: author

land afforded them. However, some conflicts did occur. The Paiute had a fierce reputation. The tribe who became known as the Modoc became known for their skill in battle as well, after conflict with whites.

The Lost River ran deep and clear through the volcanic, high-desert basin. Its source was Clear Lake. The river and area around the lake were the Modoc's favorite hunting ground, primary winter quarters, and the center of their spiritual universe. It was a small but remarkable corner of California when statehood was declared in 1850. One influential settler shared the Modoc's appreciation for this place. Jesse Carr wanted the Lost River valley for grazing his cattle even though the land wasn't particularly suited to it—between three and four thousand feet in elevation, covered in lava rocks and snow all winter, sagebrush and low grass the rest of the year. Despite the lands' inadequacies, Carr encouraged his man-in-charge, Jesse Applegate, to take possession of it. But how?

The Why

The process began with Applegate and his men fomenting several uprisings against the Modoc, which were successful. It cleared out an area where Carr allowed settlers to establish a presence year-round, working the land, allowing the cattle and sheep to graze. Though the land claims were mostly ill-gotten, the political winds blew favorably. Carr's ambition grew as local sentiment regarding the Modocs worsened considerably. So he devised a plan. He would play the long game and, if possible, have the United States government remove the Modoc—with the feds paying for the trouble.

Accelerating the inevitable confrontation, local newspaper stories about the so-called Indian Problem aroused fervent public interest. Politicians in Yreka and Weed got into the act and beat the flames of antipathy. Inevitably, the story spread even more widely to Portland and San Francisco. The inflamed citizenry demanded a solution: The Modoc must be removed or wiped out entirely.

The reasons for their removal were twofold: to create economic benefit for settlers in the formerly fallow grassland, and to make the place safe for that enterprise. This end could be easily arrived at simply by removing the Modoc to the Klamath Indian Reservation just north in Oregon. The rub in this neat solution was that no one bothered considering how the Modoc felt about it. The Modoc liked living in their homeland and did not agree that they should have to give it up or share it. They had been living there for thousands of years before the Oregon Trail and Gold Rush pioneers stumbled in. Why should they have to give up what had always been theirs?

Another problem not appreciated by the forces trying to relocate the Modoc was that they and the Klamath had an uneasy coexistence. They were similar but separate, and not especially friendly. Some would say this uneasiness continues to affect their relationship today.

In spite of these obstacles, the Modoc were relocated to the Klamath Reservation in the 1860s and each tribe attempted to make it work. This was not successful, however. The Klamath outnumbered the Modoc three to one. Food was scarce. The government's promised relief in the form of food and blankets was not forthcoming. After a particularly bleak winter in 1870 to early 1871, to avoid starving, the Modoc were forced to eat their ponies, an intolerable insult for the tribe who ordinarily took good care of their stock, especially horses.

As a result of these deprivations, the Modoc elected to return to their homeland by Lost River. Their hope was that they might do better there, if settlers might allow them to hunt, fish, and forage in their traditional way. And if they did starve to death, at least the surroundings would be familiar. But the settlers would not have it. In 1872, they formally engaged the United States military to assist them. Jesse Carr had gotten his wish.

There had been serious trouble before that. As early as the 1850s, there was violence between the whites and Modocs, including several skirmishes and campaigns around Lost River and Tule Lake. More often than not, the fighting was provoked by militias, composed of settlers and mercenaries who rode in for the fight. All the trouble that ensued was blamed on the Modoc.

Robert Aquinas McNally wrote the essential text, *The Modoc War* (Bison Books, 2017), and dates its beginning to November 29, 1872. The army made up of cavalry, soldiers, and local militia engaged the Modoc near Lost River and ordered them to surrender their arms. While many were complying with the order, a fight broke out between Scarface Charley and Lt. Boutelle of the 1st Cavalry. Each shot and missed. After that, the Modoc grabbed their weapons and, led by their chief, Kientpoos, retreated to the stronghold inside the lava beds. In the action, one soldier and two Modocs died. In the next two days, eighteen settlers would be killed, as well. The war had begun.

By mid-January of 1873, the army had accumulated a force of four hundred or so regulars. These were relatively inexperienced soldiers whose orders were to teach the Modoc a lesson and return them, by force if necessary, to the Klamath Reservation. At the outset, no one in the invading force believed the Modocs would oppose them. Their numbers and firepower were too great. In fact, many believed the Modocs would give up without a fight. This wishful thinking was an early sign of the army's chronic underestimation of the tribe's deep desire to live in their homeland.

In the First Battle of the Stronghold, three hundred soldiers opposed fifty Modoc. When they marched through the morning darkness on January 17, 1873, they did not know the Modocs had scouted their position and had been anticipating the raid for several days. Taking up positions, their powder was dry. The tribe had a spiritual advantage too. They found strength in an invocation and ceremony led by their religious leader, Cho-ocks, whom the whites called Curley Headed Doctor (see Photos).

A little like the Ghost Dance, introduced by the Northern Paiute spiritual leader Wovoka in 1889, Cho-ocks invited the spirit of the ancestors to join the fight. At intervals for five days, Cho-ocks brought everyone in the stronghold together around a pole. Holding talismans—sacred objects whose spirit brought them strength—they moved in unison. With knees bent, hopping on one foot while dragging the other, they moved as one in a circle praying for the ancestors to help them defeat every soldier and settler that would oppose them.

Fog! Fog!
Lightning! Lightning!
Whirlwind! Whirlwind!

Besides the Ghost Dance, Cho-ocks knew another trick that the power of belief could make real. It was an invisible wall, represented by a rope woven from tule fibers, dyed red. Once it was strung out on the battlefield, warriors behind it believed they were protected.

Cho-ocks unfurled the magic rope a short distance from the lava outcropping. Behind it was a labyrinth of caves, passageways, elevated perches, and protected shooting positions, known today as Captain Jack's Stronghold.

As prophesied in the Ghost Dance, on the morning of the First Battle of the Stronghold, a dense ground fog covered the desert floor. In the gray dawn, the Modoc's faith was affirmed. The gloomy, ground fog slowly lifted, revealing the soldier's positions, one by one. Behind small depressions in the sand and sage brush, the army regulars, local militia, and Native scouts were each sighted down a rifle barrel. The firing commenced. Hidden behind rocks, the Modoc changed positions often to make their small band seem larger and more intimidating as bullets rained down on the invaders.

The army and volunteers were pinned down and took a pounding, trying to return fire from an unseen enemy. The Modoc made every shot count. Each discharge from the cap and ball rifles found its mark or nearly. Even an indirect hit or deflection tore through flesh and bone. Eventually, officers signaled a retreat; by then many in their command were too badly injured to move.

Despite the rocky barrier between the sides, it was close combat. The Modoc taunted their enemy. They spoke directly to several army scouts, Native Americans whom the government employed for their tracking skills and willingness to fight. Some were Klamath, most were Warm Springs Indians from the Columbia River. The Modoc recognized them as Native People. Whose side were they on?

When it was over, the army counted thirty-five casualties and sixteen wounded. Many of the sixteen wounded soldiers required painful surgery and did not return to the field. Not a single Modoc died in the First Battle of the Stronghold. In military courses teaching battlefield strategy, the Modoc position that day is considered a textbook example of attacking from a strong defensive position.

The Why

The view from Captain Jack's Stronghold—Lava Beds National Monument, CA

After the army retreated, the red rope lay undisturbed in the brush where it had been stretched the night before. Its power was manifest. While routing the United States Army, the small band of Modocs had gotten into their head as well. Soldiers who fought in the historic battle experienced the enemy's bravery and marksmanship, which surprised them.

In the days and weeks after the First Battle, the Modoc kept their psychological advantage, but that would change. The humiliation of getting clobbered by a much smaller force provoked a lust for revenge up and down the army's ranks. They had been embarrassed and needed to redeem themselves. Between January and April that year, the army added to their number by several hundred, including a new commander, General Edward Canby.

The general's rise in the military had been achieved by a combination of perseverance, ambition, and good connections. Graduating thirtieth out of thirty-one in his West Point class, Canby overcame a few early career blunders to distinguish himself in the War Between the States without quite winning the approval of General Grant when it was all over. Seven years later, Canby was posted to his

264

new command. He moved from Virginia to the Pacific Northwest to lead the army against the Modoc. He arrived in August 1872.

After he got to the Lava Beds, the general discussed with officers how they had failed in the first big skirmish. Once the unfortunate event was related, Canby arrived at a novel strategy to defeat the enemy. It was "a gradual compression with an exhibition of force." That is, intimidating the Modoc with a show of several hundred uniformed soldiers and officers maneuvering regularly around them. This squeezing would bring the army's forces into fairly close proximity with the Modoc. In Canby's mind, the tribe's overwhelming disadvantage would be obvious and they would have to surrender.

During this campaign, a cavalry troop moving between camps discovered thirty-one horses grazing outside the stronghold and took them. The Modocs argued the horse stealing violated the terms of the cease-fire, which they did, and demanded the ponies be returned. Canby ignored the complaint—to keep the pressure on. In a way it worked, but not in the way he had hoped.

After the theft of their horses, the Modoc elected to negotiate. A government-formed Peace Commission had been created after the First Battle of the Stronghold and brought both sides together. For the meeting on April 11th, they erected a section of white canvas over the sand and sagebrush that allowed participants protection from the sun and wind. It was referred to as the Peace Tent.

Until this meeting, the army had little interest in understanding the tribe's motivations, though they had the opportunity. Several members of the army's camp, serving as translators, were Modocs. They were not consulted. Army negotiators considered the Modocs too simple, including the ones translating and working with them.

Neither Canby nor anyone else on the Peace Commission was aware that the tribe practiced a radical form of democracy, similar to the non-Natives. They elected leaders to positions based on their particular strengths. For instance, one person settled civil disputes, another individual offered spiritual guidance and, in times of conflict, an entirely different member of the tribe organized the fight. There was an important difference regarding the last responsibility and anyone elected to it. The war chief could be compelled by the majority to fight to the death or forced to take the life of another. This subtle distinction was not appreciated, if it was even known, by the other side.

Kientpoos, for most of his adult life, was recognized for his diplomatic skills and ability to resolve conflict. His gift was for settling disputes—not fighting or killing. His personality was often described as "gentle." He was elected chief during the Modoc War because, among the two hundred or so Modoc that survived, he was their most valuable player—the member they believed would best represent them in a conflict.

Astonishingly, given the outcome, the army had been warned. Days before the Peace Tent, Canby met with a Modoc interpreter, a woman named Toby Riddle. She was Kientpoos' cousin and had recently visited him and his men inside the stronghold. She told the general that the group was still angry about the theft of their horses. It was the consensus that the army had broken an agreement, which the Modoc had honored. Also, during Riddle's visit, she noticed the group as a whole was becoming increasingly desperate. Food and water were being rationed. Conditions for women, children, and elders were worse than ever. What most concerned her about this situation was that the men in the cave were not willing to cooperate to alleviate the group's suffering. Everyone in the cave seemed compelled to fight rather than surrender.

Besides Toby Riddle's pointed warning to the general, she also said she was uneasy about the meeting at the Peace Tent. Whatever he gleaned from Riddle's intelligence, Canby went ahead with the original plan: negotiate with the Modoc to effect their immediate return to the Klamath Reservation.

General Edward Richard Sprigg Canby

After the meeting, Toby Riddle returned to the barracks. There she spoke with another member of the tribe who told her an ambush was planned for the next day inside the Peace Tent. At further risk to herself, she returned to Canby's quarters to relate this last, crucial warning.

During his eight-month command of the Modoc War, the general had developed a distrust of his enemy. This lack of confidence extended to Toby and her husband, Frank Riddle. Canby felt both of them favored the tribe during negotiations, which he may have been right about. Riddle's entire culture was on the brink of destruction—her entire family. That her translations were fuller in her native language could not be helped. Deep suspicion ran both ways. The Modoc had reasons to distrust the army in general and Canby in particular, who had already gone back on his word regarding the horses.

The general was described as "confident" before he went into the negotiations on his last day. He felt he finally had Kientpoos where he wanted him—resistance was futile. The army's superior strength and size were too great. The enemy's surrender was inevitable. Any attempt from Captain Jack to prolong the fighting would be a bluff.

"The Modocs might talk such things, but they would never attempt it," Canby asserted before the meeting.

Canby's attitude toward the Modoc and Kientpoos that day in the Peace Tent was largely condescending. To him, the Modoc were completely inferior: intellectually, fewer in number, dressed shabbily, dark-skinned, and lacking a proper soldier's fighting spirit. The general believed that taking the Lost River country for settlers was the best outcome for everyone because it gave the Modoc their best opportunity—to live like whites.

Another ranking member of the commission and present in the Peace Tent was Reverend Eleazar Thomas, an influential Methodist preacher who had established a church north of San Francisco in a little town called Petaluma. Thomas might have seen the Modoc in a more nuanced light than Canby. Given his non-secular background, he might have suggested a more compassionate way of dealing with the tribe—something less forceful than pointing a loaded rifle in their direction and telling them to move. But the priest from Petaluma did not advocate for the Modoc. He referred to them as "simple children" who needed to be shown a better way—towards Christianity, an agrarian lifestyle, and adoption of other Anglo customs. Indeed, Thomas ascribed to the basic tenets of Manifest Destiny: God favored the movement and the end justified the means. The Modoc referred to Thomas as the "Sunday Doctor."

> Canby and Thomas's attitude toward Indians was paternalistic, in the word's literal meaning. They saw themselves as parents possessed of wisdom and right and the Modocs as children needing direction and salvation. The Natives had no choice but to bend to God's will and American civilization's progress.... Canby and Thomas's refusal to heed Riddle's warning that the Modocs planned to kill them arose from this same cosmic paternalism. It blinded them, too, to the Modocs' desperation. To believe Riddle and to see that the Modoc people were desperate to fend off their annihilation by any means necessary was to treat Indians as equals. That Canby, Thomas, and almost all of European America refused to do.

Robert A. McNally The Modoc Wars

When Kientpoos and his contingency arrived at the Peace Tent, they had already made the decision to fight. He was ordered by the other warriors to kill Canby or die trying. One never knows how an adversary will react when he is cornered. Canby was about to find out.

Another factor shaping events that day at the Peace Tent had occurred twenty-one years before. In 1852, to discourage pioneers from settling the Lost River country, the Modoc attacked a wagon train. If they can be believed, local accounts reported that the Modoc killed sixty-five members of an emigrant party near Tule Lake. It was dubbed the Bloody Point Massacre. Newspaper accounts blamed the Modocs, but its veracity has always been dubious. Nevertheless, it inspired a revenge attack. Carried out by civilians from Yreka, including the notorious Indian-hater Ben Wright, the retaliation was almost as deadly as the event that inspired it. The Ben Wright Massacre claimed the lives of around thirty-five Modoc.

Some of the same warriors who participated in the original wagon train attack compelled Kientpoos to shoot Canby at the Peace Tent all these years later. This group knew they would be executed for participating at Bloody Point if they surrendered, while continuing the

HORRIBLE MASSACRE

GENERAL CANBY AND OTHERS KILLED BY THE TREACHEROUS MODOCS.

Sickening Details of the Affair—Troops Ordered Forward—Indignation at Washington—New York Press on the Massacre—sorrow and Intense Feeling Everywhere.

NEW YORK, April 13.—The telegraph yesterday flashed from the Lava Beds the announcement of the treachery of the Modoc Indians by which General Canby and others met with death on Friday. The sickening details received since then confirm all that was told in the first account and add much that was not mentioned then. The dispatch of the 11th from the Lava Beds says that on Thursday afternoon, five Indians came into camp and were made presents of clothing and provisions, by the Peace Commissioners, and a message was sent out asking for a talk Friday morning at a point about a mile from the picket line. Later in the evening, Bogus Charley entered camp and told the

269

bloody back and forth would delay their date with the hangman. The young chief would have preferred to continue negotiating to buy some time, perhaps for divine intervention. Unfortunately, the tribe's collective will informed all his actions in the Peace Tent.

Though Toby Riddle had warned him of the tribe's restlessness and desperation, General Edward Canby strode across the sandy plain without his sidearm. In the shade of the white canvas tent, the Modoc stated their terms. They wished to share their homeland, peacefully. In exchange, they made one request of the commission: to allow them to continue hunting and fishing the sacred Lost River country, as their ancestors had. The general waved off the proposal saying he could not agree to any new conditions without conferring with President Grant. Kientpoos recognized the stalling tactic and knew his demands would not be considered that day or ever.

Frustrated, tired, and hungry, the young chief stood a few feet from Canby. Eyewitnesses recalled the moment. Kientpoos took a backward step, drew his gun, and squeezed the trigger. The cap burst, but the gun misfired. Whether the chief reloaded or had another pistol is not clear, but he shot again. Two other Modoc who had concealed themselves outside the tent, Barncho and Slolux, ran forward with rifles to support their chief. During the fracas, a bullet struck Canby in the left temple and lodged in his brain. The general had just enough life left in him to turn and run a short distance before another Modoc shot him in the back of the head. In the mayhem that followed, Canby received the coup de grace and had his throat cut.

While other members of the Peace Commission carried guns to the tent that day and returned fire, the Sunday Doctor was not among them. However, Reverend Eleazar Thomas was shot twice and killed in the surprise attack by a Modoc warrior named Boston Charley.

Though they struck first, the Modoc were outmanned and outgunned. They retreated from the successful ambush to the only place they might hold off their opponent—the stronghold.

April 11, 1873 was Good Friday. Even though the Modoc did not appreciate its religious significance, once the survivors' accounts were shared in newspapers across the country, public sentiment turned even more sharply against the tribe. General Canby and Dr. Thomas were celebrated as martyrs in the divine cause of Western Expansion.

Toby Riddle did what she could to preserve the peace—even during the shooting. She was able to save Commissioner Alfred Meacham by warning him moments before the attack, then interrupted it long enough to save him. Her exploits and bravery received wide attention. From that day forward, she became the most celebrated member of her tribe (see Photos). In her lifetime, she received many public accolades. Meacham wrote a book about her and spent the rest of his life giving lectures about his experience while defending Native American causes.

Winema's married name, Toby Riddle, is largely forgotten. However, her given name, Winema, is a popular place name around the Klamath Basin, including Fremont-Winema National Forest in Eastern Oregon.

After the melee at the Peace Tent and the tribe's retreat to the stronghold, the army attacked them continually from April 15th to the 17th and eventually gained the upper hand. The population of the small band of warriors had been reduced and was ripe for a conventional, military-style charge the following day. Assembling a large company of foot soldiers and some cavalry, they stormed the rocky fortress and reached it for the first time.

As they walked between the lava columns at the stronghold's exterior, each soldier had formed a mental picture of what lay within. It was something they were all looking forward to seeing—perhaps to plunder for a keepsake of their experience in the war. Instead, soldiers found the interior of the stronghold was almost empty. A few old Modoc men put down their weapons and surrendered. A larger group, who had defended the stronghold the night before, had slipped away before the army came in.

The Why

Cavalrymen and foot soldiers from Fort Bidwell bivouacked at Fort Klamath during the Modoc War.
Courtesy: Klamath County Historical Society

After being hoodwinked yet again, the soldiers took a harder look at the veteran crew who had been left to defend the stronghold and provide cover for the rest. The night before, these few Modoc elders and a few others had kept a bonfire by the entrance and shot back occasionally. This gave the impression the entire group was still inside, spoiling for a fight. The ruse had been successful, and kept the army outside long enough for the band to escape out the back. The army might have taken these last few men prisoner and questioned them—perhaps derived some information about where the rest of the band had escaped to—but the bloodlust and desire for revenge was too great. Orders were given. The prisoners were executed. Several had their scalps removed. Some of these "trophies" were shared back at camp on Sheepy Ridge.

The night before, one hundred fifty men, women, and children moved silently—taking a narrow trail between the lava flows—unseen by army sentries under an almost full moon. In the moonlight, they escaped to ice caves south of Tule Lake where water was available, and to fight another day.

Eventually, the army's numbers swelled to one thousand soldiers, cavalry, officers, and scouts, and two mighty howitzers. Finally, they would have the upper hand on this ragged band. The next confrontation would be staged in the open, without any opportunities for the Modoc to conceal themselves inside the stronghold. To the army, a new theater for battle, wherever it was, would be a vast improvement.

In preparation, on April 26th, a reconnaissance platoon of sixty-two men marched over open ground, unaware their movements were being watched. Perhaps this was a continuation of Canby's "gradual compression" strategy, which had never worked in the first place. Around noon, they broke for lunch near Tule Lake. While the men ate and rubbed their feet, the Modoc fighter Chikchikam Lupatkuelatko (aka Scarface Charlie, see Photos) and twenty-one other warriors waited behind a rock outcropping, once the shoreline of an ancient lake bed. From this concealed position, the Modoc party opened fire. Caught unaware, the barrage scattered the soldiers, several of whom

One of the last images taken of Kientpoos (above), dressed in prison fatigues after having his hair cut in preparation for his execution. (right) A professional portrait taken at a photographer's studio in Weed several years before his capture.

fled in bare feet. There were only a few rocks to take cover behind. The surprise attack turned into a turkey shoot and eventually a deadly crossfire that pinned down many of the invading force. In the end, the Modocs killed twenty members of the reconnaissance party.

Popularly known as the Battle of Sand Butte, the history of this encounter has expanded over the years. Initially, newspaper accounts described the Modoc as treacherous and cunning. The same stories described the army that day as being taken advantage of, cruelly shot down, and so on.[43]

Nowadays, there is greater balance in our understanding of The Modoc War. Deep historical research by McNally and others has explored both sides' experience. At Sand Hill, the Modoc outmaneuvered a force several times larger and did as much damage in two hours as all three days at the First Battle of the Stronghold. They marshaled their small band to take advantage of a larger, more powerful force. At the same time, they were living in conditions that would have motivated surrender in almost any other group.

The Modoc always presented a moving target, but they could not keep moving forever, and the army would not go away. With more than a thousand on one side and fifty on the other, the end was inevitable.

At the Battle of Dry Lake on May 10th, the army finally routed what was left of the tribe. Kientpoos surrendered three weeks later and was taken to Fort Klamath. Though the government described the conflict as war, Modoc prisoners were not treated like prisoners of war or soldiers. A label frequently applied to them was "murderers."

Their legal rights and representation in court was embarrassingly insufficient. They did not have a defense attorney until they were several days into the first phase of the trial. In retrospect, it would seem a defense could be mounted, arguing that they were defending themselves against cultural annihilation. It was presented at trial, but without convincing any of the jury of career military officers. The

---

43 "Disastrous Fight in the Lava Beds" *The Evansville Journal* April 30, 1873

chief and five other warriors (Schonchin John, Black Jim, Boston Charley, Barncho, and Slolux) were sentenced to death.

Before the trial, Kientpoos had his hair cut; something which other men of the tribe found embarrassing and emasculating. His haircut served a practical function: to accommodate the noose he'd soon be fitted with, allowing its fullest purchase when he dropped through the gallows. In Fort Klamath on October 3, 1873, the Modoc chief had his straight, black locks trimmed one final time before a burlap bag was placed over his head. They dropped him through the chute in front of several hundred onlookers, white settlers, and their families—many traveling from as far away as Yreka and Weed in California. Black Jim, Schonchin John, and Boston Charley were hanged from the same rough-cut, wooden gallows. Their graves and markers were prepared nearby.

Though they participated in the skirmish, evidence at trial showed neither Barncho nor Slolux fired their rifles at the Peace Tent. In the end, the army court decided to spare them the death penalty, but didn't tell them until the day of the executions.

After the hanging, the four prisoners were decapitated and had their severed heads defleshed and sent to the Army Medical Museum. Once they arrived, the skulls were measured and compared in an osteological pseudo-science study.[44] The treatment of their corpses after execution did not conform to Modoc burial practice. The Modocs possessed a deeply held belief about death and the afterlife. Specific rites were required. Warriors were placed in a buckskin or tule mat at the spot where they died then cremated with their head pointing toward the west. When a traditional burial for the four men did not occur, this created a problematic issue for their families, which officials and others outside the tribe failed to appreciate.

---

44 Phrenology draws an impossible link between skull shape and intellectual capacity. Popular in America in the mid-1800s, this flawed science was used to justify negative stereotypes and exploitation of Native and African Americans (Gould, 1981). Eventually, the Modoc men's remains made their way to a shelf in the basement of the Smithsonian Institute and sat for more than a hundred years.

The Why

Burial underground would not permit the spirit of the deceased to join their ancestors. Obviously, neither was a skull on a museum shelf consistent with a proper journey to the afterlife. The four boxes that contained the skulls of Kientpoos, Schonchin Jim, Black Jim, and Boston Charley remained inside the Smithsonian Museum until 1984 when the Modoc Chief's remains were returned to his descendants. They also received the other three warriors' remains. All were taken home and given burials consistent with tribal custom.

Sketch drawn by 2nd Lt. John S. Parke a few years after the execution of Kientpoos of the remaining gallows structure, circa 1880.
Courtesy: Klamath County Historical Society

After the Modoc War ended, estimates for the total cost to the federal government ranged as high as half a million dollars. Purchasing the land the Modoc and army fought over and then creating a government reservation for the Modoc would have cost around $20,000. And cost was the least of the factors. Besides the loss of life, the war inflicted an incalculable cultural disruption, pain, and trauma. The Modoc lost many of their most valued members while being terrorized and pushed off sacred land.

Besides the Modoc who were forced to move back to the Klamath Reservation, in 1873 another group of one hundred fifty-three Modoc were transported without their consent to a reservation in Oklahoma, the Quapaw Agency. From a train stop in Redding, California, they were loaded into boxcars—some chained. When they arrived at this barren outpost in Northeast Oklahoma, the government had neither food nor shelter for any of them. Eventually, almost half died for lack of these necessities, and probably a broken heart. Those who survived were not allowed to leave until 1909 when the federal government allowed them to return. That year, twenty-nine members of the tribe that survived the Modoc War and their displacement returned to the Klamath Basin.

Un-Breaking Your Leg and Other Causes of Historical Trauma

The effects of historical trauma were not only felt by the Modoc Tribe. A few decades after the Modoc War, another injustice acutely affected the Klamath People. It was the drawing down of the Klamath Basin marshes to create farm and grazing land for recently arrived settlers. The Klamath saw huge areas of the marshes, the heart of native culture, drained and virtually given away to whites. Robert Cole, the grandson of John Wesley Cole, summed up how this land giveaway affected him, physically.

> Did you ever break your leg? One time I got run over by a truck when I was working and broke my ankle. My body healed, but it still hurts.... You accept it because you can't do anything about it, but it's still not right. It's like a pain, you know. That's why I think we have such a high rate of alcoholism and drug use and suicide.... I think even though we broke our leg, it could be mended into a way where it wouldn't hurt. But you can't do it, because if you did, we'd have to get all the other people out of the country and they aren't gonna leave, right? The Man has caused all the problems here. We wouldn't be in this situation right now, if it wasn't for the government and Man themselves. In the nineteen

hundreds, when they first come into the area here, took the land away from the Modoc and give all the land to the farmers, we call them. They were actually veterans. So they took the land from the Indians and give it to them for fighting a war which had nothing to do with us anyway. After they give them the land, they were greedy and wanted more. So the government started draining the lakes to give them more land because they didn't have no more land to take from us. They took it all. So they started taking it from Mother Nature. They've drained two thirds of our lakes and water so they can have more land to give to those greedy people.... But like I said, it's like if you break your leg, you feel bad about it, but you really can't do anything. It's broken. The only way you could fix it is by un-breaking it. And they aren't gonna give the land back to us, so we're always gonna be in that situation. You can't un-break somebody's leg.

That is what historical trauma may have felt like to Kenneth Moore, both of whose parents were Klamath. It may explain the anger and violence he demonstrated throughout his life and the various crimes and assaults he committed, including the Crater Lake murders.

John Wesley Cole

Knowing something about John Wesley Cole's life should have been easier than Kenneth Moore. But after two years of talking to his family, they decided that their patriarch may not have even known Kenneth Moore. This makes a description of Cole, outside what is written in law enforcement or other official records, difficult. Sure, Moore named Cole as his accomplice the day of the murder, according to Oscar Arrell. After that in 1967, authorities came to Chiloquin and questioned seven people who knew Moore and Cole well; none of them suggested they didn't know each other. At the end of their lives, Moore died trying to save John Wesley Cole. It sounds like they knew each other well.

Despite all evidence to the contrary, I did not press Cole's grandson on this point or why, after more than two years, he wanted to disassociate his grandfather from Kenneth Moore. We talked about it and decided to let it go. Robert Cole, or "Clinker" as he is known to his friends, was always forthcoming any time I had a question about anything. He was a great source—explaining all about his life and his grandfather. If he says his grandfather didn't know Kenneth Moore, I don't want to contradict him outside of the record.

There are two stories about John Wesley Cole that his grandson has given me permission to share. The first describes a tragic event in his family history, a murder essentially. There is no record of it, besides his and his family's retelling through five generations of Coles since it happened in the late nineteenth century. According to Robert Cole, this is the most accurate version.

Robert Cole's great grandfather, John Cole, was John Wesley Cole's father. He did not have any tribal affiliation. His wife, Kate, was John Wesley Cole's mother. Kate's ancestry came from the Modoc Tribe.

Kate's sister and she would often go out on the marshes in a dugout canoe to gather *wokas* in the traditional way—leaning over the side of the canoe, picking from the yellow water lilies. This plant, common from Alaska to New Mexico, once covered the Klamath Basin marshes for miles. Wokas are the pods inside the waxy yellow petals. In late summer and fall, the petals fall away making the pods easier to pick. The seeds inside the pods, when dried and mashed, provide nourishment and are a staple of the Klamath's diet.

According to Robert, in the late 1800s, Kate and her sister were in the canoe gathering wokas on Agency Lake when several men approached them from the shore.

The Why

"They were dressed like soldiers or the cavalry. They ordered them to come in and paddle to shore, but they got frightened and stayed out in the water. "

Suddenly, Kate's sister fell into the bottom of the canoe. A gunshot rang out over the entire lake. She had been shot. Would Kate be next? She lay down next to her sister in the boat and watched her as she died.

After the soldiers left, Kate paddled to shore. Once home, she recounted to her family what had happened and that her sister was dead. Robert Cole retold this with painful immediacy and resentment toward the person who shot his great, great aunt. Four generations removed, the family is still affected by the circumstances of her death.

Tracing the origins of this violent episode is difficult. There are so many instances of homicide and killings of Modoc and Klamath People by settlers and the military in this time period, this single event may not have even been recorded. There is no reason to doubt it, either.

There are other known accounts of Klamath women being killed by government forces—most notably by the 1846 expedition of John C. Fremont led by Christopher (Kit) Carson. After being attacked in the middle of the night, they retaliated against a nearby Klamath fishing village, Dokdokwas. It lies where the Williamson enters Upper Klamath Lake. Fremont and his men shot and killed many of its inhabitants, including women and children, then burned the village to the ground. Historians have found no connection between the fishing village and Fremont's attackers the previous night.

There is one other story about John Wesley Cole that describes him personally, as he was engaged in a traditional activity, trapping. It was a source of income for him.

John Wesley Cole had a deep knowledge of the woods and waterways from the Williamson River west to Union Creek, his grandson remembered.

"He trapped fisher and marten around Rocky Ford to Three Creeks."

Cole built three small cabins for himself, each in a location along his trapping route. Robert called them "Cole Cabins." Each was a fourteen-foot-square log cabin—with just enough room inside for a wood stove, small table, and a bed.

One of the Cole Cabins still exists near Rocky Ford—with additions made to it over the years. Several members of the family have lived there, including Robert for a while in the 1970s. Besides the cabin at Rocky Ford, Cole built another at Three Creeks and a third by Wokas Bay. It was inside this triangle of cabins where Cole concentrated his winter trapping, which Robert Cole described.

"He lived out there and trapped. He would walk from one cabin to the next. He set out his traps then go around and check to see whatever animals he'd caught. He would take it to the next cabin. Skin it, stretch it and everything then go to the next cabin. And he just kept going all winter long for three or four or five months. However long it was. And then at the end of the spring when the snow all left, he would go in his vehicle and pick up all of his hides and stuff and take them and sell them or send them off to be sold."

At the time of this interview, Robert was seventy-seven years old. He has lived long enough to see the Williamson River where it runs by the Cole's Rocky Ford cabin change course and form a new channel in its bed.

"People don't realize it because they think in the immediate time. But when you get older you realize these things happen. Things change all the time, even though they stay the same. When people buy land, they use the river as a boundary. Well, the river changes all the time, so it's like a living boundary. It can give you more land or it can take away land, depending on which way the current flows."

For trapping in winter, John Wesley Cole had two different styles of snowshoes he made himself from cedar and rawhide. One was a "bear paw," like the style popular today. The other was his "walking shoe," which was six feet long. This extra length leant stability. It was designed for getting around safely in isolated woods buried deep in snow. Snowfall accumulations during the average Klamath winter of the early to mid- 20th century could be twice as deep as today. Robert recalled one winter he experienced many years ago.

"Eighteen feet. That's how deep the snow could be."

During an especially hard winter, the elder Cole was snowshoeing by his cabin near the Williamson River. In mid-stride, Cole walked directly over a sapling, maybe twenty feet high. It had been covered with the recent snowfall and made invisible. The snowpack suddenly gave way and Cole tumbled into the tree well. After he stood up at the bottom of the hole he'd just created, he peered through the branches at the sky above. He was buried, but still alive.

Falling in a tree well has always been an extremely dangerous way to fall.[45] Whether one lands upside down or not, movement is restricted. Extricating oneself takes a lot of energy. This may cause the trapped person to perspire excessively and become drenched in their own sweat. This invites deadly hypothermia. Robert described his grandfather in this exact situation.

"He was stuck for a day and a half."

Miraculously, John Wesley Cole did not die. Robert described how he survived.

"He got out pushing snow underneath him and raising himself up until he climbed out." ... of a frozen hole eighteen feet deep. What sort of person survives that? Most would not. Even without his grandson's possible embellishments, it's clear John Wesley Cole was strong physically and mentally.

---

45 This predicament is not uncommon in Oregon today, for snowboarders and snowshoers. In the backcountry or out-of-bounds areas beside ski resorts, recreationists occasionally fall into tree wells and may, literally, hang there upside down, suspended by their feet and the board attached to them, until someone finds them, not always alive.

The first time I spoke with Robert Cole on the phone we talked for almost three hours. I learned a lot, including how much I did not know. Nobody was cutting me any slack which, given the story and questions being asked, seemed pretty fair. In this initial conversation, Robert described his grandfather and Moore as associates who often socialized and drank together with friends. That is how I understood it. So I asked a question about Moore and Cole socializing together based on my own experience.

"Did they party in the kitchen or living room? Beer or whiskey? Watching the game or playing cards?" Trying to frame it inside something familiar, Robert set me straight.

"You're thinking of a party like a white person. They have a party like an Indian. They wanted to get together and drink. They'd chew the fat, talk about a deer they killed. Things they've done, you know, things they shouldn't have done. Who knows why, you know? It's not like some socialite said, 'Oh, let's have a party,' and you go over there so you could be around so and so. That wasn't what it was about."

My ignorance was completely out in the open now. Fortunately, we moved on to another subject.

John Wesley Cole was called a "bootlegger" by law enforcement and his family confirms this. For a time, he and his wife sold liquor on the reservation. Cole leant money with terms to people he knew. Other than that, John Wesley Cole stayed between the lines observing the laws of Klamath County during his lifetime. There is one small exception. It appeared in Klamath Falls' evening paper, with a vernacular tone like something Mark Twain might have written for the *Territorial Enterprise*, but not quite so amusing.

> Ssh! No use to swear. You might just as well keep still and forget fishing for the rest of that day. If you don't believe it, ask Ted Markwardt of Chiloquin. That, according to him is the penalty of having a good boat and a good motor. Marion Barnes, game warden,

commandeered Markwardt's boat in just such manner Thursday and brought to justice one John Cole, an Indian, and accused him of robbing the nest of wild ducks of their eggs and young birds for the purpose of selling them later. A violator of the law brought to the bar of justice, but Markwardt swears that it spoiled his fishing just the same.

The Evening Herald May 25, 1932

Before the establishment of game laws, Cole's violation was the sort of activity his tribe had done for thousands of years, gathering duck eggs for food.

The Relationship Between Moore and Cole

Relying on law enforcement records, we know that, according to Oscar Arrell on the day he died, Kenneth Moore admitted to killing Jones and Culhane, and that John W. Cole was with him. Everything else in the investigation that links Moore and Cole is predicated on Arrell's confession and Hazel Arrell's interview with the Marion County Sheriff about it in early 1967.

Based on this intelligence, the FBI and Oregon State Police sent representatives to Chiloquin on September 13, 1967. Of the seven persons they spoke with that day, all of them knew Moore and Cole, including the immediate family members of each. Everyone spoke about the men in terms that strongly suggested they were well acquainted. No one claimed that Moore and Cole did not know each other. If they were strangers, someone would have said so, which should have been reflected in the report.

On consecutive pages, in the last few pages of the FBI file, there are nearly identically worded negative fingerprint tests for Moore and Cole. The fingerprint analysis was also a result of Arrell's confession.

I asked Robert Cole once, given all that connected his grandfather and Kenneth Moore in the record pertaining to the Crater Lake murders, did he think it was possible that they had done it. He repeated something he'd told me before.

"You're asking about things that aren't there. Time has erased them."

In a different interview with another person who lived in Chiloquin and knew Kenneth Moore, I asked the same question. Had Moore and Cole committed the murders in Crater Park?

"Nobody talks. That isn't our way. If they knew today, they wouldn't tell it."

And that would be a suitable ending for this story were it not for one final document in the official record linking Kenneth Moore and John Wesley Cole—one last piece of punctuation at the end—almost as unsettling as the double murder which they have been accused of. This last interconnection of the two men is described in an OSP report and repeated in the last few pages of the FBI file (see Section Three title page). The circumstances were unusual: a tragic event and coda for the story.

John Wesley Cole and Kenneth Moore were together the night they died. The second great coincidence in this story.

12 | The Frozen Marsh

When Oscar "Whitey" Arrell died on December 9, 1966, the person he used his last words on Earth to describe, Kenneth Moore, had been dead for four years, eight months, and three days. The man he said was with him the day of the Crater Lake murders, John Wesley Cole, had also been dead for the exact same length of time.

According to an old Oregon State Police report dated April 2, 1962, Kenneth Moore and John Wesley Cole died together—on or around March 28th. Just like the Eberleins finding the Pontiac at the overlook, Moore and Cole dying together sounds like fiction. The circumstances of their passing was reported by Trooper L.G. Bergmann who, by 1962, had achieved the rank of corporal. He had been present the day Al Jones and Charles Culhane were found in the woods by the overlook. His four-page officer's report about the Crater Lake murders case remains one of the most informative documents from that day. Almost ten years later, Bergmann would write the report detailing where Kenneth Moore and John Wesley Cole died—on a soggy, almost frozen dirt road miles from anywhere.

The official cause of death was listed as "exposure and exhaustion." The temperature in Klamath Falls on March 28, 1962 dipped to 18° Fahrenheit. Wind chill brought it much lower—one of the coldest nights of a long, hard winter. It was especially cold on Military Crossing Road, out on the marsh where their bodies were found. Besides the chilling cold, road conditions were bad. A recent freeze had thawed enough to make the road muddy, and in places, impassable.

Bergmann surely filed a report about the deaths of Moore and Cole on the marsh, but it has never surfaced. The only official Oregon State Police record of their passing is a memorandum written by Capt. Raymond Howard. This was shared with the 1967 Chiloquin interviewers, Gray and Christianson, as background about the men they were investigating.

> A check of our files disclosed Case #168596, a report submitted by Corporal L. G. Bergmann dated April 2, 1962 which concerns the death of John Wesley Cole and Kenneth Moore, both of Chiloquin, Oregon. These two subjects were found frozen to death 4.4 miles east of Highway 97 in the vicinity of the Upper Klamath Marsh Road and Military Crossing Road. Their deaths were attributed to exposure and freezing and there was no indication of violence being involved.
>
> **R. G. Howard, Captain**
> **Memorandum (Supplemental Information) 7/25/67**

More recently, a web search revealed this story in a Salem newspaper.

2 Die of Exposure After Mire in Mud

KLAMATH FALLS (UPI) — Two Chiloquin men died of apparent exposure and exhaustion sometime Tuesday night after their station wagon became mired in the mud about 55 miles north of here, state police said.

Investigating officers said John L. Cole, 83, and Kenneth Moore, 58, were last seen alive near Agency Lake Tuesday afternoon. Their vehicle became mired on a back road known as the "Old Military Crossing" east of Highway 97.

Police said they had driven to the Klamath Marsh area to watch evening flights of ducks and geese. When their vehicle became stuck Moore walked to Chiloquin where he secured a four-wheel drive vehicle and started back with some other persons. People involved told officers that this vehicle also became mired. After it was freed Moore said he was going on to Cole and the others returned to Chiloquin.

In the meantime, Cole had decided to try to walk out. Bodies of the two men were found two miles apart Wednesday morning by men from the Klamath Agency. Even four-wheel drive vehicles had difficulty reaching the area to bring out the bodies. There were places where water was 15 inches deep on the roadbed.

The bodies were recovered about 2:30 p.m. Wednesday.

The Capitol Journal *March 29, 1962 p.1*

When the rescue party that Kenneth Moore organized got its vehicle stuck in the frozen marsh, it must have been a moment of truth for all of them. It was freezing cold. An 83-year-old man, a tribal member whom they all wanted to save, might be dying out there. But they might also die trying to save him. The more sensible and perhaps frightened among them turned around, walked out, and lived to tell about it. Kenneth Moore knew that walking the opposite direction to save his friend could be deadly, but he did it anyway. Faced with a life or death situation, Kenneth Moore made the hard choice, putting himself at grave risk. Why did he do it? Was it just a bad decision? Or did he feel a sense of responsibility to save his friend? We can never know exactly what bound Moore to Cole that night, but it was tight.

There was a snowstorm. The temperature was below freezing. The ground on the marsh was slushy and wet—worse than if it were frozen solid. After their friends turned back, rescue was impossible. It was too dangerous. No one was coming out that night to save them.

The moon was bright enough to light the marsh—almost two-thirds full. Moore and Cole walked toward each other, possibly at the same time. Or it could be that Cole died before Moore returned with the rescue party. Eventually both men succumbed to the elements in an area of utter desolation: two miles away from each other and more than four miles from the highway.

The stretch of Military Crossing Road 4.4 miles east of Interstate 97—looking west. One of the most remote stretches of road in Klamath County.

The Frozen Marsh

They each experienced a similar end. One that has sometimes been described as "not as painful" as other causes of death, but how would anyone know that, unless they themselves had died from exposure?

Unrelenting cold and wetness penetrated their clothes and boots. Cole was all alone. So was Moore. If he did call out his friend, his energy was wasted. Voices don't carry two miles in a snowstorm over a wet, wooded marsh. Kenneth Moore's last words, spoken or shouted, were written on the wind.

Finally, a similar sensation overcame them both, much more pleasant than the freezing cold. As hypothermia set in, the bitter sting of winter became a gentle caress. In those last few minutes before sleep became irresistible and their hearts ceased beating, did either man think about that warm July afternoon ten years before or the secret they shared and would take to their death?

Photos

The photo at left was taken on July 21, 1952, before Albert Jones and Charles Culhane were removed and taken to the medical examiner. This image belongs to the Park Service who kept a file containing other photographs and records. It was lost or taken from the dispatch center between 2000 and 2010.
Courtesy: Stephen Mark

The photo below is of the same scene but taken in March 2020. The split fir under which Jones and Culhane lay in the top photo is on the far right, casting the shadow across the frame. If you look carefully, both photos reveal where the trunk splits into two separate trees.

photo: author

At the top of the trunk below the split is the blazemark scar carved on July 21, 1952 to make the scene distinguishable. This allowed investigators to return and look for evidence the next few days. These woods are quite ordinary. Without this blazemark, it would have been difficult to find this spot. It is even more difficult today. The author (below) wishes anyone who visits this place be respectful and considerate of the men who died here.

photos: author

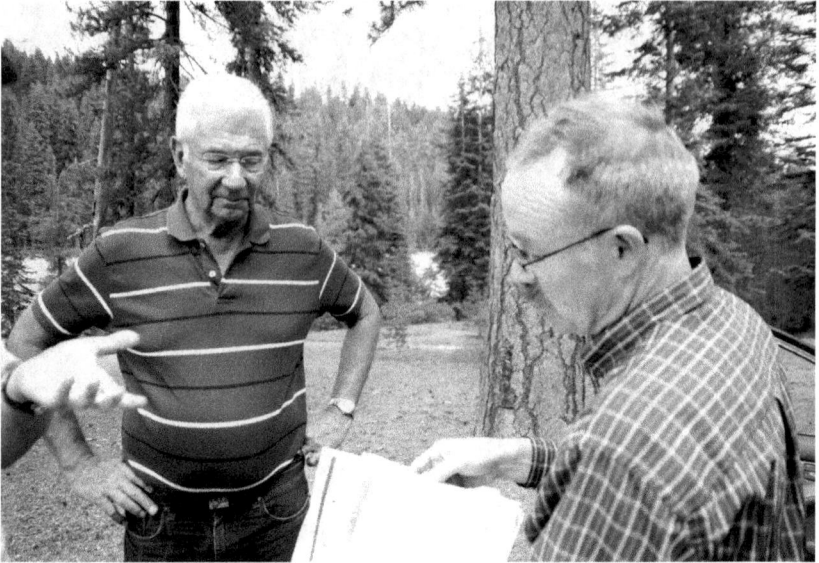

Alan Eberlein (left) with Crater Lake National Park Historian Stephen Mark in July 2013. Behind them is the ponderosa pine beside which Albert Jones' Pontiac was found abandoned on July 19, 1952.
photo: author

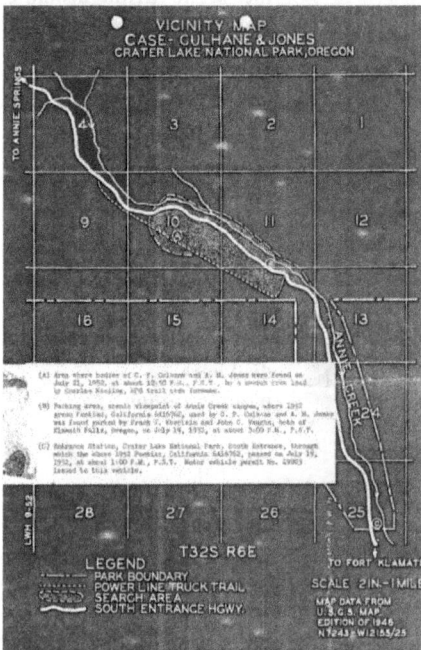

Map created by CLNP during the investigation to show the locations of the two scenes and the south gate entrance. Curiously, the first scene where Jones and Culhane were kidnapped and their Pontiac left alone at the Annie Creek Canyon Overlook is about a mile south (B) of the actual location.
Courtesy: Stephen Mark

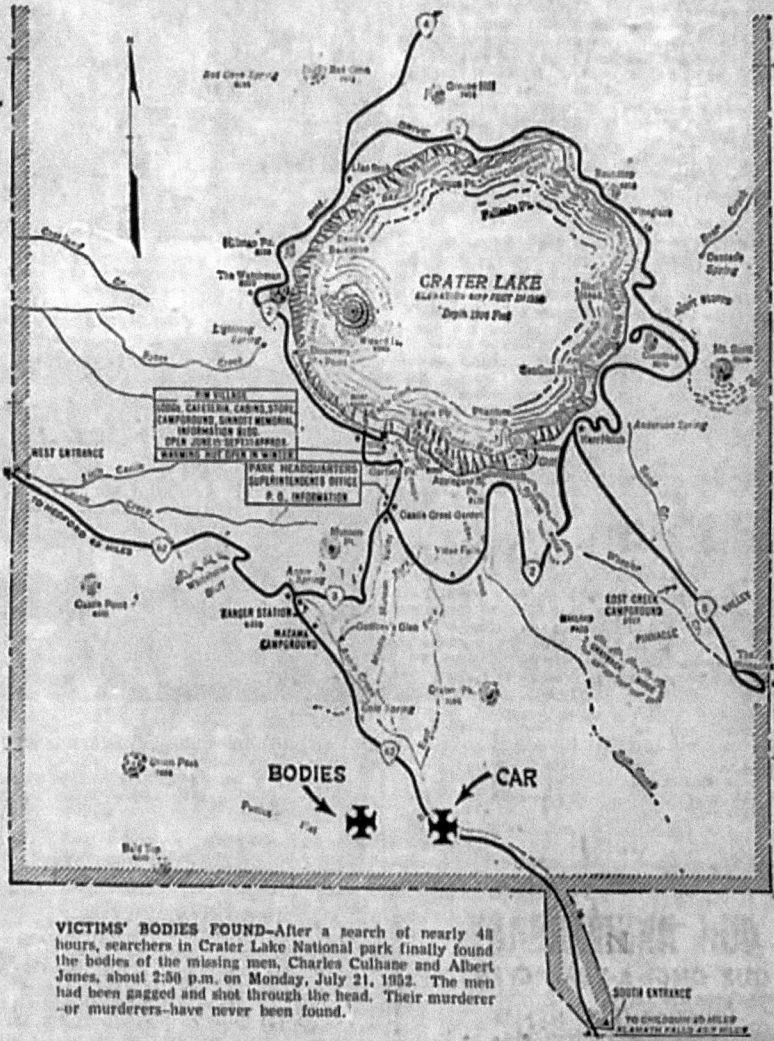

MEDFORD MAIL TRIBUNE

SECTION B   MEDFORD, OREGON, SUNDAY, NOVEMBER 11, 1962   PAGES 1 to 8

CRATER LAKE

BODIES

CAR

VICTIMS' BODIES FOUND—After a search of nearly 48 hours, searchers in Crater Lake National park finally found the bodies of the missing men, Charles Culhane and Albert Jones, about 2:50 p.m. on Monday, July 21, 1952. The men had been gagged and shot through the head. Their murderer —or murderers—have never been found.

Courtesy: Medford Mail Tribune

295

WARNING: GRAPHIC IMAGES

Charles Culhane was shot in the right cheek (left) an inch below the corner of his mouth.
Courtesy: OSP

These two scene photos illustrate the proximity of the men to the small lodgepole or jackpines to which they might have been tied and left had the robbery not escalated to murder.
Courtesy: OSP

Courtesy: OSP

Image that appeared in both the *Klamath Falls Herald and News* and *Medford Mail Tribune*. Jones' shoes are outlined in the lower left corner.

298

REPORT TO OFFICIALS
OF VIOLATION OF GENERAL RULES BY INMATE

To {Superintendent, WARDEN and DEPUTY WARDEN:

Date October 6th, 1934

Please be advised that:

Name _____ Moore _____ Number 13037

This man continually stalling on job. Spoken to by guard several times without result - very tough and resentful - reprimanded by Yard Captain to no avail. After being taken to Yard Captain by guard made the remark, "Now, I hope you are satisfied.

Place: Yard   Time: 9:45 A.M.

(Give Location, Time and Details)

Form No. 55 MD---12 80   Signed _____ Ramsay

Oregon State Prison document among Kenneth Moore's Department of Corrections file. This violation report contains the only words Moore is known to have spoken (in anger to a yard captain named Ramsay).
Courtesy: Oregon Dept. of Corrections

299

FEDERAL BUREAU OF INVESTIGATION
U. S. DEPARTMENT OF JUSTICE
COMMUNICATIONS SECTION

AUG 3 1952

TELETYPE

FBI, LOS ANGELES   8-3-52   2-04 AM

DIRECTOR, FBI AND SACS, PORTLAND AND PHOENIX G I R URGENT

UNSUB., CHARLES CULHANE, VIC., A. M. JONES, VIC., CGR-MURDER. COLTON
CALIF. PD ADVISED TWELVE THIRTYFIVE AM INSTANT THAT SHELL CREDIT CARD
FOUR ONE EIGHT ONE EIGHT SIX WAS USED BY UNIDENTIFIED SUBJECT USING
ALIAS A.M. JONES TO MAKE PURCHASE AT SEVEN THIRTY AM ON AUG. TWO,
FIFTYTWO AT SHELL SERVICE STATION COLTON, CALIF. DESCRIPTION UNKNOWN
BUT SUBJ PROCEEDED EAST ON HIGHWAY NINE NINE DRIVING CRYSLER TWO-DOOR
SEDAN YEAR AND COLOR UNKNOWN BEARING OREGON LIC. ONE NINE THREE ZERO
DASH ONE ONE THREE. PHOENIX ADVISE ARIZ. STATE POLICE THAT FEDERAL
WARRANT HAS BEEN ISSUED TO HOLD ALL SUBJECTS AND CONTACT SHELL SERVICE
STATIONS ON MAIN HIGHWAYS. LA HAS ALERTED CALIF. ARIZ. BORDER PATROL
AND LOCAL LAW ENFORCEMENT AGENCIES, ALSO INTERVIEWING SERVICE STATION
ATTENDANTS ON DUTY. REQUEST PORTLAND FURNISH LA AND PHOENIX ANY FURT
IDENTIFYING DATA RE INSTANT CAR.

RECORDED - 47   1 20 - 18550 - 49

CARSON

PX AND PD TO BE ADVISED   EX. - 69

The breathless, all caps teletype message of August 3, 1952 describing a vehicle in Colton, California that purportedly used Albert Jones' Shell credit card to pay for gas there. When the FBI followed up they found the source of the information to be unreliable and the information impossible to substantiate.

LOST RIVER MURDERERS.

I certify that L. HELLER has this day taken the Photographs of the above
Modoc Indians, prisoners under my charge.
Capt. C. B. THROCKMORTON, 4th U. S. Artillery, Officer of the Day.
I am cognizant of the above fact. GEN. JEFF. C. DAVIS, U. S. A.

After their surrender, captured Modocs were not considered war criminals legally
or by the public. In many cases their treatment and sentences were much worse
for it. Pictured left to right are Curly Headed Jack, Wheum, and Buckskin Doctor.
These three were among the fifty or so warriors who participated in the Modoc War
under Kientpoos aka Captain Jack. This image is often found under the title "Lost
River Murderers."
Courtesy: Huntington Library

Chikclikam Lipolkuelatk, aka Scarface Charley, led a life fraught with turmoil and loss—witnessing the genocide of his tribe while participating in several of the bloodiest battles in the Modoc Wars, including the Battle of Sand Hill, a surprise attack which he led. In later years, he developed a reputation as a skilled craftsman, building traditional furniture. He lived to be forty-six years old.
Courtesy: Merriam Library

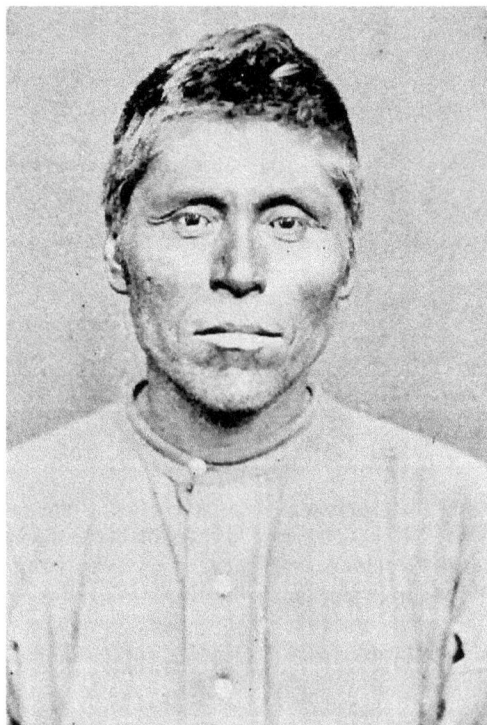

Curley Headed Doctor was the Modoc's spiritual leader during the time of the Modoc War. He is often described as a shaman. His given name was Cho-ocks. He lived from 1828 to 1890. Like Kientpoos, Cho-ocks desired to live in peace with white settlers.
Courtesy: Library of Congress

Illustrated by MUYBRIDGE, Published by BRADLEY & RULOFSON.

THE MODOC WAR.

1624—A—Mrs. Riddell, (TOBY), (the Squaw who cautioned General Canby of his impending fate), and Riddell her husband.

Photograph taken at the army camp near the Lava Beds in 1873. Toby Riddle (Winema) is standing between Capt. Oliver Applegate (left) and her husband, Frank Riddle (right). Middle row: Lac-el-es and Martha Mainstake (l to r). Front row: Me-hu-no-lush and Sau-kaa-dush (l to r). Though she was celebrated in her lifetime, this plate is a sad example of how she could yet be the object of derision and casual insult, referring to her as "Squaw."

Reverend Eleazar Thomas, a Methodist minister from Petaluma, California died along with General Edward Canby on April 11, 1873 while attempting to force the Modoc to move from their ancestral land to the Klamath Indian Reservation, a tribe with whom the Modoc did not share good relations historically. Thomas' paternalistic attitude was considered condescending by the tribe who referred to him as the "Sunday Doctor." His death on Good Friday made him a martyr for the cause of Indian Removal. Courtesy: Press Democrat

Kientpoos' grave (with Modoc warriors "Boston Charley," Schonchiss, and "Black Jim"). The first photograph shows them in their original burial place. They were removed to a second location by the Fort Klamath Museum (below).

Bibliography

Abbey, Loren and Zibura, Pamela *A Massacre of Innocents* iUniverse 2015

American Indian Policy Review Commission Task Force "Report of Terminated and Non Federally Recognized Indians" U.S. Government Printing Office 1976

Barker, M.A.R. *Klamath Texts* University of California Press 1963

Brave Heart, Dr. Maria Yellow Horse "How Trauma Gets Passed Down Through Generations" 2014

Brown, Dee Bury My Heart at Wounded Knee MacMillan 1971

Brown-Rice, Kathleen "Examining the Theory of Historical Trauma Among Native Americans" The Professional Counselor Electronic Journal 2014

Bureau of Land Management "Klamath River Basin Study" Summary Report December 2016

Byrd, Mike "The Corpse as a Scene" Miami-Dade Police Department

Carpenter, Marc James "Pioneer Problems 'Wanton Murder', Indian War Veterans and Oregon's Violent History" Oregon Historical Quarterly, Summer 2020

Chiu, Peggy (Trust for Public Land) "Stewards of Their Lands: A Case Study for the Klamath Tribes, Oregon" 2007

Compton, Jim *Spirit in the Rock* Washington State University Press 2017

Cook, Philip J. "Robbery Violence" Journal of Criminal Law and Criminology Summer 1987

Cooper, Alexia and. Smith, Erica L. "Homicide Trends in the United States, 1980-2008" U. S. Department of Justice November 2011

Cressman, Luther S. *The Sandal and the Cave: The Indians of Oregon* Oregon State University Press, 2005

Eberlein, Alan The Crater Lake Murders of July, 1952 (personal account) September 2011

Eberlein, Frank The Crater Lake Murders of July, 1952 (personal account) 1952

Federal Bureau of Investigation File Volumes 1-7 December 2015

Gentry, Curt J. Edgar Hoover: The Man and His Secrets Norton 2001

Gould, Stephen J. *The Mismeasure of Man* W.W. Norton & Co. 1981

Grann, David Killers of the Flower Moon: The Osage Murders and the Birth of the FBI Doubleday 2017

Grattan, Rebecca E. et al "A History of Trauma is Associated with Aggression, Depression, Non-Suicidal Self-Injury Behavior, and Suicide Ideation in First-Episode Psychosis" 2019

Gregory, Regina "EcoTipping Points Project Models for Success in a Time of Crisis" March 2017

Hallock, Louis W. "Report of Murder of C.P. Culhane and A.M. Jones in Crater Lake National Park on or about July 19, 1952"

Kroeber, Alfred Louis *Handbook of the Indians of California* Dover Publications 1925

Leslie, Jack *Decathlon of Death* Tarquin Books 1979

Lewis, David G. PhD *Klamath Tribal Termination* essay 2007

Margolin, Malcolm *The Way We Lived* Heyday Books and the California Historical Society 1981

Matthiessen, Peter *In the Spirit of Crazy Horse* Viking 1983

Mayfield, Thomas Jefferson Indian Summer Traditional Life Among the Choinumne Indians of California's San Joaquin Valley Heyday Books 1993

McNally, Robert Aquinas The Modoc War: A Story of Genocide at the Dawn of America's Gilded Age

Meacham, A.B. Wigwam And War-Path: The Modoc Indian War 1872-3, By An Active Eyewitness Leonaur Ltd. 2013

Most, Stephen *Klamath Basin Project (1906)* Oregon Historical Society

Murray, Keith A., *The Modocs and Their War* University of Oklahoma Press, 1959

Ousey, Cheryl "Crater Lake Murders: The Unsolved Murders of Albert Marston Jones and Charles Patrick Culhane on July 19, 1952 in Crater Lake National Park" August 2001

Pevar, Stephen L. The Rights of Indians and Tribes: The Basic ACLU Guide to Indians and Tribal Rights 1992

Reisner, Mark Cadillac Desert: the American West and Its Disappearing Water Penguin 1993

Robbins, William G. *Lower Klamath Lake* Oregon Historical Society

Smith, Hellen Crume Stories Along the Sprague: Sprague Valley Elders Talk to Young People about Their Lives Impact Publications 2006

Other Media:

https://chiloquin.com/chiloquin-home/chiloquin-history/

Ball and O'Neill "Square Pegs and Round Holes: Understanding Historical Trauma in Two Native American Communities" 2016

Hatcher, Gail *Open Letter from the Klamath Tribes* (to Warren Buffet) August 19, 2020

Murder Accountability Project Half of Native American homicides not reported to FBI March 2019

Truth About Fur "How are Trapped Animals Killed?" truthaboutfur. com

About the Author

Monty Orrick has worked for twenty-five years as a TV news photojournalist in Oregon. Always happy to be nominated (for anything), he received four Emmy nominations. With Tim Gordon, he wrote a book about that crazy profession, "Feeding the Beast"—a handbook for professionals and journalism students to learn to tell better stories.

In 2011, he first came across the story of the Crater Lake murders. He could not let it go—or was it the other way around? He effectively solved the case ten years later. For anyone interested in a meaningful discussion about it, there is a dedicated Facebook page:

https://m.facebook.com/profile.php?id=100093321581643

Besides his two books, Monty has published a handful of campfire stories about his misadventures fly fishing and backpacking in the Sierras. His other chief talents are watching baseball and listening to records.